D1121570

THE CEMETERIES
OF
NEW ORLEANS

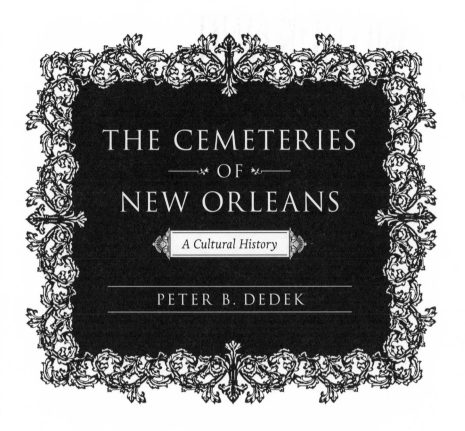

THE CEMETERIES
— OF —
NEW ORLEANS

A Cultural History

PETER B. DEDEK

Louisiana State University Press
Baton Rouge

Published by Louisiana State University Press
Copyright © 2017 by Louisiana State University Press
All rights reserved
Manufactured in the United States of America
First printing

Designer: Michelle A. Neustrom
Typefaces: MillerText and Trajon Pro
Printer and binder: McNaughton & Gunn, Inc.

All photographs in Appendix A were taken by the author.

Library of Congress Cataloging-in-Publication Data
Names: Dedek, Peter B., 1964– author.
Title: The cemeteries of New Orleans : a cultural history / Peter B. Dedek.
Description: Baton Rouge : Louisiana State University Press, [2017] | Includes bibliographi-
    cal references and index.
Identifiers: LCCN 2016041524| ISBN 978-0-8071-6610-9 (cloth : alk. paper) | ISBN 978-0-
    8071-6611-6 (pdf) | ISBN 978-0-8071-6612-3 (epub) | ISBN 978-0-8071-6613-0 (mobi)
Subjects: LCSH: Cemeteries—Louisiana—New Orleans—History. | Sepulchral
    monuments—Louisiana—New Orleans—History. | Tombs—Louisiana—New Orleans—
    History. | Burial—Louisiana—New Orleans—History. | New Orleans (La.)—Social life and
    customs. | New Orleans (La.) —Buildings, structures, etc.
Classification: LCC F379.N562 A23 2017 | DDC 363.7/50976335—dc23
LC record available at https://lccn.loc.gov/2016041524

The paper in this book meets the guidelines for permanence and durability of the Committee
on Production Guidelines for Book Longevity of the Council on Library Resources. ∞

To the people of New Orleans, living and dead

CONTENTS

PREFACE

For over two centuries, the dead of New Orleans have been interred in aboveground tombs arranged along the sun-bleached avenues of miniature cities. With their strange appearance and a fanciful variety of tombs and monuments, the city's historic cemeteries have long caught the attention of visitors and residents alike. Many tourists have found them perplexing, describing them as exotic "cities of the dead," ghoulish reminders of mortality, and the strange products of a foreign Creole culture. The cemeteries of New Orleans strike tourists as so unusual because they have more in common with cemeteries in Spain, France, and the Caribbean than they do with other burial grounds in the United States. Although most authors and tour guides cite but one reason for the diverse aboveground architectural tombs—the high water table that made most graves fill with water as soon as they were excavated—there are other reasons the cemeteries developed the way they did, reasons that shed light on the fascinating history of the city, its climate, geography, and the many cultures that have created and sustained it.

The cemeteries of New Orleans are not solely places to bury and mourn the dead. They are an integral aspect of the city and part of its distinctive culture. In these walled sanctuaries, life and death intersect. The people of New Orleans (like many in south Louisiana) celebrate an annual holiday in their cemeteries. They use them as places of prayer and religious ritual in which some pray for the souls of the dead while others summon their spirits to alter the fates of the living. The cemeteries have hosted colorful parades and elaborate ceremonies. They have been venues of charity, community building, social one-upmanship, and racial discrimination. Historic cemeteries can be found in nearly every neighborhood as quiet neighbors to many who live in the city. They reflect New Orleans's history and chronicle its triumphs and tragedies in brick, marble, granite, and iron.

Although they stand as bold reminders of the inevitability of death, the cemeteries also reveal the manner in which the people buried there lived. In the nineteenth century, prosperous French-speaking Creoles who dwelled in brick and stucco houses in and around the French Quarter usually found rest in densely packed brick or stucco tombs belonging to their family. Members of the working class who lived in Creole cottages or shotgun houses often were laid to rest within the narrow cells of a wall tomb or in the vaults of tombs constructed by benevolent societies, and the poor, who often lived in small cottages or cabins on the fringes of the city, commonly found obscure, water-filled graves. A person's position in society was most often expressed by the manner in which he or she was buried, but this is not always obvious to visitors to the older cemeteries today. Many of the tombs built by benevolent societies in which their mostly working-class members were interred are significantly more imposing and ornate than the smaller and often plainer family tombs where the affluent found rest. The memory of so many others—the poor, the enslaved, the victims of epidemics—is lost altogether in unmarked graves in paupers' burial grounds and in the soil beneath the tombs of the historic walled cemeteries. Nothing commemorates their having lived at all.

Since childhood, I have been fascinated with historic burial grounds. They can be picturesque churchyards that chronicle birth and death on leaning slabs of slate or marble, or lonely fields of mostly forgotten gravestones and monuments tucked away on the back streets of cities and towns. Others are beautiful, manicured parks, architectural galleries displaying styles and decoration from throughout the ages in marble and granite— sprawling sculpture gardens guarded by triumphant stone angels created at a time when death was commemorated with artistry, taste, and elegance.

Accustomed to the eastern churchyards and garden cemeteries of New York and New England, I found St. Louis Cemetery Number 1, the oldest existing cemetery in New Orleans, curious and captivating. Why, I wondered, did the people of this city bury their dead in what looked like diminutive houses or temples, or in multivaulted mausoleums, or in ovenlike niches in cemetery walls? Were these cemeteries French? Was New Orleans the only place where such cities of the dead could be found? I wondered who had designed them and what craftspeople had cut the stone details that made many of the tombs so ornate and interesting. And finally, I asked why the fronts of some of the tombs I saw had been piled high with offerings of coins, alcohol, lipstick, and other common items. It was only after years of living in New Orleans and the receipt of a doctorate in history that I began to discover the answers to these questions.

Unlike most works about cemeteries, this book does not focus on the well-known people buried within them, but rather on those who designed, built, visited, mourned, and worked in these burial grounds. It examines the role of the cemeteries within the context of the diverse cultures and the fascinating history of New Orleans. These chapters trace how the cemeteries evolved from the founding of the city in 1718 until around 1920. In addition, chapter 7 discusses the degree to which the cemeteries have been preserved and maintained from their early years up to the present and offers insights into how they might be better conserved in the future. It is my hope that this volume will inspire greater appreciation of the historic cemeteries of New Orleans, and that this will encourage stronger efforts to ensure their preservation.

I would like to thank Emily Ford for her generous assistance in this endeavor, and also Margaret Lovecraft for her support and her patience.

THE CEMETERIES
OF
NEW ORLEANS

FROM MUD AND CRAWFISH
TO CITIES OF THE DEAD

New Orleans's cemeteries did not start out as cities of the dead. From 1724, when the first known public cemetery in the city opened, until the first decade of the nineteenth century, New Orleans's main burial ground was a desolate field with a few wooden or metal crosses marking mostly underground graves. In the 1700s, only a small number of elite who were allowed to be interred inside St. Louis Church in the medieval Catholic tradition could avoid being buried in soggy soil littered with the bones of their predecessors. From their humble beginnings, New Orleans's cemeteries evolved along with the city. They started small and informal and, like the city itself, eventually grew more substantial, sophisticated, and picturesque.

When the French founded New Orleans in 1718, it was one of the most remote and dangerous places imaginable. The tiny colonial outpost occupied a strip of land between a great river and seemingly endless, forested swamps. It was isolated, rife with disease, and prone to flooding. A small number of French settlers had occupied the general area since 1699, when Pierre Le Moyne d'Iberville (Sieur d'Iberville), a French Canadian soldier and explorer, and his brother, Jean-Baptiste Le Moyne de Bienville, discovered the mouth of the Mississippi River on *Mardi gras* of that year. The party established a camp, which Iberville prophetically named Pointe du Mardi Gras. The French government under Louis XIV had sent explorers in search of the entrance to the Mississippi River so he could claim this potentially important strategic position for France before the British or the Spanish had a chance to occupy it.[1]

The Louisiana colony was the result of a vast financial scheme concocted in 1715 by John Law, a Scottish professional gambler and unorthodox economic theorist who had worked his way into French high society. Against all odds, Law managed to establish himself as the power behind the throne. Louis XIV had died that year, ending his 72-year reign, one of the longest in history. This freed the French nobility of his tyrannical oversight and gave Law his chance. The only heir to the French crown young enough to have survived the long-lived monarch was his five-year-old great-grandson. Until Louis XV had the chance to mature sufficiently to assume his duties as king of France, Philippe II, the Duc d'Orléans, would rule as regent. At the time, France was experiencing a severe economic depression, and the Crown was nearly bankrupt. Law, who had known the Duc d'Orléans for decades and had a legendary gift of persuasion, convinced the duke to place much of the French economy in his hands.[2]

With d'Orléans's blessing, Law printed vast amounts of paper money, not fully backed by gold as was the usual practice at the time, and pursued an expansionist economic policy based mainly on credit.[3] Law needed a way to convince investors he would be able to develop the resources required to back his promises of future prosperity. The Louisiana colony was the ideal confidence scheme for Law (fig. 1.1). Few had any knowledge of the area, and western European powers, particularly Spain, the Netherlands, France, and England, had already reaped great fortunes through trade, plunder, resource extraction, and slavery in the New World, making another colonial venture seem promising. Backed by the French regent, Law's "Company of the West" set out to develop agriculture, mining, and the fur trade in Louisiana. To grow the colony and create profits for investors, who included many of the most influential people in France, Law needed to persuade thousands of potential French settlers to leave home and try their luck in Louisiana.

In 1717, Sieur de Bienville brought a group of about fifty men to the future site of New Orleans to clear trees and build housing with the intent of establishing a permanent French settlement there. The new city would guard the mouth of the Mississippi from a point nearly one hundred miles upstream from the Gulf where the river made a sweeping curve. This would allow French gunners positioned in new fortifications on the natural levee a clear shot at any ships approaching the settlement from either upstream or downstream, ensuring that the English or the Spanish would not be able to take the position easily. Named for John Law's benefactor, the Duc d'Orléans, La Nouvelle Orléans welcomed its first settlers, mostly soldiers

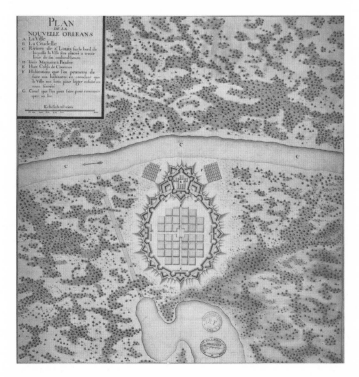

Fig. 1.1. Utopian "map" from 1718 of the planned city of New Orleans with imaginary fortifications, imaginary streets, and little basis in reality. Courtesy Bibliothèque national de France.

and convicts, in June of 1718. Three years later, chief engineer Le Blond de La Tour and his assistant, Adrien de Pauger, laid out the city as a rectilinear grid of streets beside the river to create some semblance of order in a hostile wilderness. They mistakenly believed the location Bienville had chosen was upriver and inland enough to be safe from hurricanes.

It did not take long for word to get back to France that Louisiana was little more than an elaborate hoax, and no gold and few economic opportunities were to be had in the struggling colony. Louisiana offered settlers sweltering summers, pernicious hunger, rampant disease, and little else. Once they understood the truth about the colony, even impoverished people who were already facing starvation in France refused to emigrate. This caused Law and his allies to resort to rounding up petty criminals, prostitutes, and indigent workers and forcing them onto ships to make the hazardous journey across the Atlantic. In its first years, New Orleans was essentially a New World penal colony and trading post for France.

The colony experienced such a shortage of women suited for marriage that John Law's company started offering cash benefits to any reputable woman or girl willing to immigrate. The company would pay for each woman's passage and promised a small stipend if she agreed to be housed at the Ursuline Convent after arriving in the colony and to earnestly seek a husband. Over a number of years, the company recruited "shiploads" of young women in this manner.[4] Many of them had been educated in convents in France and had come from respectable families. They became known as *filles à la cassette* (casket girls) because colonists thought the trunks they brought from France containing their trousseaux looked like caskets.[5] Regardless of their backgrounds, many would-be colonists did not survive the journey, and many more died within days or weeks of arrival from diseases abetted by poor sanitation, inadequate supplies, and the area's swampy environment.[6]

According to many published sources, the copious number of people who died in New Orleans during its first few years were buried in the natural levee along the river. This was essentially the only place one could excavate deeply enough to conceal a body where the resulting hole would not soon fill with water. Unlike in most places in the world, the riverbanks in southern Louisiana provide the highest ground in the area, because rivers there have deposited silt along their banks over thousands of years, gradually building up land a few feet higher in elevation than the surrounding swamps.

Within five years of its debut, Law's entire economic program, including his efforts to develop Louisiana, collapsed in what was dubbed the "Mississippi bubble." The fall bankrupted most of his investors and drove France into economic chaos. Despite the demise of the misguided economic experiment that had driven the colonization project in Louisiana, the French crown persisted in maintaining the undermanned and undersupplied outpost.

Although the colony received few supplies and suffered from frequent epidemics, it continued to expand. By 1721, the settlement had a convent, at least one store, and a hundred or so houses. A census from November 1721 recorded that the city contained 21 Indian slaves, 172 black slaves, 29 white servants, 38 white children, 65 white women, and 145 white men, for a total of 470 people. Although the area was hit by a hurricane that destroyed many buildings in 1722, the colony survived, and its population expanded further. In 1732, a census reported 893 people living in New Orleans. Despite additional floods, epidemics, and mismanagement, this growth did not abate. By 1756, over four thousand people lived in the city, with the population increasing to about seven thousand by the 1760s.[7]

In addition to burials in or near the levee, it is probable that some early interments were made on land near the Place d'Armes (present-day Jackson Square). In 1800, when Spain was in charge of Louisiana, the acting civil governor stated, "When the colony was established, the dead were being buried where the Cabildo building is today, and due to the increase in population, the cemetery was moved."[8] The Spanish governor went on to say that early on, the cemetery was relocated to a block at the corner of Bienville and Chartres streets, "the second block from the levee"; however, no existing map from the time shows a cemetery in either of those locations. Without archaeological evidence, it is impossible to determine where the earliest cemeteries may have been located.

An 1859 article in New Orleans's *Daily Picayune* alleges that an early cemetery had once existed in an area north of the intersection of Orleans and Rampart streets, just outside the boundaries of the city at that time and roughly where the City Auditorium sits today in Armstrong Park. Its author writes, "It stood where now lies the head of the Old Basin, or Canal Carondelet; and old inhabitants remember the excitement created when the Basin was dug, and coffins were cut by the spades, their dead contents rolling out into the trench."[9] The existence of a cemetery at this location has not been revealed by other sources, although the newspaper account of the discovery of the bodies as being in living memory at the time lends some credence to the story. The same article correctly places New Orleans's first verified cemetery in a block at the intersection of St. Peter's and Burgundy streets. An issue that complicates any search for early cemeteries is that the maps from the time are not particularly reliable. Many of the maps of the city created between 1725 and 1789 show no cemetery at all, while another, dating from 1755 by Thierry, depicts a cemetery occupying a full block several blocks downriver from the Place d'Armes, which is indicated on no other extant map.

Within a few years of the city's founding, its rising population and high mortality rate made the establishment of a designated burial ground necessary. Church burial was limited to a fortunate few, making the creation of a cemetery necessary even for many of the city's well-to-do residents. Despite this need, it appears that French officials took their time to act. The earliest known plan of the city, drawn by Le Blond de La Tour in May 1722, shows no cemetery, nor does de Pauger's plan of 1724.[10]

A 1725 map includes the known cemetery that occupied half of the block bounded by present-day Burgundy Street, St. Peter's Street, and what would eventually become Rampart Street. The map indicates that the cemetery was located within what were probably mostly fictional city fortifications, and the streets surrounding the cemetery on the 1725 map may also have been speculative. A 1731 map depicts the cemetery in roughly the same location, but set in a field clearly outside the city with a diagonal path leading to it from what appears to be a fortifying wall or berm (fig. 1.2). In addition to evidence from these early maps, a document in the Archives nationales in Paris states that "by the year of 1724, the local cemetery was still unfenced, hence unprotected from runaway animals," causing Father Raphael to refuse to permit bodies to continue receiving a Christian burial there. Within a year, workers had surrounded the cemetery with a wooden fence, and burials resumed.[11] The 1731 map shows the cemetery bordered by a dotted line that appears to be a wooden fence.

It is very likely that all burials in the St. Peter's Street Cemetery were below ground. Only ditches and the fence surrounded it until 1743, when a group of volunteer parishioners constructed a five-foot-high brick wall around the entire burial ground, which now occupied the entire block.[12] Records indicate that the cemetery comprised "twelve lots of 70 feet front 120 feet deep."[13]

Apparently, most everyone in the city used the St. Peter's Street Cemetery, which appears not to have been segregated by race. In 1984, archaeologist Shannon Dawdy excavated within the bounds of the former cemetery and found the remains of Africans, Europeans, Native Americans, and individuals of mixed race buried in close proximity. Anthropologist Jordan Krummel reported that the only burial objects recovered from the old cemetery during that excavation were two saint medals, a "jewel-set" rosary, and a glass-encased depiction of the Virgin Mary, all found in the grave of a man who died in his forties and was determined to have been born in the Congo due to the distinctive notching seen on his teeth.[14]

During the time the St. Peter's Street Cemetery was in use, proprietorship of the Louisiana colony transferred from France to Spain. France

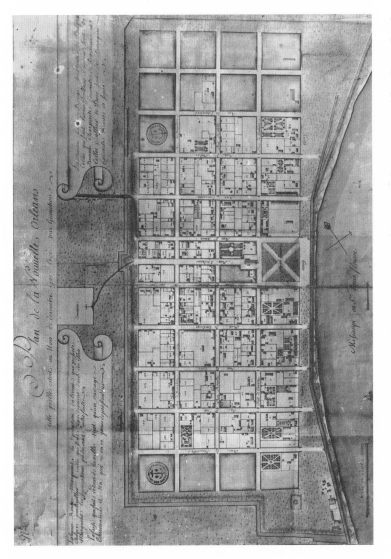

FIG. 1.2. Map of New Orleans, 1731. St. Peter's Street Cemetery can be seen at the top center with a diagonal path leading to it from the city's fortifications. Courtesy The Historic New Orleans Collection, acc. no. 1974.25.18.135.

ceded the territory in 1762, although the Spanish did not take actual possession of New Orleans, its capital, until 1769. The Spanish presence would have a significant influence on how the city's cemeteries developed.

By the 1780s, the St. Peter's Street Cemetery had become overcrowded, and the city had grown up around it. Not only was the burial ground filled with human remains, but body parts of farm animals could also be found there. Archaeologists have discovered pig, goat, and cattle bones in the area once occupied by the cemetery, indicating that it was used as a place for butchers to slaughter animals and dump their remains, an activity that must have contributed to its foul and unhealthy atmosphere.[15] In 1788, the Cabildo, the legislative body that functioned as city council when New Orleans was under Spanish rule, decided that the old burial ground threatened public health and prohibited further burials there. However, in the absence of a viable cemetery to replace it, burials continued at the St. Peter's Street site.[16]

Tragedy struck New Orleans in 1788. A hurricane hit the city, the indigo crop failed, and the previous winter had been unseasonably cold, threatening the food supply. Adding to that, on Good Friday of that year, a fire devastated around 80 percent of the city, including St. Louis Church, every bakery in town, and hundreds of residences.[17] Before much rebuilding could be completed, a flood caused by a breach in the levee submerged the city's three lowest-lying streets for several months.

The crop failures, fire, and flood weakened the population. Although few people died in the Good Friday fire itself, poor living conditions triggered a deadly outbreak of an unknown disease (possibly cholera) late in 1788. The resulting deaths helped spur the Cabildo to create St. Louis Cemetery Number 1, New Orleans's oldest surviving burial ground. Increased pressure on the already overcrowded St. Peter's Street Cemetery had caused it to become ever more unsanitary.[18] Around this time, Antonio de Sedella, a local Capuchin priest, wrote, "Whilst passing the cemetery having myself perceived a fetid smell, I sought information from the neighbors and they affirmed that these foul odors have been very often perceived this year, the consequence is that we are looking for another burial ground where the dead will produce no deleterious effects and the corpses could be buried there inside of eight days."[19] The Cabildo agreed. In October 1788, the governing body declared, "There are a great number of people buried in the cemetery, so many that there is no room for any more; and at the time of digging the graves, the remains of other deceased are found, which not only cause annoyance but it also produces a bad odor, which due to the proximity to the city may be cause for infection with grave danger to the public's health, with several epidemics of diseases which have been experienced throughout the summer, as well as at the present time."[20]

The problem of unhealthy and overcrowded cemeteries was not unique to New Orleans. In the late 1700s and early 1800s, other municipalities founded new cemeteries outside the city for health reasons, especially those cities located in areas particularly prone to disease. A city with an exceptionally tragic history of epidemics, Port-au-Prince in Saint-Domingue (Haiti), established a large cemetery on the edge of town in the early 1790s to accommodate hundreds of English soldiers killed by a yellow fever epidemic during the opening years of the Haitian Revolution. The countless victims of other illnesses followed. Although in ruins today, in the mid-nineteenth century the cemetery had streets lined with trees, aboveground tombs, and mausoleums, making it resemble the "cities of the dead" of New Orleans.[21]

Rampant disease also spurred the creation of an early suburban cemetery on the opposite side of the world, in Calcutta, India, where the English colonists, who were highly susceptible to local epidemics, created the South Park Street Cemetery in 1767. The new cemetery replaced an old, overcrowded church graveyard near the center of Calcutta.[22] The colonists eventually built many ostentatious, freestanding tombs at the South Park Street Cemetery throughout the years it was in use. Tropical and semitropical cities like Port-au-Prince, Calcutta, and New Orleans built early suburban cemeteries sooner than cities in northern regions that were less prone to epidemics.

Although not as susceptible to disease as places in the tropics, cities in Europe, such as Paris and Madrid, also suffered from periodic fires and epidemics, and had high death rates in the late 1700s. Like New Orleans, these cities had old, unsanitary cemeteries overflowing with the dead. In the late eighteenth century, attitudes about burial were beginning to change across Europe and its colonies. In 1785, the imperial Spanish government passed a law requiring municipalities to move cemeteries outside the city limits for health reasons. Although it would take decades for most cities in the Spanish Empire to comply with the law and create new suburban burial sites, the Cabildo asked for, and received, permission from the Spanish king to create a new cemetery only three years after the royal decree.[23]

After St. Louis Cemetery Number 1 (then known as the St. Louis Cemetery) opened in 1789, the old St. Peter's Street Cemetery continued to be used, at least sporadically, for over a decade. In one such instance, a break in the levee caused the new cemetery to flood in the summer of 1797, and the Cabildo begrudgingly allowed burials to resume in the St. Peter's Street Cemetery for a period.[24] Illustrating the slow transition in use between the two burial grounds, an 1801 map created by Carlos Trudeau shows both the "new" cemetery outside the city fortifications and the "ancient" cemetery within them (fig. 1.3).

In 1800, a conflict arose between the city and the Catholic Church as to which entity owned the St. Peter's Cemetery and would have the right to sell the property off as building lots.[25] The Cabildo eventually won, and by 1802 the twelve lots it had platted in the city block the cemetery had once occupied had been sold to developers. At first, development proceeded slowly. A map from 1816 shows only three buildings in the area that had comprised the old cemetery. By the 1820s, however, the cemetery had been completely built over and largely forgotten.[26] Apparently, despite its closure, not all, if any, bodies were transferred from the St. Peter's Cemetery to St. Louis Number 1. Construction workers dug up some twenty-two coffins on the site in 1910, and a century later in 2011, the owner of a house in the block was surprised to discover fifteen eighteenth-century coffins while excavating for a small swimming pool in his garden.[27]

At first, St. Louis Number 1 looked much like its predecessor, except that the newer cemetery was located farther from the natural levee on even lower and wetter ground. St. Louis Number 1 was laid out as a "300 foot Square" area behind the site of the Charity Hospital at the time. A wooden fence enclosed a field of mud punctuated by watery, underground burials. At the time that the new cemetery was in its planning stages, the Cabildo had promised to raise the level of the site by three feet above grade to ensure dry burials and also planned to build a brick wall around it, but did neither, ensuring that gravediggers would routinely strike water close to the surface.[28] Floodwaters covered the entire area some of the time. Twelve years after the cemetery was created, Don Luis de Peñalver y Cárdenas, the diocesan bishop, proposed building an elevated "highway" from the city ramparts to the cemetery so that mourners and the clergy "dressed with their sacred ornaments" would not have to wade through standing water and mud to reach the cemetery, but this plan was never carried out, either.[29]

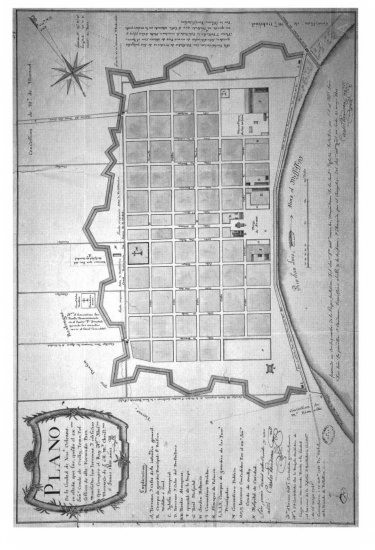

FIG. 1.3. The 1801 map created by Carlos Trudeau showing both the old St. Peter's Street Cemetery (within the street grid) and the new St. Louis Cemetery (outside the fortifications on the upper left) during the decade or so during which they coexisted. A small military cemetery is also depicted at the far right, on the corner of present-day Royal Street and Esplanade Avenue. Courtesy Archivo General de Indias, Madrid, Spain.

The earliest American visitor known to have published an account of a New Orleans cemetery was John Pintard, a New York merchant of French Huguenot descent who visited the city in 1801, two years before the Louisiana Purchase. Pintard was contemplating moving to New Orleans in the hope of taking advantage of the economic opportunities there and rebuilding a fortune he had lost some years earlier in New York. Although Pintard decided to return home and face his creditors, he left a fascinating account of his time in Louisiana, and particularly of his visit to St. Louis Number 1, which was barely twelve years old at the time.

He found a place vastly different from the "city of the dead" experienced by countless tourists since. Pintard entered the cemetery located "without [outside of] the fortifications and near the Baron Carondelet canal" by means of "a broken palisade." Within the "melancholy enclosure," Pintard saw that "not a single grave stone marked the remains of either the noble or the ignoble dead—Over some few, brick arches were turned—at the head of every grave was planted an iron or wooden cross, some of the iron ones were indented with the names of the lifeless tenants."[30] Despite his observation that "water appears on digging in any place one foot below the surface," Pintard in this description implies that most, if not all, of the burials were subterranean with little to mark them. His observations appear to have been accurate. In 1800, the attorney general of the Spanish colony recommended that "graves be very deep," indicating that aboveground interment was not common at that time.[31]

The few "brick arches" Pintard mentions may have been rudimentary aboveground tombs created by building a simple brick vault around a coffin rather than burying it, but even these appear not to have been numerous. The wrought-iron cross marking the Antoine Bonabel grave, which can still be seen in St. Louis Number 1, has a death date of 1800, and therefore must have been present during Pintard's visit (fig. 1.4). That marker has the oldest known death date of any existing grave or tomb in New Orleans. Judging from Pintard's observation, wrought-iron crosses such as this predated significant aboveground tombs in New Orleans cemeteries. At least one tomb, perhaps one of the "brick arches" Pintard describes, may have been present in the cemetery in 1801 when he visited it. In 1920, a reporter for the *Times-Picayune* described seeing the "Wiltz family tomb" marked "1797," and called it the oldest death date in the cemetery at that time.[32]

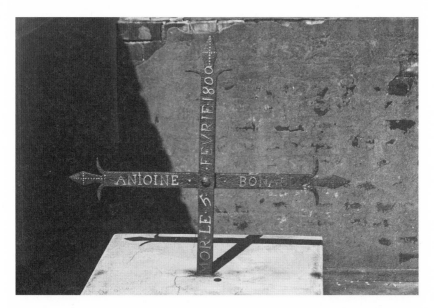

Fɪɢ. 1.4. The wrought-iron cross on the Antoine Bonabel grave, St. Louis Cemetery Number 1, dated 1800, has the oldest known death date of any existing grave marker in New Orleans. Photo by author, 2008.

As with many early visitors to New Orleans, Pintard was disturbed by the prospect of a watery grave. Being in St. Louis Number 1 prompted him to comment, "Give my bones to terra firma I pray—." He also noted that "heretics" (such as himself, as he was a Protestant) were not permitted burial within the barren enclosure of consecrated ground that he so objected to. They were "deposited indiscriminately without the burial place." This situation did not endure for long, however. Only a few years later, in 1804, a graveyard for Protestants was established "adjacent to that of the Catholics."[33]

Having found the waterlogged cemetery repugnant, Pintard adds, "It is of little consequence whether one's carcase [*sic*] is given prey to crayfish on land—or the catfish of the Mississippi . . . a body is speedily transmitigated in crayfish or catfish—dressed by a French cook & feasted upon by a greasy monk—a fair lady—a petit maitre or a savage who in their turn supply some future banquet—." Pintard's thoughts on mortality and a strange form of cannibalism while standing in St. Louis Number 1 were but the first recorded of many similar observations. The fact that St. Louis Number 1 was established at a lower elevation farther from the river and closer to the water table and crawfish habitat than the St. Peter's Street Cemetery probably accelerated the switch to aboveground burial that took place in New Orleans in the first years of the nineteenth century.

If we believe Pintard, few aboveground burials existed in St. Louis Number 1 in 1801. However, by the time English-American architect Benjamin Henry Latrobe visited the cemetery in 1818, it had numerous, albeit simple, aboveground tombs made of brick "plaistered [*sic*] over, so as to have a very solid and permanent appearance."[34] Buttressing Latrobe's observations, New Orleans City Council session notes indicate that tomb building was common by 1816. When the council had to create a temporary cemetery on higher ground than St. Louis Number 1 due to a flood, it mandated that any bodies buried at the new location would have to be moved to the St. Louis Cemetery after the floodwaters receded and that "no tombs of any kind shall be placed" in the temporary burial ground.[35]

Tomb building had been underway since at least 1804. A transcript of the New Orleans City Council meeting on December 8, 1804, records a complaint by an Anthony Orso who was "intending to erect a tomb to the memory of his late father" in the cemetery.[36] Orso was unhappy that the church had charged him a fee of $100 (approximately $1,500 in 2016 dollars) to allow his project to go forward. The city council concluded that the church had the right to exact the tax on the tomb and that "Mr. Orso must comply with the existing custom."[37] This is likely the first extant public record of anyone building a tomb in New Orleans, and the fact that Orso was surprised enough at the fee to bring it to the city council indicates that few people had endeavored to build significant tombs prior to this time.

Another factor that helped spur tomb building was the recurring prohibitions against burial of clergy and high-status individuals within St. Louis Church, which was elevated to the status of a cathedral in 1794. The government in New Orleans attempted to prevent burial in the cathedral in 1794, 1803, and again in 1804, but interments continued there until at least 1805.[38] By the first decade of the nineteenth century, city records show that the practice was increasingly frowned upon, giving the elite no alternative except burial in the soggy ground or entombment within the cemetery.

It took over a decade to finally enforce prohibitions against interment in St. Louis Cathedral, because the custom of burying in church buildings was deeply ingrained in Catholic Church tradition and in the cultures of many of the peoples that had settled in the city. In early Christian times (AD 380–600) freestanding tombs, similar in design to those constructed by the pre-Christian Romans, were still being built in most parts of Europe. Higher-status Christians were either interred in tombs in suburban and rural cemeteries like their pagan forebears or were buried in vast underground catacombs.[39] After AD 380, however, the ancient cemeteries and catacombs were gradually abandoned, and new burial areas sprang up around the graves of known Christian martyrs and saints. Many early churches occupied the sites of saintly graves, and Christians desired to be laid to rest as close to a local saint's bones as possible, as they believed this would bring their souls closer to God and heaven.

By the beginning of the Middle Ages (c. AD 600), the construction of freestanding tombs had ceased entirely except for the resting places of some members of the high nobility, kings, and popes, and most of these were either next to or inside churches.[40] For many at this time, ornate tombs had become associated with worldliness and vanity. Many of the upper class chose to be buried under the floor in a church building itself, as they would be in St. Louis Church early in New Orleans's history, and likewise in churches and cathedrals all over Europe and the Americas. Over time, the floors and walls of Catholic and even many Protestant churches became covered with grave markers, and tombs buttressed their walls both inside and out. The suburban cemetery was not resurrected until the late 1700s, with New Orleans helping to pioneer its new creation.

Many authors and tour guides attribute the development of aboveground burial in New Orleans solely to the area's high water table. Supporting this notion, countless observers have made note of flooded graves ever since Pintard's visit in 1801. Groundwater was certainly a major factor; however, the fact that for the first eighty-five years of the city's existence most, if not all, burial in the city was subterranean indicates that other reasons exist.

One explanation for the early practice of burial in New Orleans is that digging graves is less expensive than tomb construction. Few in the city could afford to build tombs in the 1700s, as most people were simply struggling to survive. Those who could have done so were usually buried in the church. However, once a larger segment of the city's population began to enjoy greater economic security by the end of the 1700s, aboveground burial in New Orleans became the norm, not purely out of necessity, but because in the cultures of the peoples that had established the city, tombs had long functioned as status symbols.

France and Spain, the two colonial powers that dominated New Orleans's early history, were both Catholic countries that practiced aboveground interment. Although people came to New Orleans from many other parts of the world—particularly Africa, the Caribbean, and later Ireland and Italy—and Native Americans had a significant presence in the city in the 1700s and early 1800s, the Catholic Church controlled burial practices well into the nineteenth century. The Church repressed the burial traditions of some of the peoples that resided in Louisiana, particularly those of African origin. Although West Africans arrived in New Orleans as slaves at least as early as 1719, their traditional burial practices had little effect on the form New Orleans cemeteries would take. African Americans would, however, influence the ways in which New Orleans cemeteries have been viewed and used throughout their history.[41]

In a departure from other parts of the Americas, in Louisiana under the French and Spanish, enslaved African Americans and even free blacks were not allowed to bury their loved ones without strict Church oversight. Article XI of the Black Code (*Code Noir*) enacted in March 1724 by the French authorities required slave masters to bury their Christian slaves in consecrated ground, and Article II of the *Code Noir* required that all slaves be instructed and baptized in the Catholic Church, causing the vast majority of burials of African Americans to be overseen by Church authorities.[42]

The Spanish colonial rulers were even more determined than the French to Christianize slaves.[43] This allowed few burial customs brought from Africa to survive, except for a number of funeral customs which were to influence New Orleans funerals throughout the city's history. The Church made sure that when the authorities caught anyone performing unlawful burials, the body would be disinterred and reburied in consecrated ground with Catholic rites.[44] The Church policy appears to have been effective. Thirteen African American skeletons buried between ca. 1724 and 1810 in the St. Peter's Street Cemetery and excavated in the 1980s showed no evidence of African burial practices at all.[45] Church oversight also left little opportunity for early African-influenced grave design in Louisiana. Later on, as people from the Caribbean, both white and black, immigrated into New Orleans, especially during and after the Haitian revolution (1791–1804), a number

Fig. 1.5. Engraving depicting the Cemetery of the Holy Innocents in Paris, around the year 1550, by Theodor J. H. Hoffbauer. Bones lay scattered all over the ground, and the charnel houses to the left were piled high with human remains.

of African and Caribbean burial rites, especially those related to Voodoo, were indeed imported and practiced (see chapter 5).

Although controlled by Spain after 1769 and by the United States after 1803, New Orleans, especially Catholic New Orleans, had close ties with France. Significant parallels exist between the development of cemeteries in France and those in New Orleans. Paris went through a transition from relying on an overcrowded, unsanitary urban cemetery to the creation of cemeteries outside the city limits at roughly the same time as New Orleans, although on a far grander scale.

Until the first decade of the nineteenth century, most of the dead in Paris were deposited at the Cemetery of the Holy Innocents, an urban burial ground that had been in use since at least 1186 (fig. 1.5). The crowded Parisian cemetery had few individually marked graves and, in some ways was a more urban, vastly larger version of the St. Louis Cemetery Pintard described in 1801 and the St. Peter's Street Cemetery before it. Like the earliest burial grounds of New Orleans, the Cemetery of the Holy Innocents was crowded and dirty. Bodies were commonly piled up as they awaited burial, and they often ended up occupying mass graves.

Houses surrounded the cemetery, and its neighbors used the graveyard as a dumping ground for garbage and human waste. This made it
insufferably foul, even to observers at the time who were accustomed to
strong smells in cities because of the constant presence of organic waste
of all kinds festering in their streets.[46] Noxious vapors from the cemetery
sometimes overcame people living nearby. In 1780, a vile gas emanating
from a mass grave in the Cemetery of the Holy Innocents in which sixteen hundred bodies had recently been placed began venting into the base-
ments of houses surrounding it, making a number of people deathly ill.
Shortly thereafter, city authorities concluded that the cemetery needed to
be closed.[47]

In 1765, the city of Paris had passed an ordinance requiring that all
burial grounds be moved outside the city, but little came of it. The king
issued a royal decree that covered the entire nation in 1776; however, im-
plementation of such laws was still not forthcoming, and burial in many
existing urban graveyards and inside churches continued until Emperor
Napoleon Bonaparte finally enforced existing law and required the termi-
nation of intramural burials in 1804. Like the St. Peter's Street Cemetery in
New Orleans, many old urban cemeteries in France and Spain were closed
and built over around this time. Closed in 1786, the Cemetery of the Holy
Innocents became the site of an urban market. The bones of the millions of
people interred there and in other urban graveyards in Paris were removed
and rehoused collectively and anonymously in the Paris catacombs.[48] In
Pintard's time, the barren quality of the St. Louis Cemetery was actually
the norm in many parts of Europe, particularly in countries bordering the
Mediterranean, but that was changing.

The first graves in the large, sanitary suburban cemeteries Napoleon
created in Paris starting in 1804 were mostly underground burials marked
with crosses or simple headstones; however, in the decades that followed,
Parisian families built their cemeteries over with vast neighborhoods of
stunning architectural monuments. The most significant of these new cemeteries, Le Père Lachaise, would influence the evolution of New Orleans
cemeteries in the 1830s and throughout the rest of the nineteenth century.

At the time the Paris suburban cemeteries were being created and developed, the neoclassical style, based on Greek, Roman, and Renaissance
architecture, had dominated art and design in Europe for several decades.
This formal, orderly system of architectural design and decoration was

the product of an eighteenth-century fascination with ancient Greek and Roman art and architecture. The explosion of interest in classical design stemmed, in part, from the discovery and initial excavations of the ancient Roman city of Herculaneum in 1738 and its neighboring city of Pompeii in 1748. In AD 79, an eruption of Mount Vesuvius had buried the two cities in volcanic ash, causing them to be abandoned and forgotten. Although ash, heat, and gases badly damaged both cities, the eruption preserved what was left under protective layers of ash and pumice. Scholarly books about excavations at the two cities—such as the nine illustrated volumes of *Le Antichità di Ercolano* (*Antiquities of Herculaneum*) assembled by the Accademia Ercolanese (between 1757 and 1792), which were translated and republished in English and French; and the four volumes of *The Antiquities of Athens*, by James Stuart and Nicholas Revett (1762)—captured the interest of the intellectual elite of Europe, including many architects.[49] As the neoclassical period took hold, architects and tomb designers also looked to earlier works on classical architecture, such as *De Architectura* (published in English as *Ten Books on Architecture*) by the ancient Roman architect Vitruvius Pollio, written around 15 BC, and *I quattro libri dell'architettura* (*Four Books of Architecture*) by the late Italian Renaissance architect Andrea Palladio, published in 1570.

The etchings of Giovanni Battista Piranesi (1720–1778) also provided inspiration. A Venetian artist, Piranesi moved to Rome and created prints of its ancient ruins and monuments, which he sold. His depictions were often romantic fantasies, the product of the artist's rich imagination as much as accurate renditions of the ruins themselves. Piranesi, who considered himself an architect as much as an artist, also drew up original architectural fantasies based on the language of classical architecture, including his imaginative (and extraordinarily inaccurate) depiction of the ancient Roman necropolis along the Appian Way (fig. 1.6).

Piranesi's prints were widely distributed as young, affluent members of the upper and middle classes from Continental Europe, Great Britain, and the Western Hemisphere took "Grand Tours" of Italy, where they would buy souvenirs, such as reproductions of classical sculptures and prints by Piranesi and other Italian artists. Some of these tourists examined and recorded images directly from ancient Roman ruins, and many would go on to finance, design, and construct buildings inspired by the images and memories they had collected in Italy and other parts of southern Europe

FIG. 1.6. *Appian Way*, etching by Piranesi and frontispiece for *Le antichità Romane*, vol. II (1784). Fantasies such as this would inspire nineteenth-century tomb designers.

after they returned home. This resulted in the construction of neoclassical buildings and tombs throughout Western Europe and the Americas.

Images of classical architecture such as Piranesi's grand and creative conceptions inspired Western European architects to experiment with ancient forms and motifs. Two significant eighteenth-century French architects, Claude-Nicolas Ledoux (1736–1806) and Etienne-Louis Boullée (1728–1799), took inspiration from Piranesi when creating their bold neoclassical designs. Ledoux and especially Boullée were interested in designing tombs and memorial structures, because these could be more easily adapted to their inventive, monumental style than could most functional buildings. The two architects omitted much of the customary classical ornament and emphasized the basic architectural forms and proportions of classical architecture, often reducing the structures they designed to grand and austere compositions of cubes, spheres, cones, cylinders, barrel vaults, and columns. The work of Ledoux and Boullée had a significant impact on the funerary design of the nineteenth century, particularly in France and, by extension, New Orleans. As cemeteries developed during the first two decades of the 1800s, the neoclassical monument or tomb became the norm for the affluent throughout the Western world.

FIG. 1.7. Woman in mourning placing a wreath on her husband's neoclassical memorial. From J. J. Chalon, *Twenty-four Subjects Exhibiting the Costume of Paris: The Incidents Taken from Nature* (London: Rodwell and Martin, 1822).

Napoleon, who saw his empire as a French revival of the ancient Roman Empire, encouraged neoclassical design in everything: gardens, architecture, interiors, furniture, and tombs (fig. 1.7). Many of the monuments built in the new cemeteries around Paris therefore emulated ancient Roman precedents. The idea of a suburban cemetery itself had an ancient Roman precedent. Early in their history, the Romans had outlawed burial within cities for health reasons, and the empire continued to enforce the policy throughout its existence for everyone but a select few in the elite. As a result, necropolises sprang up along the highways outside Roman cities and towns. Ruins of these were observed in the eighteenth and nineteenth centuries.[50] Even though most areas of Italy had no concerns about high

FIG. 1.8. Tombs in Pompeii, dating from the first century AD. Photo by author, 2012.

water tables, the Romans chose to build aboveground tombs and mausoleums to house the ashes or bodies of their deceased loved ones.

To the ancient Romans, a person's afterlife began in the tomb. They believed that if funerary rights, including cremation or burial, were not done correctly, the dead would haunt the living. To ensure the dead made their way safely to the underworld and remained there, Romans made honors to the deceased on a regular basis in the years and decades following their deaths. The ancient Roman tomb acted as the point of contact between the living and the dead. Roman tombs functioned as places of prayer and memory. Because of their religious purpose, the tombs themselves often mimicked temple architecture and contained shrines and altars. A similar attitude toward the role of tombs in the fate of the spirits of the dead would eventually be reflected in New Orleans cemeteries (figs. 1.8, 1.9).

In the Roman tradition, surviving relatives and friends prayed and left food and drink at tombs, especially on Feralia, which took place on February 21. Families held banquets at tombs after a funeral and on death anniversaries and on a number of holidays. During the Feast of the Roses in May, survivors decorated family tombs with flowers.[51] All Saints' Day

FIG. 1.9. Nineteenth-century tombs in St. Louis Cemetery Number 2. Photo by author, 2013.

celebrations on November 1—when New Orleanians, like others in southern Louisiana, have traditionally visited the tombs of their ancestors, left flowers, and sometimes served food and drink there—reflect these ancient practices (see chapter 5).

Like many ancient Roman tombs, the design of some nineteenth-century tombs in Europe, Latin America, and New Orleans included altars on their facades or within their interiors. An 1853 description of a fictional scene at a New Orleans tomb illustrates this: "'What is he doing?' we whispered. . . . 'Renewing the chaplets of flowers, with which he is wont to deck his wife's tomb.' . . . 'He has done this every Sunday evening for twenty years. His wife was never interred beneath the soil. . . . She reposes in a mausoleum first erected over her remains. If you noticed, there is a small recess or chamber in the sepulchral tenement. . . . The chamber is furnished with an altar, a crucifix, images and vases, and there are two chairs for the bereaved.'"[52]

Unlike most architectural monuments in ancient Rome, such as temples and civic buildings, tombs there were usually not designed by architects, but stood as vernacular and vague interpretations of classical architecture. Similarly, tombs in New Orleans cemeteries were also mostly

FIG. 1.10. Pedestal tomb, ca. 1835, in St. Louis Cemetery Number 2. Photo by author, 2013.

informal, vernacular structures, especially before the arrival of the French architect Jacques Nicolas Bussière de Pouilly in the 1830s. Benjamin Latrobe noted the vernacular tombs in St. Louis Number 1 that he saw in 1818 as "crowded close together" and made of brick "much larger than necessary to enclose a single coffin."[53] The tombs Latrobe depicted in his sketchbook rested on a pedestal to elevate them above the ground, a quality they shared with many ancient Roman temples and tombs (figs. 1.10, 1.11). Roman tombs came in a number of distinct forms, including towers, pyramids, tumuli (earth-sheltered, cone-shaped graves), cylinders, rectangular temples, circular temples, marble benches, freestanding sarcophagi, and columns, all of which would eventually be imitated in New Orleans's cemeteries in some form or another (see Appendix A).

While the rich of ancient Rome usually built aboveground family tombs, from the time of Augustus (27 BC–AD 14), the remains of many working-class citizens ended up in unsavory suburban crematoria called "the Kitchens." To avoid being disposed of in such places, working-class

Fɪɢ. 1.11. Tomb in Pompeii, first century AD. Photo by author, 2012.

Romans formed fraternal societies that built communal mausoleums called *columbaria* (Latin for "dovecote"), which ensured a proper burial or site for cremated ashes for their members (fig. 1.12). In the nineteenth and early twentieth centuries, benevolent societies in New Orleans practiced a strikingly similar tradition of constructing communal society tombs to house the remains of their members in a respectful manner (see chap. 4).

Although many columbaria were subterranean or built into the sides of hills, and usually each ovenlike niche held the ashes of a person rather than his or her body, the columbaria resemble the oven tombs that have existed in New Orleans cemeteries since at least 1818 (figs. 1.13, 1.14).[54] When the

FIG. 1.12. Piranesi etching from *The Roman Antiquities*, vol. 2, Plate XVI (1756), inscriptions and fragments of the burial chambers of the Family Arrunzia.

early Church forbade cremation, the niches became large enough to hold a coffin.

By the time Benjamin Latrobe visited St. Louis Cemetery Number 1 in 1818, the people of New Orleans had begun to view burial in a hole filled with water as repugnant. When he visited the Protestant area of the cemetery that had been created in 1804, Latrobe observed "tombs of much the same construction [as in the Catholic section]," but he also saw "two or three graves opened & expecting their tenants: 8 or 9 inches below the surface they were filled with water & were not three feet deep." Like Pintard before him, he could not help but notice that "the ground was everywhere perforated by the crawfish—the amphibious lobster. . . . I have, indeed, seen them in their usual attitude of defiance in the gutters of the streets." He then goes on to propose cremation as a way of avoiding the burial of bodies "as food for worms & crawfish"—worms if the body were placed in an aboveground tomb, crawfish if buried in the ground.[55]

As the population of New Orleans grew, a relatively inexpensive yet respectable and dry means of putting to rest large numbers of people had to be found. The answer was not difficult to discover: the Spanish had ruled

FIG. 1.13. Ancient Roman columbaria in Ostia Antiqua, Italy, near Rome. Photo by author, 2012.

FIG. 1.14. Oven wall vaults, 1830, in St. Louis Cemetery Number 2. Photo by author, 2013.

Louisiana for three decades, and Spain had a long tradition of large-scale aboveground burial. Spain was a Roman province for hundreds of years, and ancient Roman burial traditions formed the basis of Spanish burial practices and tomb design. The oven tombs, also known as *fours* ("ovens" in French), that appeared in St. Louis Number 1 sometime between 1801 and 1818 when Latrobe described them are based on a Spanish adaptation of the ancient Roman columbaria. These wall tombs follow a traditional Spanish burial custom that existed in Spain at the time it ruled Louisiana.[56]

Recalling her tour of Spain in 1899, author Katherine Bates wrote: "Very strange is the look of a Spanish cemetery, with its ranges of high, deep walls, wherein the coffins are thrust end-wise, each above each, to the altitude of perhaps a dozen layers. These cells are sometimes purchased outright, sometimes rented for ten years, or five, or one. When the friends of the quiet tenant pay his dues no longer, forth he goes to the general ditch, *osario común*, and leaves his room for another. Such wall graves are characteristically Spanish, this mode of burial in the Peninsula being of long antiquity."[57]

Today, historic cemeteries with massive walls of oven and wall tombs can be found in many Spanish cities, such as San Isidro Cemetery in Madrid, opened in 1811 (fig. 1.15); Granada Municipal Cemetery in Granada, opened in 1805; and the old cemetery at Comillas, Spain, built into the ruins of a medieval church overlooking the Bay of Biscay sometime after 1648 (fig. 1.16).[58]

Latrobe provided the first surviving description of the oven tombs of New Orleans: "In one corner of the Catholic burying ground are two sets of Catacombs, of three stories each, roughly built, & occupying much more room than necessary. Many of the Catacombs were occupied, but not in regular succession."[59] Edward Henry Durell (1810–1887), a Harvard-trained lawyer and native of New Hampshire who visited St. Louis Number 1 in the early 1840s after moving to New Orleans, described the oven tombs more succinctly: "Each [cemetery] is enclosed with a brick wall of arched cavities or ovens . . . made just large enough to admit a single coffin, and raised tier upon tier to a height of about twelve feet, with a thickness of ten" (fig. 1.17).[60]

Observers from the East like Durell were accustomed to well-defined grave plots with clearly marked, individual gravestones. Many Anglo tourists found it strange that so many of the oven vaults were sealed yet unmarked. One such writer commented, "Hundreds of them . . . have no

FIG. 1.15. Oven vaults in San Isidro Cemetery, Madrid. Photo by author, 2014.

FIG. 1.16. Oven tombs in the old cemetery at Comillas in northern Spain. Photo by author, 2014.

FIG. 1.17. Oven tombs in St. Louis Cemetery Number 1. Over the past two centuries, the structure has been significantly altered and has also sunken into the ground, concealing most of the first tier of vaults. Photo by author, 2013.

names at all on them, or only scrawl, made with a stick or some rude instrument in the fresh mortar."[61] Another visitor noted, "The only space for an epitaph is about two feet square. . . . [Some] were walled up with brick, and there was nothing to tell who moldered within."[62] In an 1833 article in the *Louisiana Courier,* a reporter provides a somber impression of the *fours* in St. Louis Number 1: "The doors of these ovens were filled with bricks and plastered over. On some of them there were inscriptions, on marble perhaps. Many of these ovens were open mouthed—warning visitors of their fate, almost as it were, inviting them to enter."[63] Another writer expressed a similar sentiment in 1864: "As you enter these cemeteries, along the outer wall seem arranged large brick ovens, four ranges high, in which is deposited a coffin. . . . At first sight these graves made me shudder as many of these burial ovens have become dilapidated, and you feel as if you were among the bones of the dead."[64] Commenting on a posthumous anonymity that bothered tourists but that people in New Orleans seemed to find acceptable, a visitor to the Protestant Girod Street Cemetery in 1845 observed, "In one of the side walls, is a tomb stone of plain white marble, with only the words 'My Husband!' engraved upon it."[65]

Oven-style tombs can be found in former Spanish colonies other than Louisiana—Cuba, for example. Until the 1959 Cuban Revolution and the subsequent US trade embargo on Cuba, New Orleans and Havana enjoyed a thriving trade relationship that linked the two cities economically and culturally for nearly two centuries.[66] Havana's early cemeteries developed at about the same time and in a similar manner as cemeteries in New Orleans.

As in New Orleans, the moneyed citizens of Havana clung to the tradition of church burials into the early nineteenth century, and it was not until 1806 that Bishop Juan de Espada (1756–1832) opened Havana's first suburban cemetery, originally known as the General Cemetery and later as the Espada Cemetery. Espada, a champion of public works projects such as draining swamps and building cemeteries, created the cemetery primarily to promote public health. He advocated going back to ancient Roman and early Christian methods of burial in place of interment in churches, because he, like many of his educated contemporaries, believed the practice helped spread disease.[67]

Favoring the neoclassical style, Espada hired a formally trained French neoclassical architect named Etienne Sulpice Hallet (1760–1825) to design the new cemetery for the people of Havana, both rich and poor, located a mile outside the city. Hallet had emigrated from France to the United States, where he supervised construction work on the US Capitol; however, President Washington had dismissed him for making unauthorized changes to the building's design and not consulting with his superiors. Hallet's elegant Havana cemetery enclosed a large, rectangular space with thick walls accessed through a neoclassical gateway.[68]

Espada Cemetery's graves, some of which had operable marble lids, were often reused, as vaults are in New Orleans, but the bones of former occupants were not concealed in a space beneath the tomb as they usually are in the Crescent City. In 1843, a reporter for the *Daily Picayune* described the Espada Cemetery: "In each of the four corners there is raised a pyramid-like pile of human bones bleached to snowy whiteness, and the sun shining through the eyeless sockets of fleshless skulls. To a person of nervous temperament the sight must not be very pleasing."[69]

Although it had underground burials at first, the Espada Cemetery was expanded in 1845, at which time thousands of oven tombs, very similar to those of New Orleans, were added to accommodate the increasing number of dead in the growing city.[70] A visitor described the cemetery around 1900, noting that the inside "consists of tiers of masonry niches for the reception of the bodies. There are about 12,000 of these compartments, but this figure by no means represents the number of interments here, since it was the custom to rent the tombs for a term of years, and at the expiration of the time the bones were removed and thrown into the *osario* or bone pit."[71] The Espada Cemetery was abandoned around 1870 and demolished in 1901. It was replaced by the Cristobal Colon Cemetery, which, like its predecessor, has a lot in common with the cemeteries of New Orleans. The Cristobal Colon Cemetery particularly resembles Cypress Grove and the Metairie Cemetery (see chapters 2 and 6).

Espada and his associates planned and constructed Havana's Espada Cemetery at about the time St. Louis Number 1 was being transformed from a field of dirt and crosses into a burgeoning necropolis of tombs. Because of the close connection between Havana and New Orleans, and the Spanish tradition of building oven-style graves, the cemeteries of New Orleans and those of Cuba and other former Spanish Caribbean colonies share many features. The practice of aboveground burial is common throughout the Caribbean and Central and South America, in both wet and dry regions. For instance, the General Cemetery established in 1821 in Santiago, Chile, contains many aboveground wall and family tombs, and La Recoleta Cemetery, opened in 1822 in Buenos Aires, Argentina, has many tombs that are nearly indistinguishable from those in New Orleans cemeteries arrayed along its sloping avenues (fig. 1.18).

Construction of both oven and family tombs in St. Louis Number 1 proliferated in the 1820s. In 1826, a tourist from Massachusetts named Timothy Flint published a chronicle of his visit to St. Louis Number 1. He writes: "The old Catholic cemetery is completely covered either with graves or monuments. The monuments are uniformly either of white marble, or plaster, or painted white, and by the brilliant moonlight evenings of this mild climate, this city of the dead . . . makes an impressive appearance."[72]

In 1817, seven or so years before Flint's visit, the population of New Orleans had reached about thirty-three thousand, a significant increase from a mere six thousand in 1803. This growth was mainly due to an influx

FIG. 1.18. La Recoleta Cemetery, Buenos Aires, Argentina. Photo by Liam Quinn/Flickr.

of free blacks and French colonial whites fleeing the slave insurrection in Saint-Domingue, and of Americans coming to the city after the 1803 Louisiana Purchase. The city's population reached forty-one thousand in 1820, and New Orleans mayor Joseph Roffignac found the city's only cemetery so overcrowded and unsanitary that he forbade burials there in the summer months. Where people were supposed to inter bodies in the summer was not clear, because no alternative burial ground existed. Like others before them, the New Orleans City Council held the belief that harmful "miasmas" emanating from cemeteries spread yellow fever, cholera, and other dreaded diseases. The council voted to establish a new cemetery farther from the city in that same year.

The resulting cemetery, St. Louis Cemetery Number 2, was first proposed in 1819, built on land purchased in 1821, and opened in 1823. Covering more territory, the new cemetery would be the site of many more tombs than St. Louis Number 1. St. Louis Number 2 was laid out in a more formal, classically inspired manner, echoing the design of Havana's Espada Cemetery, with a wide, straight avenue down the center that ran the entire length of the cemetery's four city blocks. Instead of being arranged irregularly along crooked alleys as in St. Louis Number 1, the tombs of St. Louis Number 2 were lined up uniformly along the central street, with other tombs sited in a somewhat less orderly fashion behind them. Originally, the cemetery comprised a single rectangle running from Canal Street all the way to St. Louis Street; however, the cemetery was split into four separate blocks when Iberville, Bienville, and Conti streets were cut through.[73] In 1846, the Archdiocese of New Orleans sold the block closest to Canal Street, which had seen few burials anyway, fearing that close proximity to busy Canal Street would pose a health hazard.

Like St. Louis Number 1, thick walls containing oven vaults surrounded the new cemetery; however, St. Louis Number 2 had a far greater number of them. Also as with St. Louis Number 1, both whites and blacks used the new cemetery, but its final block, between Iberville and Bienville streets, was mostly African American, while the other two sections were predominantly white.[74]

By the 1830s, the tombs in both St. Louis Number 1 and St. Louis Number 2 were becoming more architecturally sophisticated. The Reverend Joseph H. Ingraham visited New Orleans from New York in the mid-1830s and later published his observations about the city and its cemeteries. Describing St. Louis Number 2, he writes: "Many of the tombs were constructed like, and several were, indeed miniature Grecian temples; while others resembled French or Spanish edifices, like those found in 'old Castile.' . . . All were perfectly white, arranged with the most perfect regularity, and distant little more than a foot from each other" (fig. 1.19).[75] When Ingraham subsequently stopped at St. Louis Number 1, the "old Catholic cemetery," the only comment he recorded was that it was "crowded with tombs without displaying the systematic arrangement observed in the one [St. Louis Number 2] I had just left."[76] When discussing St. Louis Number 2, Ingraham diverged from his predecessors when he cited a possible reason for the construction of oven tombs besides the high water table: "By a casual estimate I judged there were about eighteen hundred apertures in this vast pile of tombs. This method . . . might serve as a hint to city land-economists."[77]

Christ Church, which had operated the Protestant section of St. Louis Number 1, opened the Girod Street Cemetery in 1822. The need for a new Protestant cemetery became apparent in 1821, when the city decided to demolish part of the Protestant section of St. Louis Number 1, then the only Protestant burial ground in the city, to make room for a new roadway

FIG. 1.19. Varied nineteenth-century tombs in St. Louis Cemetery Number 2, exhibiting the density that once existed throughout the cemetery. Photo by author, 2014.

(later named Treme Street). The Christ Church congregation took the opportunity to establish a larger place to bury Protestants in New Orleans. It bought land outside town at the edge of the Faubourg St. Mary (now part of the central business district) to create the cemetery, which would not only accommodate members of Christ Church but also allow the dead from any Christian denomination other than Catholicism to be buried there. Catholics soon came to know the Girod Street Cemetery as the Cimetière des Hérétiques (Cemetery of the Heretics).[78]

In addition to pressure caused by road building through St. Louis Number 1, severe yellow fever outbreaks in 1819 and 1822 helped trigger the creation of the Girod Street Cemetery and St. Louis Number 2.[79] In 1819, at the height of what was probably the worst outbreak of yellow fever and perhaps the worst epidemic of any kind the city had yet seen, the New Orleans City Council appointed a committee "to the effect of establishing cemeteries at a greater distance from the City and the Faubourgs [early neighborhoods established outside of what is now the French Quarter] than those existing at present."[80]

The emotional and practical impetus for creating the new cemeteries was obvious. Liliane Crete relates a historical account of the abysmal conditions at St. Louis Number 1 in 1822: "The bodies were hastily trundled off to the cemetery to avoid contagion. At the gates of the cemetery, an incongruously festive atmosphere reigned. Street vendors had collected there to cry their savory wares. Inside the gates the stench was overwhelming, the spectacle horrific. Open graves filled with muddy water were everywhere as were mounds of bones and disorderly heaps of coffins."[81] As a result of these conditions, thousands of oven tombs were built in the Girod Street Cemetery and St. Louis Number 2 in an attempt to provide proper, sanitary burials for victims of epidemics as well as for other deceased members of the city's growing population.

In the 1820s, the names of recent arrivals marked many New Orleans graves, as newcomers seem to have been more susceptible to yellow fever and cholera than natives of the city. Timothy Flint wrote in 1826: "In the Protestant burial grounds I was affected to read great numbers of names of men who died in the prime of life from Boston, Salam [sic] and vicinity. Multitudes of adventurous young men from New England have here found rest, and it is generally recorded that they died 'du fievre jaune' of yellow fever."[82] During a visit to the Girod Street Cemetery in the early 1830s, Reverend Ingraham also identified with his fellow Protestant northerners who had fallen victim to epidemics: "Here molder the remains of thousands, who, leaving their distant homes, buoyant with all hopes and visions of youth, have been suddenly cut down under a foreign sun, and in the springtime of youth. . . . So New Orleans continues, and will long continue to be, the charnel-house of the pride and nobleness of New England."[83]

Like St. Louis Number 1 and St. Louis Number 2, the walls that surrounded the Girod Street Cemetery contained hundreds of oven tombs with family tombs and the larger society tombs built within the area they enclosed. A writer from Philadelphia (C. W. Kenworthy) calling himself "a Physician of New Orleans" described the Girod Street Cemetery in 1854: "The tombs are all built above ground after the usual style of New Orleans cemeteries, chiefly of brick, with ovens or vaults for single coffins or for family use."[84] The writer also states that, like many other New Orleans cemeteries, the Girod Street Cemetery was prone to flooding: "The cemetery has been much flooded in rainy seasons, and the water constantly stands in the open ditches and drains about the grounds, in the driest weather cov-

FIG. 1.20. Vaults in Girod Street Cemetery, 1885. The vaults were lined oppressively along an alley. Many observers described the Girod Street Cemetery as lacking the charm of the early Catholic cemeteries. Illustration from *Souvenir of New Orleans and the Exposition* (New Orleans: L. Schwarz, ca. 1885).

ered with a green slimy matter. . . . The undertakers have frequently floated about the paths of this cemetery in a boat to bury the dead."[85]

Many observers were impressed with the Girod Street Cemetery, but not favorably. In 1833, a mere eleven years after the cemetery had been opened, a reporter for the *Courier* visited and observed: "The tombs are badly covered. The ovens were badly plastered. There is little like neatness, prosperity and even decency. The whole is shameful; and the Americans would not tolerate it if they made this their abiding place and not the place to alight and make money in."[86] A traveler who visited the Protestant cemetery in 1845 described it as being less ostentatious than the Catholic cemeteries: "There is little of the display here that is found in the other grounds. Tombs that, apparently, were commenced with a resolution to show honor to the departed, have been left without a stone to record the name of the neglected tenant" (fig. 1.20).[87]

While the St. Louis cemeteries continued to be in reasonably good repair well into the nineteenth century, the Girod Street Cemetery never received the same level of care. It is likely that, as the *Courier* pointed out in 1833, the Catholic families with deep roots in the city usually had more of a commitment to maintaining tombs for the benefit of their descendants than did many Protestants, who had migrated to the city primarily to find economic opportunities and did not know how long they might remain there.

᠀

Although the cemeteries of New Orleans started out as desolate burial grounds resembling the urban cemeteries of medieval Europe, by 1830 they had evolved into "cities of the dead" rather than into churchyards or urban graveyards with individual tombstones and monuments like cemeteries in most parts of the United States. The most common explanation for the aboveground burials is the city's high water table. Although New Orleanians practiced belowground burials during the city's early years, they did so only out of necessity, as the city was small and not very affluent in the 1700s. Only after the St. Peter's Street Cemetery had closed around 1800, and St. Louis Cemetery Number 1—located farther from the river on soggier soil than its predecessor—became the only available cemetery, did aboveground tombs begin to appear.

This does not mean that the people of New Orleans were particularly attached to subterranean burial. If they had been as dedicated to belowground burials as most other Americans were, they would, as the Cabildo recommended in the late 1780s, have raised the level of St. Louis Number 1 and subsequent cemeteries. Alternatively, they might have built individual graves up. In early years, they rarely did so except in Jewish cemeteries such as the Gates of Mercy Cemetery, which was established in 1828. Despite the high water table, Jewish burial grounds contain no aboveground tombs because Jewish tradition requires in-ground interment. In waterlogged New Orleans, Jews built up the ground around their graves with copings in order to elevate the level of the buried coffins above the water table. Had they had been so motivated, New Orleanians of other faiths could have done likewise.

The eighteenth-century practice of underground burial among New Orleans Catholics was primarily due to a lack of financial resources. Early New Orleanians struggling for survival did not have the luxury of financing or designing the construction of tombs. The few that could afford it were still being interred in the church building. At the time tombs started to appear, the city's economy was expanding. Eli Whitney's invention of the cotton gin and Etienne de Boré's successful effort to granulate sugar from local sugarcane in the 1790s spurred the growth of the slavery-based Louisiana plantation economy, with New Orleans functioning as its primary port and financial hub. The 1803 Louisiana Purchase accelerated this process, creating the wealth required for tomb building, and tombs began to appear around that time.[88]

The Catholic Church also helped shape the famous cemeteries of New Orleans. Catholic cultures in Europe had a long tradition of tomb building by elite families and individuals. In building aboveground tombs, the citizens of New Orleans were perpetuating the methods of interment practiced by their ancestors. In New Orleans, if one could not be buried inside the church, the most prestigious burial was in a tomb located in a cemetery. Tombs functioned not only as dry places to inter the dead, but as indicators of social status that strengthened family and class identities. In the early 1800s, New Orleans's largely French-speaking population began to find inspiration in the fanciful, largely neoclassical tombs of Père Lachaise Cemetery in Paris, a place with dry soil where burials marked by simple gravestones would have sufficed. Instead, French citizens who could afford it chose to build funerary structures, and the people of New Orleans followed suit.

Another factor that shaped the character of New Orleans cemeteries is geography. For most of its history, New Orleans occupied a limited area of dry ground surrounded by swamps and bordered by the river. Until the levees and water pumps of the twentieth century were constructed, buildable land, even buildable land prone to flooding, was at a premium. Exacerbating this, the city experienced explosive growth after the Louisiana Purchase, and the urbanized area kept swallowing up existing cemeteries that had been purposely located outside the city only decades earlier. This transformed them into walled urban refuges for the dead in which reusable ovens and family tombs provided a space-efficient burial option at a time when cremation was forbidden by the Catholic Church and rarely practiced. With their size limited, the historic intramural cemeteries grew dense and urban in nature.

Historically, the cemeteries of New Orleans went through three developmental phases. During the first, the dead were buried below ground in an enclosure at the edge of town. In the second, which started between

1800 and 1810, New Orleanians began constructing simple, vernacular freestanding tombs and walls of oven tombs based on historic Spanish and French precedents. During the third phase, which started in the 1820s, a larger population, greater prosperity, and the arrival of J. N. B. de Pouilly and other professionally trained and cultured immigrants caused the free-standing tombs of the rich to become more substantial, ornate, and neo-classical. At the same time, the many oven tombs in the cemeteries continued to provide a respectable, less costly resting place for those who did not have access to a family tomb. The society tombs, which guaranteed an even more affordable, aboveground burial to the members of the benevolent associations that built them (see chapter 5), emerged during this third phase.

TEMPLES OF LILLIPUT
The Mid-Nineteenth Century

B ecause of the high mortality rate in nineteenth-century America, the
unfortunate presence of death affected every stage of people's lives,
making the creation and maintenance of cemeteries of utmost importance.
The material standard of living of many New Orleanians rose in the middle decades of the 1800s as the economy thrived and the city's population
grew, mainly due to immigration from foreign countries and other parts of
the United States. In this prosperous environment, social prestige became
increasingly associated with the size and design of a family's tomb. For the
rich, a traditional, humble brick-and-stucco sepulcher no longer sufficed.
Many were willing to pay for marble-clad mausoleums and stone grave
markers that were both flamboyant and monumental. A tomb finished in
marble imported from Italy or other distant places expressed a family's
social status because of the material's inherent beauty, its durability compared to stucco, and its high cost. The many substantial family tombs and
society mausoleums being commissioned in New Orleans provided ample
opportunity for the use of fine materials, sophisticated ornament, and a
grand scale. With a greater variety of available materials and increasing
numbers of rich clients, architects and other tomb designers sought out
stylistic prototypes that were more impressive than the traditional tombs
found in the city before the 1830s.

A major innovator of ornate, revivalist tomb design in New Orleans,
the talented J. N. B. de Pouilly (1804–1875) arrived in the city from Paris
in 1833. De Pouilly immigrated from one of the most sophisticated cities in the world to a rough and bustling port city not far from the American frontier. When he disembarked in New Orleans, he found an affluent

segment of the population ready to utilize his knowledge of Parisian architecture. Although New Orleans had been under American control for thirty years at the time he arrived and had been ruled by Spain for nearly forty years before that, many of the city's people still spoke French and had strong cultural ties to France. And many New Orleanians, particularly the French-speaking Creoles who lived mainly in and around the French Quarter, were eager to follow the latest French fashions, at least to a point. Up to this time, most tombs, and most New Orleans architecture as a whole, had been designed in a vernacular mix of styles based loosely on the classical language of architecture filtered through France, Spain, the Caribbean, and other parts of the United States.

De Pouilly had received architectural training in France, although it has not been determined where he studied. It is possible he attended the famous Ecole des Beaux-Arts in Paris, but no record of his ever being a student there has been found.[1] He may have just visited the Ecole and studied at the Ecole Polytechnique or another secondary design school in France. Regardless of where he acquired it, de Pouilly began applying the architectural knowledge he had gained in Europe and demonstrated his talent soon after he arrived in the Crescent City. He drew the plans for many city landmarks, including, most famously, the 1853 expansion and reconstruction of St. Louis Cathedral on Jackson Square. He also designed the grand New Orleans Exchange Hotel (1835; demolished); St. Augustine Church, at Bayou Road and St. Claude Street (1842); and Citizen's Bank, on Toulouse Street (1837; demolished). However, he is best known for his funerary architecture.[2]

The collapse of two of his buildings cut de Pouilly's architectural career short. In 1850, the central tower of St. Louis Cathedral fell during construction, destroying much of the church's roof and walls. Then, in 1854, came the deathblow to de Pouilly's architectural ambitions when part of the Orleans Theatre, which he had renovated in 1845, collapsed, killing several people and injuring about forty others. Although his contractors were probably to blame, de Pouilly would never serve as superintending architect on a nonfunerary project again.[3] Another reason he is not well known for his civic architecture is that, with the obvious exception of St. Louis Cathedral, most of the buildings he designed for the living have been lost, while at least twenty-four examples of his cemetery work have survived.

The funerary architecture de Pouilly brought from France represented a shift from the homespun tomb design New Orleanians were accustomed to. His work, for both the living and the dead, deviated from the strict neoclassicism of the eighteenth and early nineteenth centuries, which was based on rational, Enlightenment concepts. De Pouilly's work gravitated toward the more eclectic midcentury revivalist mode of design, which involved the reinterpretation of a number of diverse historical architectural styles.

As the Romantic movement swept through Europe in the early nineteenth century, its emotional, eclectic sensibilities began to be reflected in architecture. Represented by philosophers such as Jean-Jacques Rousseau and Henry David Thoreau, Romanticism emphasized intuition and human emotions over rational thought, and valued the dramatic beauty of nature over that of orderly human creations. Before the Romantic era, most people saw nature as a dangerous obstacle to human progress to be conquered. Mountains were impediments to agriculture and travel, and ancient ruins were sources of cheap building stone. The Romantics appreciated nature for its own sake and built on the sensibilities of the earlier neoclassicists, such as Piranesi, to value ruins of all sorts as picturesque sources of inspiration. Romantic aesthetics influenced the designs of de Pouilly's tombs, which were more sophisticated and avant-garde than anything that existed in New Orleans cemeteries at the time he arrived.

In Paris, de Pouilly's contemporary architect Henri Labrouste (1801–1875) led a group of architects and architecture students at the Ecole des Beaux-Arts that broke away from traditional neoclassicism, which mostly mimicked the forms, decor, and proportions of ancient Roman and Renaissance architecture with only minor modifications. Labrouste and his colleagues experimented with stylistic innovations based on a wider range of historical influences and also tried new architectural engineering methods, such as expanding the use of cast iron. The resulting "Neo-Grec" architecture emphasized the application of diverse types of architectural decoration to a structure while allowing its materials, method of construction, and functional purpose to determine the basic form, rather than relying on historical precedents to dictate the overall shape a building would take.[4] The use of new building technologies allowed for larger, more durable, and sophisticated structures. New applications of cast iron even extended to the construction of funerary architecture. A number of mid-nineteenth-century tombs in New Orleans were made entirely of cast-iron components manufactured in a factory, assembled onsite, and painted to mimic white marble.

The "picturesque" Neo-Grec style that emerged from the Paris architectural scene was more expressive and fanciful than its neoclassical predecessor. Architects such as de Pouilly took the language of classical architecture (the Greco-Roman orders, arches, temple fronts, domes, and the like) and added new forms and motifs from historical styles and periods other than Greece, Rome, and the Italian Renaissance. De Pouilly and his colleagues used detailed architectural reference books, such as J. N. L. Durand's *Précis des leçons d'architecture données à l'Ecole Polytechnique* (1805) and *Recueil et parallèle des édifices de tout genre, anciens et modernes* (1800), to help inspire their novel architectural compositions.[5]

Because of their mostly symbolic function, these new architectural concepts could be expressed more freely in tomb design than in conventional architecture, where functional considerations and clients with preconceptions and conservative tastes often diluted architectural innovation. The majority of de Pouilly's tombs drew inspiration from various classical forms, such as Roman tombs, sarcophagi, classical temples, and Greco-Roman columns, and also from different sources, such as gothic churches and ancient Egyptian temples. Adding to his visual language, de Pouilly had visited and made detailed drawings of monuments at Père Lachaise Cemetery before coming to New Orleans and found many of the precedents for his tomb designs there.[6]

Père Lachaise was laid out in 1804 on the former estate of the Jesuit priest François de la Chaise, Louis XIV's confessor for whom the cemetery was named. The burial ground first occupied a hilly, forty-two-acre site, which was later enlarged. Architect Alexandre-Théodore Brongniart designed the grounds with curving roads and walks to resemble an aristocratic English garden of the period (fig. 2.1).

As mentioned in the previous chapter, like St. Louis Cemetery Number 1, Père Lachaise saw the construction of few aboveground funerary structures during its first two decades.[7] The site was still in a largely pastoral state in the 1820s when the cemetery helped inspire the creation of the American and English garden cemeteries that would emerge in the 1830s (see chapter 6).[8] However, the rural character of Père Lachaise soon changed as families started building architectural tombs and grave markers there, many of which resembled miniature classical temples or gothic Christian chapels. More and more tombs filled Père Lachaise, eventually giving the cemetery a dense, urban appearance. A visitor wrote of the

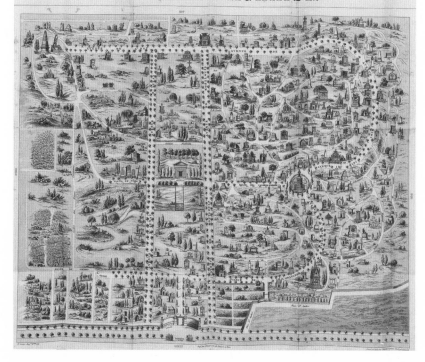

FIG. 2.1. Map of Le Père Lachaise Cemetery, showing its romantic, parklike layout. From M. A. Henry, *Le Père Lachaise historique, monumental et biographique* (Paris: M. A. Henry, 1852).

cemetery in 1836: "Everywhere the tombs are thick, very thick."[9] As Père Lachaise was built up, it came to resemble a hilly version of New Orleans cemeteries (figs. 2.2, 2.3). The dead of the French middle classes were being interred in a more hygienic, respectful, and extravagant manner than ever before. For the first time in history, the bourgeoisie could have the sort of tombs formerly reserved for the nobility.

Although most of its initial occupants were drawn from the middle class, Père Lachaise soon became popular with the rich as well. When Napoleon outlawed burial in churches, he forced the upper class to find alternative places to bury its dead, which spurred the construction of tombs, a process that was happening in New Orleans at the same time. Because of the increasing opulence and expense of the tombs the rich built, architects

FIG. 2.2. Tombs lining a street in Père Lachaise Cemetery. Photo by author, 2013.

FIG. 2.3. Tombs lining a street in St. Louis Cemetery Number 1. Photo by author, 2013.

Fig. 2.4. Burial in Père Lachaise Cemetery. Engraving in Augustus Pugin and Charles Heath, *Paris and Its Environs* (London: Jennings and Chaplin, 1831).

grew interested in designing them, adding to the sophistication, architectural interest, and picturesque quality of Parisian cemeteries (fig. 2.4).

In the first decades of the nineteenth century, French tomb designers had looked to ancient precedents from Greece and Rome when designing funerary architecture, in part because many of the medieval aristocratic tombs and monuments had been destroyed during the French Revolution, depriving them of traditional French architectural precedents to work with. By 1830, the novel concepts of the more eclectic Neo-Grec school began to influence French cemetery architecture. Père Lachaise became an artistic necropolis that recalled Europe's classical roots but also showcased its latest architectural trends, attracting attention and tourists.

Although the tombs of Père Lachaise inspired de Pouilly, the tombs he designed in New Orleans were not identical to them. A major difference is

FIG. 2.5. Nineteenth-century tomblike chapel grave markers in Père Lachaise Cemetery. Photo by author, 2013.

that most French funerary structures had no practical purpose. With some exceptions, the French buried their dead in subterranean vaults located underneath the tomblike structures themselves, which served as elaborate grave markers with diminutive chapels inside usually containing an altar, crosses, candles, and other religious paraphernalia, but no burial vaults. Although the structures in Parisian cemeteries resemble mausoleums at first glance, they are mostly picturesque funerary follies. When de Pouilly and other tomb designers inspired by French cemeteries worked in New Orleans, they had to adapt their designs to include aboveground vaults. This made the New Orleans tombs more substantial than many of their French counterparts (figs. 2.5, 2.6).

In addition, de Pouilly's initial drawings of tombs at Père Lachaise were often more elaborate and stylistically innovative than were his designs as built. This reflected budget constraints, the traditional tastes of many of his clients in New Orleans, and the aesthetics and skills of local tomb builders. Despite the differences, it is not difficult to recognize the drawings in his sketchbook that formed the basis for the designs of a number of his surviving tombs.

FIG. 2.6. Nineteenth-century tombs in St. Louis Cemetery Number 3. Photo by author, 2013.

A further departure was in the choice of building material. The French used stone to construct their tombs, but because of the rarity of suitable building stone in Louisiana and on the Gulf Coast as a whole, New Orleanians usually constructed their tombs out of brick. Most tombs built before 1850 were either brick forms covered with stucco or, in more elaborate examples, brick structures sheathed in marble slabs that gave the illusion that the tomb was constructed completely of stone. A good number of early tombs had marble only on their front facades. The *Louisiana Courier* describes the brick tombs in St. Louis Number 1 as they appeared in 1833: "The tombs are chiefly or all made of brick, some plastered over, others not" (fig. 2.7).[10] By the mid-1830s, stone-clad tombs began to appear.

Another significant contrast is that tombs in Père Lachaise were meant to provide a permanent resting place for their inhabitants, whereas New Orleans tombs were reused on a regular basis—a practice adopted from Spain, the Caribbean, and medieval France. Undertakers could add new bodies to occupied vaults so long as a minimum of a year and a day had passed since the previous interment in a particular vault. During the process of a new burial, any remnants of a coffin from the previous burial were

FAMILY TOMB, BUILT IN 1811.

FIG. 2.7. Old brick tombs built in 1811, St. Louis Cemetery Number 1. Drawing from C. W. Kenworthy, *History of the Yellow Fever in New Orleans, during the Summer of 1853* . . . (Philadelphia and St. Louis: C. W. Kenworthy, 1854). Courtesy Louisiana Research Collection, Tulane University.

removed and burned, or otherwise disposed of. The bones of the former resident were pushed to the back of the vault itself in the case of oven vaults and most society tombs, or were pushed down a shaft into a dedicated space (called a *caveau*) located beneath the tomb in most family tombs. Tombs were reused quite frequently, a fact that unsettled many tourists from northern Europe and areas of the United States outside of southern Louisiana. In New Orleans, cemetery design and usage rendered the body's impermanence an obvious fact, a reality most Victorians were trying to make less apparent in their cemeteries.

De Pouilly and his contemporaries transformed parts of the cemeteries of New Orleans, especially St. Louis Number 1 and Section Two of St. Louis Number 2, from cities of brick and stucco to ones of marble and cast iron. De Pouilly applied his knowledge of Neo-Grec and other revival styles to many prominent New Orleans mausoleums. Judging from the innovative qualities of the 130 tomb designs dated from 1843 to 1874 included in a surviving sketchbook of over three hundred architectural drawings he created and labeled "3 Nouvelle Orléans," de Pouilly was a prolific and inventive designer. After the mid-1850s, as his architectural career waned, he continued to design tombs, including his own resting place, which he completed a year or so before his death.

The revival styles that characterized de Pouilly's work in New Orleans cemeteries came from a variety of influences in addition to those of Henri Labrouste and the Ecole des Beaux-Arts. In the mid-nineteenth century, three major revival styles—Greek revival (ca. 1820–60), gothic revival (ca. 1830–80), and Egyptian revival (ca. 1820–50)—were commonly used to design tombs in New Orleans and throughout the United States. De Pouilly employed all three of these styles liberally in his cemetery work.

The temples of the ancient Greeks, such as the Doric Parthenon and the Ionic Temple of Athena Nike in Athens, inspired enthusiasts of the Greek revival style. Although earlier architects like Benjamin Latrobe and Thomas Jefferson had included Greek elements in many of their neoclassical buildings, the Greek revival style did not truly emerge until the 1820s.[11] One impetus for its popularity, the Greek war for independence against the Ottoman Empire (1822–30), created sympathy for the Greek cause in the West, especially in the United States, which identified the Greek revolution with its own fight for independence. Since ancient Greece was the birthplace of democracy, Americans saw Greece as one of the forebears of the American form of government. After the Greeks finally won their struggle in 1832, it became easier for people from the West to visit and record ancient Greek monuments, inspiring additional interest in this ancient architecture.

Greek revival emphasizes the aesthetics and forms of ancient Greek architecture over those of the Romans. Because Greek houses and temples were nearly always rectangular in plan, most Greek revival buildings and tombs have rectangular footprints. Because the Greeks rarely used the arch, Greek revival buildings and tombs almost never include them. Although they can appear quite similar, Greek revival buildings rarely possess the architectural flourishes commonly found in eighteenth- and early nineteenth-century neoclassical buildings, such as fanlights, curved porches, balustrades, and broken pediments. When the style first became popular, most historians believed Greek temples had originally been left white rather than painted in a variety of colors as they actually were. Greek revival structures were therefore usually finished in plain white or light gray stone, white painted stucco or wood, or brick with white trim.

FIG. 2.8. The Cambon (*left*, 1875) and Berens-DeBouchel (*right*, 1871) tombs in St. Louis Cemetery Number 3, modeled after Greek temples and constructed by tomb builder Florville Foy. A marble exterior and decorative motifs such as fluted columns and an anthemion located above the pediment give these tombs the architectural distinction connoting social status that their owners desired to express. Photo by author, 2013.

With its common use of stone facades, thick columns, small windows, and simple geometry, the style was well suited to tomb design. Greek revival tombs were often more strictly Greek than buildings done in the style, which had to include practical adaptations, such as glass windows and chimneys. The style's simple features were dignified and fairly easy to execute in stuccoed brick or stone. Greek revival tombs normally took the Greek temple form, with temple-front porticos featuring a triangular pediment and an entablature supported by columns in one of the three Greek orders: Doric, Ionic, or Corinthian (fig. 2.8).

De Pouilly modeled his Peniston-Duplantier tomb (1842, St. Louis Cemetery Number 2) on a Greek temple, using the Doric order with fluted columns and triglyphs and metopes in its frieze, with a pediment above. Interestingly, the tomb has crosses incised in the metopes identifying it as a Christian structure, even though it was closely modeled on a pagan temple. The structure has bronze doors protecting the vaults within and

FIG. 2.9. The Peniston-Duplantier tomb (1842), by J. N. B. de Pouilly, St. Louis Cemetery Number 2. Photo by author, 2013.

is surrounded by a classically inspired geometric iron fence (fig. 2.9). The Jean-Baptiste Plauché tomb (1845, St. Louis Number 2), also by de Pouilly, is in the Greek revival style as well (fig. 2.10).

Another popular mid-nineteenth-century revival style, gothic revival, emerged in the 1830s and was likewise used extensively in cemeteries. English author and architect A. W. N. Pugin (1812–1852) helped popularize the gothic revival style. Pugin, who was a convert to Catholicism, promoted the medieval cathedral as an alternative historical model to the ancient pagan temple for nineteenth-century revivalist architecture. Pugin and his allies argued that it was inappropriate for modern Christians to use pagan monuments as precedents for their civic buildings, churches, houses, and tombs. Instead, they favored the forms and decorative schemes developed

Fig. 2.10. The Jean-Baptiste Plauché tomb (1845), by de Pouilly, St. Louis Cemetery Number 2. Photo by author, 2013.

during the gothic period as exhibited by the great cathedrals of Europe, such as Notre Dame and Westminster Abbey. Respected English writer and artist John Ruskin supported Pugin's advocacy of gothic revival architecture, furthering its acceptance and popularity. Andrew Jackson Downing (1815–1852) helped promote the style in the United States with his popular house-plan books.

Although gothic features were originally developed to achieve the greatest possible height in medieval cathedrals and to allow the maximum amount of natural light into their interiors, nineteenth-century architects and tomb designers utilized iconic gothic features—such as buttresses, pinnacles, pointed arches, rib vaults, and stained-glass windows—as purely decorative elements to create an atmosphere of reverence and piety. Like

FIG. 2.11. The J. W. Caballero tomb (1860), by de Pouilly, St. Louis Cemetery Number 2. A novel example of the gothic revival style, the tomb possesses gothic features such as a pointed, scalloped arch above its entrance and pinnacles and crockets along its roofline. It lacks the pointed openings and buttresses evident in most gothic revival tombs. Photo by author, 2013.

the Neo-Grec, gothic architecture appealed to the prevailing Romantic sensibilities. Many nineteenth-century Romantics saw the Middle Ages as a more natural and moral time and favored its architecture because of its pre-industrial origins and picturesque appearance. Naturally, gothic features were well suited to cemetery architecture, given that high-status people had been buried in gothic-style tombs in or near gothic-style churches and cathedrals for hundreds of years. With their Christian associations, gothic-style tombs functioned as dignified and religious settings for nineteenth-century mourners to contemplate and remember loved ones.

Gothic revival tombs can be found in most New Orleans cemeteries. De Pouilly used the gothic revival style when designing the J. W. Caballero family tomb (1860, St. Louis Number 2; fig. 2.11), which he modeled on an image in his sketchbook.

A third revival style used extensively in mid-nineteenth-century cemeteries drew inspiration from ancient Egyptian temples and tombs. With its exotic features and iconic imagery, ancient Egyptian architecture captured the imagination of architects and tomb designers in the first half of the nineteenth century. Largely forgotten until General Napoleon Bonaparte invaded Egypt in 1798 with his army and a team of antiquarians, Egyptian decorative motifs soon appeared on the furniture and interiors of Napoleon's French Empire style (1804–15). In the decades that followed, the Empire style influenced design across the Western world, even in countries that had been among Napoleon's bitterest enemies.

Around 1830, the Egyptian revival style became particularly popular in the United States because of its visual power and symbolic meanings. Although Egyptian revival architecture did not evoke Christian traditions as gothic revival did, the style did suggest permanence and strength.[12] Used sparingly in a limited number of building types, Egyptian revival was seen mainly in prisons, courthouses, and churches. Egyptian revival design is found in cemeteries more than anywhere else.[13]

The Egyptians were especially known for building pyramids and other elaborate tombs, and their architecture became closely associated with funerary monuments. New Orleans has several impressive examples of Egyptian-inspired cemetery architecture. One is the pyramidal Varney Tomb (ca. 1813, St. Louis Number 1). Another is the gate to Cypress Grove Cemetery (1840; fig. 2.12), designed by Frederick Wilkinson. Wilkinson received inspiration for his design from the Egyptian revival gate of Mount Auburn Cemetery in Cambridge, Massachusetts. The Mount Auburn gate, designed by Dr. Jacob Bigelow (see chapter 6), was constructed from wood in 1831 and later replaced by a stone version in 1843.[14] An engraving of the Cypress Grove gate in an 1845 tour book closely resembles the Mount Auburn gate; however, Wilkinson's gate as it was built lacks the monolithic cornice above the columns shown in the engraving, and its columns appear to be of a different design.[15]

The best surviving example of a nineteenth-century Egyptian revival tomb in New Orleans is the Grailhe tomb in St. Louis Number 2 (1850),

FIG. 2.12. Entrance to Cypress Grove Cemetery (1840), designed by Frederick Wilkinson. The columns, although square, are abstractions of those of an ancient Egyptian temple. Photo by author, 2013.

designed by de Pouilly. The Grailhe tomb is not a typical example of Egyptian revival. De Pouilly abstracts its ancient Egyptian decorations, giving the structure a more geometric and modern aesthetic than is usually the case with Egyptian revival architecture. Although based on ancient Egyptian motifs, the tomb's decorations were etched into the stone, forming an abstract composition of simple lines. If one were to remove many of the tomb's decorative motifs from the Egyptian revival context of the tomb, they would be difficult to recognize as being Egyptian at all.[16] The cast-iron fence that surrounds the tomb is simple and geometric and is more inspired by ancient Rome than by ancient Egypt. Unfortunately, sometime after 2003, looters stole its original bronze doors (fig. 2.13).

With the emergence of the revival styles and aided by de Pouilly's influence, fashion overtook necessity and thrift in the tombs of the well-to-do in New Orleans by the 1840s. Tombs became increasingly elaborate and stylish. C. W. Kenworthy of Philadelphia described family tombs in the older cemeteries in 1853:

Chiefly built of brick and plastered or stuccoed. . . . Some of these are of iron, some of granite, others of brown sand stone and marble. Many of them, especially in the French cemeteries, are very handsome and appropriate. . . . Many of them are quite fanciful in form, and much the larger portion are decorated with various emblems of the regard of the living for their departed friends . . . the numerous little images of Cupids and kneeling saints in Plaster of Paris, most of them half washed away.[17]

The same author describes the large tombs constructed by benevolent societies, which were increasing in number at the time: "The society tombs of large size containing many vaults or ovens [are] constructed in various ornamental styles" (see chapter 4). He continues, "The French and Catholic cemeteries within the limits of the city are all highly interesting to a stranger, and present many things which seem extremely curious and singular to a Protestant American."[18] Mark Twain was similarly captivated by the architectural interest of the cemeteries—their mix of older, vernacular tombs and the more elaborate recent additions. In *Life on the Mississippi* he relates: "They bury their dead in vaults . . . and when one moves through the midst of a thousand or so of them . . . the phrase 'city of the dead' has all at once a meaning to him. Many of the cemeteries are beautiful and are kept in perfect order. . . . If those people down there would live as neatly while they are alive as they do after they are dead, they would find many advantages to it."[19]

The stylistic sophistication of the cemeteries of mid-nineteenth-century New Orleans caught the attention of many English-speaking Victorian visitors. These elaborate burial sites contrasted with, and often outshone, the cemeteries and churchyards they were familiar with. With aboveground burials in imposing, freestanding family and society tombs in a density found nowhere else in the United States, the cemeteries came to be among the city's most visited tourist attractions.

Writing in 1840, a visitor from Ohio commented: "[We] visited the Catholic cemetery which I consider one of the most beautiful curiosities of New Orleans. It is a perfect miniature of a handsome city of the dead."[20] In 1845, another Ohioan exclaimed: "I wandered through the streets of New Orleans and saw many strange and beautiful objects before I started home; but the memory which dwells most sacredly in my remembrance, and keeps the greenest corner of my heart, is that brief sojourn to the Cemetery

Fig. 2.13. The Grailhe family tomb (1850), by de Pouilly, St. Louis Cemetery Number 2. The tomb features abstracted Egyptian motifs, including a cavetto cornice and cavetto lintel over the entrance, a vulture-winged sun disc symbol, battered walls, and attached (squared) clustered lotus columns. Photo by author, 2013.

of St. Louis."[21] In 1851, another American tourist declared: "To a stranger to New Orleans there are no greater objects of curiosity than the French Graveyards."[22] An English visitor added his voice in 1855: "The cemeteries of New Orleans are peculiar to the city and are visited by all strangers."[23] Echoing the sentiments of other visitors with an added twist, in 1883 Mark Twain penned his well-known remark: "There is no architecture in New Orleans, except in the cemeteries."[24]

In the early 1830s, Rev. Joseph Ingraham followed a funeral procession and discovered the "new burial place" (St. Louis Number 2). He was favorably impressed: "When I entered the gateway, I was struck with surprise and admiration. Though destitute of trees, the cemetery is certainly more deserving, from its peculiarly novel and unique appearance, of the attention of strangers, than (with the exception of that at New-Haven and Mount Auburn) any other in the United States."[25] He found a much more varied and sophisticated architectural environment than earlier visitors had described in St. Louis Number 1: "A broad avenue or street extends nearly an eighth of a mile in length; and on either side of this are innumerable isolated tombs, of all sizes, shapes, and descriptions, built above ground. The idea of a Lilliputian city was at first suggested to my mind on looking down this extensive avenue. The tombs in their various and fantastic styles of architecture—if I may apply the term to these tiny edifices— resembled cathedrals with towers, Moorish dwellings, temples, chapels, palaces, mosques—substituting the cross for the crescent—and structures of almost every kind."[26] While Ingraham may have exaggerated the exotic nature of the tomb designs he described to impress his readers up north, his observations show that St. Louis Number 2 developed quickly and was built with more architectural variety than the older tombs in St. Louis Number 1 (fig. 2.14).

In 1838, the *Daily Picayune* described St. Louis Number 2 in a similar manner: "In its very appearance it is a *City of the Dead.* Its streets, inter-

FIG. 2.14. A surviving block of Ingraham's "Lilliputian city" in St. Louis Cemetery Number 2. Photo by author, 2015.

secting each other at right angles, the neat little edifices, constructed for the last home of humanity; here and there one overtopping its neighbors, and glittering with the rich gildings of the crucifix or with some magnificent escutcheon; the splendid railing which encloses some of these mansions, and the willow trees, scattered over the ground; all these, together within the surrounding wall, unite in impressing one with the idea of a miniature city."[27]

The advances in tomb design seen in St. Louis Number 2 and other cemeteries during the mid-nineteenth century did not extend to the funerary needs of all of the residents of the city. Not all New Orleans cemeteries were "miniature cities" where bodies were neatly buried in costly vaults. Kenworthy described a cemetery he visited in 1854 called "Cypress Grove Number 2," a "potter's field" located in the "immediate vicinity of the Fireman's, the Odd Fellows' and the St. Patrick's Cemetery." He provides a rare glimpse into a nineteenth-century New Orleans indigent cemetery:

> One-half of the ground is appropriated for the poor and unfortunate, who have no "oven" or tomb provided for their reception . . . and the other half is under the immediate direction of the Charity Hospital. . . . There are few well marked or well protected graves, and no ovens or tombs above ground. . . . On the left can be seen trenches or "winrows" as some have called them, where hundreds upon hundreds of bodies lie with not so much as a stick to mark their place. . . . The single graves are, great numbers of them, are marked with sticks and crosses, bearing some rude inscription; but there is not a single stone monument or other durable material, in the whole field, which no doubt contains eight or ten thousand bodies. . . . Besides the sticks and crosses . . . there are a few surrounded by neat wooden railings, painted white, and others have a substantial board placed at the head and foot, with carefully painted letters on them.[28]

Kenworthy makes an additional observation about his visit to Cypress Grove Number 2 reminiscent of the sentiments Benjamin Latrobe had expressed over forty years earlier in relation to crawfish in St. Louis Number 1: "One portion . . . is quite overgrown with tall, thick, blackberry bushes. . . . These bushes bear a rich harvest of fruit which the poor wretches from the city, who are soon to lie in the same soil, do not hesitate

Fig. 2.15. Potter's field, Cypress Grove Cemetery Number 2. Drawing from C. W. Kenworthy, *History of the Yellow Fever in New Orleans, during the Summer of 1853* . . . (Philadelphia and St. Louis: C. W. Kenworthy, 1854). Courtesy Louisiana Research Collection, Tulane University.

to gather and eat . . . as if they were grown in a pleasure garden instead of an epidemic cemetery" (fig. 2.15).[29]

Holt Cemetery, a municipal burial site founded in 1879 in the area now known as Mid City, is another New Orleans cemetery that does not match the "city of the dead" description. Although in recent decades, the cemetery has been used for the burial of mostly low-income individuals, research done in the 1990s indicates that earlier in its history, Holt was the site of burials of people from a wide variety of ethnicities, religions, and walks of life. Early in its history, some Protestants may have chosen Holt for religious rather than financial reasons due to a shortage of plots in non-Catholic cemeteries in the city at the time.[30] By 1908, however, the *Daily Picayune* described Holt as a "paupers" cemetery.[31]

Today, the cemetery contains the graves of "veterans to famous jazz musicians to victims of epidemics and violent inner city crime."[32] Much of its history is not evident when one visits. All of the burials are belowground, and most are marked with folk art crosses, stones, toys, and other diverse objects often made of perishable materials that quickly degrade in the hu-

FIG. 2.16. Holt Cemetery. Photo by author, 2013.

mid climate, giving Holt a strikingly transient and different character from other existing New Orleans cemeteries (fig. 2.16).

Holt and the earlier potter's fields show more influence of African burial traditions than the Catholic, Protestant, and fraternal and municipal cemeteries. With burials underground, and mourners free to mark the graves of their loved ones as they wish, the potter's fields manifest African burial traditions. Archaeologist Ross W. Jamieson writes, "The surface material placed above the grave appears to be the most enduring material marker of African influences in the New World."[33] In Holt and other cemeteries throughout America, African Americans continued the African tradition of marking graves with various types of ceramics, bottles, and similar objects. An early example of such practices is a blue shell-edged plate dated 1800–1818 found above the burial of an African American in South Carolina. The *Journal of American Folklore* documented African American graves in South Carolina with "oyster shells, white pebbles, ceramics, glass bottles," and other "bric-a-brac" atop them in 1892. Sometimes a miniature house was built on top of the grave to protect the funerary items. The grave goods may have been ritually broken to symbolize the deceased's break with life and to keep them from haunting the living.[34] A 1905 article describing a scene in one of the "old French cemeteries" on All Saints' Day offers a glimpse into how African Americans in New Orleans marked the graves of their loved ones at the beginning of the twentieth century:

> It was a grave unmarked by a marble monument. The wooden headboard had long since had washed from it the original inscription. By the side of it sat an old negro woman. . . . Her eyes were fixed on a fluttering white ribbon freshly placed on the monument. It bore, in painfully formed letters cut out of gilt paper and pasted on the satin background, "To My Daughter." The row of tiny shells at the base of the monument traced the one word. "Felice" and "Mother" was formed from evergreen branches arranged near the base of the grave.[35]

FIG. 2.17. Although modern, the grave goods found at Holt Cemetery reflect ancient African burial traditions. Photo by author, 2015.

FIG. 2.18. A perishable coping grave at Holt. Photo by author, 2015.

The markers and items left on graves at Holt Cemetery resemble these descriptions but with more modern objects (figs. 2.17, 2.18).

Unlike the potter's fields, which tourists rarely saw, the urban cemeteries visitors encountered after 1830 contained densely packed, substantial tombs, many with significantly more ornamentation than those Latrobe had witnessed in 1818. Three major influences transformed the early plain box tombs, step tombs, platform tombs, and gabled pediment tombs into the highly decorated artistic temples and chapels for the dead for which New Orleans became known. The first was the arrival of de Pouilly and other European designers and artists, the second was the new aesthetic standards brought by the many Europeans and easterners arriving in the city, and the third was the greater supply of relatively affordable building stone made available by advances in shipping and the eventual arrival of railroads that linked New Orleans to the rest of the continent in the early 1860s.

Between 1800 and the 1860s, most New Orleans cemeteries were transformed from dismal burial grounds to impressive silent cities with a variety of tomb forms and styles (see Appendix A) reflecting a revolution in design. There were tombs mimicking historic architectural icons such as Egyptian, Greek, and Roman temples, classical sarcophagi, pyramids, Romanesque and gothic churches, classical columns, and obelisks. Because of the city's preponderance of aboveground tombs, and because many of its people were willing and able to pay for increasingly extravagant burial sites, tomb designers were able to realize a more architecturally spectacular vision than they would in most cemeteries elsewhere in the United States, giving birth to the city's historic cemeteries as we know them today.

THE ARCHITECTURE
AND ART OF DEATH
The Builders and Decorators

Prior to the Civil War, New Orleans was essentially an island. The city's only land connections to the rest of North America were narrow roads that ran in a vaguely northward direction along the natural levees on both sides of the Mississippi River. Until 1812, when the first steam riverboat arrived, sailing vessels served the city. Virtually everyone and everything arrived and departed on ships.

A lack of good building stone and the city's isolation limited locally produced building materials essentially to wood, bricks, and lime-based stucco. Until the late nineteenth century, local manufacturers produced almost all of the brick used in the city. These bricks came in two basic varieties, one made from clay taken from the banks of the Mississippi River and the other made from clay collected from the shores of Lake Pontchartrain and from various locations in St. Tammany Parish. The Pontchartrain brick is tannish-orange and soft; the Mississippi brick red-orange and somewhat harder.[1] Both types are vulnerable to moisture and erosion if left unprotected by stucco or otherwise shielded from the elements (fig. 3.1).

Most New Orleans tombs constructed before the mid-nineteenth century were simple structures made of these soft local bricks and covered by protective lime-based stucco, which was usually lime-washed white, vaguely mimicking stone. In addition to white, from at least as early as the 1830s, some tombs in St. Louis Number 1 and the other early cemeteries were lime-washed in earthen colors, such as rusty red, pale yellow, pink, lamp black, and tan. Tombs finished in these colors can be seen in an 1834 watercolor of St. Louis Number 1 by John H. B. Latrobe. Tomb builders used colored lime-wash into the first decades of the twentieth century.[2]

FIG. 3.1. A decayed tomb in St. Louis Cemetery Number 2. Once the lime-wash and the underlying stucco have weathered and fallen away, the structures of brick tombs such as this begin to erode and crumble, resulting in the eventual loss of the tomb if action is not taken. Photo by author, 2015.

The majority of early New Orleans tombs contain one or more above-ground burial chambers, each capped by a brick barrel vault. In some cases, rather than constructing the roofs above individual burial chambers as brick vaults, tomb builders procured slate, mainly imported from France or Wales or shipped in from Pennsylvania, for use as horizontal dividers between individual stacked vaults (much like the floors between stories of a building; fig. 3.2). Slates also provide the underlying structure of many tomb roofs.[3] Some tombs originally possessed only one or two chambers, but at some point after they were constructed, their owners added additional vaults above them, making the tomb taller.[4] This sometimes happened to a single tomb more than once, resulting in successive layers of vaults with the earliest one at the bottom. Over time, many of the older tombs have sunk inches or even a foot or two into New Orleans's "loamy and clayey" soils, concealing their original bases.[5]

Early tombs have a flat, sloped, or curved stucco roof, sometimes with stepping or a shallow gable. Some include a false front with a parapet wall

FIG. 3.2. A degraded pediment tomb in St. Louis Cemetery Number 2. Because of the deterioration of the facade and the loss of its closure tablets (marble or granite slabs placed over vault openings with the names of the deceased etched into them), the horizontal slate dividers between the tomb's burial chambers are left visible. Photo by author, 2013.

often topped by a pediment (see Appendix A).[6] Many of the gabled tombs have decorative cornices and pilasters formed from stucco or, in more elaborate and expensive examples, a cut marble veneer (fig. 3.3).[7] The people who built these tombs were local masons, many of them enslaved in times prior to emancipation, who probably worked on other kinds of building projects in addition to tombs. Construction of the early brick tombs required that the builders be experienced bricklayers or masons, but they did not have to possess the specialized skills of a stonecutter.

A high level of skill was required to hand carve marble closure tablets and other tomb components and ornaments rendered in stone, which sometimes included original sculpture (fig. 3.4). When a closure tablet became filled with the names and dates of the deceased after a tomb's vaults

FIG. 3.3. Ruined brick tomb with marble veneer in St. Louis Cemetery Number 2, exposing the interior structure. Photo by author, 2015.

had been filled multiple times, the old tablet would be relocated to the side of the tomb to continue commemorating the dead within the tomb, and a marble cutter crafted a new tablet ready to receive the names and dates of newcomers and affixed it to the front.

By the 1830s, tomb and funerary monument designers such as the architect J. N. B. de Pouilly employed diverse materials, including marble, brick, stucco, bronze, and iron, to execute their designs. At this time, the more expensive and prestigious tombs began to be decorated with high-quality sculpture, artful relief, and refined architectural motifs. This created opportunity for marble cutters, tomb builders, sculptors, and ironworkers. With a growing population and increasing prosperity, marble yards operated by artisans who designed and built tombs, handcrafted funerary sculpture, carved closure tablets, and fabricated tomb decorations sprang up around the city's cemeteries.

In addition to providing tombs for a city that had a generally high death rate throughout the nineteenth century, these craftspeople had to scramble to provide tombs for the victims of the epidemics that struck the city on a regular basis. During the height of an outbreak, the dead were interred

FIG. 3.4. Marble sculpture on the roof of a tomb in St. Louis Cemetery Number 2. Most of these pieces were not signed, or in some instances the signature may have worn off. Surviving funerary sculpture such as this attests to the talent of the many stonecutters who worked in the city in the 1800s. Photo by author, 2013.

quickly to avoid the bodies of lost loved ones piling up at cemetery gates and being taken away by the authorities and hastily thrown into a mass grave. Although these artisans' businesses benefited from the increased mortality caused by the high incidence of yellow fever and other diseases, their occupation put them at high risk of contracting the diseases themselves. During the summer months, when epidemics usually occurred and those who could left for the countryside or fled to the North, tomb builders and people in related occupations, such as undertakers and sextons, had to remain in the city and face the risks.[8]

Before the 1860s, funerary stonecutters used expensive marble imported from Italy to craft into stone sheathing for the outsides of tombs, closure tablets, and sculpture. As the number of steamboats arriving in the city multiplied in the middle of the nineteenth century, and New Orleans became accessible by railroad in 1861 when the New Orleans, Jackson & Great Northern Railroad reached the city, building stone became less expensive and more common in the city.[9] With more shipping options, a larger supply and greater variety of building stone allowed for increasingly sophisticated tomb designs. In addition to Italian marble, after the Civil War, builders started importing marble from Alabama and Rutland, Vermont, which often undercut the price of the Italian product.[10] As the century progressed, greater quantities of marble and other kinds of stone, such as granite, became available for tomb construction and decoration. As the city's economy gradually recovered after the end of the Civil War, increased access to raw materials helped bring opportunity and wealth into the city, further spurring demand for impressive tombs. In the late nineteenth century, tombs were often sheathed with or even built entirely of stone. Exclusively stone tombs, which with few exceptions appeared late in the century, had heavy masonry bases and thick walls and solid roofs made up of stone blocks and slabs. By the 1890s, such tombs were usually built of granite rather than marble.

The nineteenth-century stonecutters of New Orleans came from a variety of backgrounds. Many of the earliest of these craftsmen were immigrants trained in Europe, while others were free people of color whose ancestry, at least on their mothers' side, went back for generations in New Orleans. Although hundreds of people cut stone and built tombs in New Orleans in the nineteenth and early twentieth centuries, this chapter describes a representative sample of these artisans. In a 2013 study of Lafayette Cemetery Number 1, preservationist Emily Ford recorded over forty different craftspeople who had signed closure tablets or entire tombs in that cemetery alone, and many of the tombs examined in that cemetery had not been signed at all.[11] Although the majority of these artisans are virtually unknown today, some of the most prolific and creative of the stone carvers and tomb builders who worked in the cemeteries of New Orleans left a legacy that can be traced. One of the earliest of these was Paul Hippolyte Monsseaux.

An immigrant from France who moved to New Orleans sometime during the 1830s, P. H. Monsseaux (1809–1874) designed and constructed a significant number of early tombs in the city's cemeteries, particularly in those favored by the city's French-speaking residents, often referred to as Creoles. Some scholars argue that for much of its history the term "Creole" simply meant "native to Louisiana," but the exact meaning of the term has been a subject of debate.[12] "Creole" as used in this chapter refers to people native to Louisiana who have French, Spanish, or African roots or a combination thereof.

Monsseaux was part of the generation of marble cutters that established the stonecutting business in New Orleans. At a time when Monsseaux's business was well established, an 1851 city directory described him as a "marble cutter & Sculpter & Lime Dealer" located at St. Louis and Robinson Streets.[13] Ten years later, the 1861 *Gardner City Directory* listed his business simply as a "marble yard" at the same address, which was across the street from St. Louis Cemetery Number 2, where he built many of his tombs.[14] Monsseaux's signature appears on a good number of the more architecturally significant structures in New Orleans cemeteries that date from the mid-nineteenth century, meaning his company either designed a tomb or built it or both. Like most stonecutters, he designed and crafted entire tombs or sometimes just carved the closure tablet. The majority of his freestanding tombs were brick structures covered with stucco with only their plaques being of cut marble imported from Italy.

However, he did build stone slab tombs as well. De Pouilly, who developed a close and enduring business relationship with Monsseaux, designed many of his more ostentatious funerary commissions. Examples of de Pouilly tombs built by Monsseaux in St. Louis Number 2 include the Fauche family tomb (1836); the Peniston-Duplantier family tomb (1842; see fig. 2.9); the Dupeire family tomb (1842); the Sociedad Iberia de Beneficencia Mutual mausoleum (1848); and the Grailhe family tomb (1850; see fig. 2.13).[15] Drawings of many of the most substantial tombs built by Monsseaux appear in de Pouilly's sketchbook. Along with de Pouilly, Monsseaux belonged to a group of designers and artisans that contributed to the increase in architectural and artistic sophistication of the early New Orleans cemeteries. Monsseaux was buried in a tomb in St. Louis Number 2, Square 2, an area of the cemetery where significant examples of his work can still be found.

Another prolific early tomb builder who was a contemporary of both de Pouilly and Monsseaux was Newton Richards (1805–1874). Born in New Hampshire, Richards arrived in New Orleans in 1831 at the age of twenty-six, after being trained as a stonecutter in Boston and working in New York City for a time. Upon arrival, he started a business as a "stone

FIG. 3.5. The Greek revival Lacoste family tomb (1849), designed by de Pouilly and built of granite by Newton Richards, St. Louis Cemetery Number 2. Photo by author, 2015.

dealer" cutting and selling imported marble for use in building facades and cemetery architecture. Like Monsseaux, he located his marble yard near St. Louis Cemetery Number 2.[16]

In addition to his cemetery work, Richards designed the colossal Battle of New Orleans Monument that can still be seen on the site of the 1815 battle, which occurred in Chalmette just east and downriver of New Orleans.[17] Perhaps inspired by architect Robert Mills's 1833 design of the Washington Monument, in 1855 Richards proposed the construction of a large obelisk made of stone blocks. The 150-foot-tall monument, which had key doorways with cavetto lintels facing in all four directions, reflected the Egyptian revival style sometimes used in the cemetery monuments and tombs with which Richards was familiar.[18] Although the project was not completed in his lifetime, according to a local newspaper Richards was a

FIG. 3.6. The Robinson family tomb in Cypress Grove Cemetery, designed and built by Newton Richards around 1862. This classically inspired tomb has an intact cast iron fence. Unfortunately, similar fences have been looted from many other tombs in this and other historic cemeteries around the city. Photo by author, 2015.

"man of considerable energy" who "infused new life into our mechanics, builders, and property owners."[19] He used much of this "considerable energy" to construct a great number of tombs, many out of granite, which was unusual so early in the century. Among the funerary works he built are the Greek revival Lacoste family tomb in St. Louis Number 2, designed by de Pouilly and built in 1849 (fig. 3.5); the Edward Duncan tomb in St. Louis Number 2, built in 1858; and the Robinson family tomb, located in Cypress Grove Cemetery and built around 1862 (fig. 3.6).

Monsseaux was an immigrant from France, and Richards had come from New England; however, some of the tomb builders of the mid-nineteenth century were native to the city. A number of these were people of color. Free people of color played an important role in the life of antebellum New Orleans. Before emancipation, New Orleans had three basic castes or social ranks based on race: enslaved blacks, free people of color, and whites. In Louisiana, free people of color were sometimes known as black Creoles.

Aside from south Louisiana, the social division among blacks, whites, and Indians was much more clearly defined in the United States than in Latin America or the Caribbean, where people intermingled more freely and formed more complex racial identities. Prior to American independence, whites in the English colonies of North America developed a strict concept of racism to justify their enslavement of Africans, and by the time of the drafting of the US Constitution in 1787, whites generally believed that Africans were meant to be enslaved because of "natural law"—a position that attempted to justify the inherent contradiction between the idea that "all men are created equal" and the fact that the Constitution allowed a large proportion of the population to continue to suffer under slavery.[20] Although racial identity in the American colonies was mostly based on a person's appearance, the legal definition of who was considered white or black gradually became more and more restrictive. By the end of the nineteenth century, people with as little as one thirty-second African blood were considered to be "black" in some American states. For much of New Orleans's history, however, the concept of race involved more subtle gradations between black and white than elsewhere in the United States. Terms such as "mulatto" (half-white, half-black), "quadroon" (one-quarter black and three-quarters white), and "octoroon" (one-eighth black and seven-eighths white) illustrate this.

Links to Caribbean, French, and Spanish culture and legal systems help account for the less rigid concept of race in New Orleans. French and Spanish colonial law made it easier for slaves to be emancipated there than in other areas of what would become the United States. The skills that many enslaved African Americans possessed, such as carpentry, blacksmithing, masonry, and stonecutting, allowed some to buy their freedom.[21] The influx of refugees fleeing the Haitian Revolution (1791–1804) also increased the number of free people of color in New Orleans significantly. By the time of the Civil War, Louisiana had far more free blacks than any other southern state. The 1860 census reported around 11,000 free people of color living in New Orleans, compared to only 355 in the entire state of Texas, 753 in Mississippi, and 114 in Arkansas. The total number residing in the state of Louisiana was 18,647.[22]

Although certainly not accepted as the norm, mixed-race couples were viewed with more tolerance in Louisiana than in other parts of the American South. In early French Louisiana, the population of white women was so sparse that white men often put racial bias aside and married women of other ethnicities. The early French "pragmatic Capuchin friars" started recognizing mixed marriages in the mid-1700s, although their Spanish successors reversed the policy sometime after 1762.[23]

The practice of wealthy whites taking wives and mistresses with African heritage, sometimes after attending the so-called quadroon balls, known as *plaçage*, has long been incorporated into the lore of New Orleans. At these events, women of color were presented to white males, who would often initiate relationships and sometimes start families with them. Some white men maintained two families, one black Creole and the other white. In these interracial relationships, the woman did not enjoy the social or legal protections of marriage, although the man was normally obligated to provide for her and her children's future at least to some degree.[24] Although quadroon balls are often romanticized and portrayed as having been high-class affairs resulting in long-term relationships between upper-class white men and elegant black Creole women dressed in fine clothes and presented in grand style, many of these events were little more than markets for prostitution involving white men and poor female immigrants, from St. Dominique and other places, who were just trying to survive.[25]

The Louisiana racial caste system was reflected in its cemeteries. Until after the Civil War, in most New Orleans cemeteries prosperous black Creoles were buried in a manner indistinguishable from whites, often in the same cemeteries and even in the same blocks of tombs and oven crypts (see chapter 5), while all but a handful of enslaved blacks received in-ground burial in indigent cemeteries, such as Cypress Grove Number 2, or in unmarked locations. Until Reconstruction (1862–77) ended in New Orleans,[26] cemeteries were segregated mostly by socioeconomic factors, with the moneyed usually buried in family tombs, members of the working class in ovens or society tomb vaults (see chapter 4), and the poor ending up in potter's fields. Because of slavery prior to the war, and due to the general economic disparity between blacks and whites, the majority of those buried in potter's fields were black.

All people of color enjoyed increased rights during the Reconstruction years; however, white rule was again imposed in Louisiana with the Compromise of 1877, when federal troops that had been supporting the state's Reconstruction government withdrew. Subsequent Jim Crow segregation laws made no distinction between blacks and Creoles of color, and the special status of black Creoles quickly eroded. Before the Civil War, many black Creoles had the opportunity to develop gainful careers doing skilled labor and owning businesses. Not only were many free people of color buried in the same cemeteries as whites; they also helped design and build them. The best-known of the black Creole marble cutters and tomb builders was Florville Foy (1820–1903).

Florville was the son of Prosper Foy (1790–1878), a white immigrant from France who had fought in the Napoleonic wars and come to New Orleans by way of Saint-Domingue and who had served in the Battle of New Orleans.[27] In addition to being a marble cutter, sculptor, art and architecture teacher, and builder, the elder Foy belonged to the local intellectual elite and was an amateur historian who wrote articles for the *New Orleans Bee*. Architect Benjamin H. Latrobe was the godfather to one of his children. Foy owned a plantation in St. James Parish and possessed numerous slaves.[28]

Prosper Foy entered a long-term relationship with Eloise Aubrey, a free woman of color.[29] The two had at least three children together, including Florville. When Florville reached the appropriate age, Prosper sent him to France to study, a fairly common practice among the well-to-do white fathers of black Creole children. Upon his return, Florville started working in the marble business alongside his father. They set up shop on Basin Street near St. Louis Number 1, and Prosper taught Florville the marble-cutting trade. Father and son worked together for a few years, after which the elder Foy retired from the business. In 1842, Florville opened his own studio on Rampart Street, which specialized in tomb design, decoration, and construction in brick and stone.[30]

Because of Florville's skill, and likely the fact that his father was a French immigrant like himself, J. N. B. de Pouilly began hiring him to execute some of the elaborate tombs he designed. De Pouilly's patronage bolstered Florville's prestige and helped make him one of the more successful tomb builders and marble cutters in New Orleans at the time (fig. 3.7).

Foy's obituary attested to his status as a successful and prolific tomb builder: "The handiwork of Florville Foy is to be found in most every cemetery of the city. In the old St. Louis burial ground, rows of his tombs are to be seen, and it is not too unusual to note clusters of them together. . . . His stone-cutting shops were busy beehives of industry. He was devoted to the art and originated many of the designs which brought him the greatest

Fig. 3.7. The refined, gothic revival–style Antoine Abat family tomb, St. Louis Cemetery Number 2. Signed "Florville Foy 1851." Photo by author, 2015.

favor."[31] He was known for his artistry and sometimes carved his graceful signature medallion of flowers on his marble closure tablets (fig. 3.8).

Foy's reputation spread to other parts of the Gulf Coast, such as Biloxi, Mississippi, and Pensacola, Florida, where he received commissions to construct tombs. In 1851, he built the John Hunt Tomb in St. Michael's Cemetery, a Catholic burial ground in Pensacola. The tomb, which is signed "F. Foy" rather than "Florville," the signature he usually used in New Orleans, looks like a family tomb that could be found in most any nineteenth-century New Orleans cemetery. Rendered in the classical revival style, the marble sepulcher features a carved sarcophagus positioned on the roof, inverted torches in the corners, and a wreath centered in its pediment. His signature can also be found on at least two marble closure tablets in the same Florida cemetery. His signed work also exists in the old

FIG. 3.8. Iconic flower medallion on a closure tablet signed by Florville Foy, St. Louis Cemetery Number 2. Photo by author, 2015.

cemetery in Biloxi. (Tombs and closure tablets by other New Orleans tomb builders, such as P. H. Monsseaux, have also been discovered in historic Florida cemeteries.)[32]

At the height of his business, Foy employed at least eight artisans at his studio and marble yard on Rampart Street. In most years, his enterprise grossed over $20,000 annually (approximately $440,000 in 2016 dollars).[33] In the 1830s and 1840s, Foy lived well and took his place in the society of white and black Creole artisans and business owners. Florville's circle of friends included painter Paul E. Poincy and poet Camille Thierry, who both contributed to *Les Cenelles*, the first book of poetry published by people of color in the United States.[34] He lived in a large apartment over his studio and, as was common for prosperous black Creoles in antebellum New Orleans, he owned slaves. One of his two enslaved housekeepers remained with him until his death. From about 1850, Foy lived with Louisa Whittaker, a white woman whom he could not marry because interracial marriages were illegal in Louisiana until after the Civil War. In 1885, when both were in their sixties, the two were finally wed, and they remained together until January 1902, when Louisa died tragically after intense heat from a stove caught her clothing on fire.[35]

Foy had interests that went beyond his funerary marble business. Like his father, he engaged in agriculture and raised prizewinning animals at a farm he owned outside the city.[36] In an 1892 advertisement in the *Daily Picayune*, he offered "Berkshire and Poland pigs and angora goats" for sale.[37] The gradual transition from independent stonecutting studios to larger operations that used mechanical tools and precut stone elements brought in by train eventually drove out many skilled craftsmen, who worked on a relatively small scale, mostly by hand. Despite this, Foy managed to keep his studio open until his death in 1903.

Florville Foy was one of a group of black Creoles who constructed tombs mostly for the city's French-speaking population. Among his fellows were Eugene and Daniel Warburg, the sons of Daniel Samuel Warburg (1789–1860), a white commission merchant who immigrated to New Orleans in 1821. The elder Warburg was a member of a prosperous Jewish family from Hamburg, Germany. Soon after he arrived in New Orleans, Warburg purchased Marie Rose Blondeau (ca. 1804–1837), an enslaved woman of mixed race who had been born in Cuba. He pursued a relationship with her, and in 1826, she gave birth to a son, Eugene, who was born into slavery. Warburg freed Eugene when he was four years old and also emancipated Marie at some time before her next child was born. Daniel Warburg came into the world as a free person of color in 1836. Like Prosper Foy, Daniel Samuel Warburg had many business interests. He was not only a merchant, but also a land speculator who made a fortune buying, selling, and developing Louisiana real estate in the 1830s. He was also an eccentric inventor who tried unsuccessfully to market his novel theories on how to improve marine navigation, and he concocted a set of mathematical formulas in the belief they could be used to win lotteries.[38]

Like Prosper Foy, Warburg saw to it that his Creole sons were educated. He probably had ambitious plans for his sons' education in Europe, but he lost much of his fortune in the Panic of 1837 and during the subsequent economic depression, forcing him to focus less on formal education and more on preparing his sons to learn a practical means of supporting themselves. He decided to have them trained in the trade of marble cutting and sculpting funerary art.[39] Although their education was cut short by their father's financial problems, both Eugene and Daniel were literate, and Eugene was reported to have written French well.

The late 1830s was a difficult time for the Warburgs. Marie Rose died in 1837 at age thirty-three, leaving the now-motherless brothers living with their father.[40] Because of his monetary losses, Warburg moved his family out of the fashionable French Quarter to the less prestigious Third Municipality, closer to where the Foys lived. Luckily, he had managed to retain enough of his properties to support himself into old age.

Eugene Warburg studied sculpture with Philippe Garbeille, a Frenchman who had been schooled in Paris and was reputed to be the best sculptor in New Orleans at the time. Although he focused his ambitions on high art, Eugene also did cemetery work to support himself. An 1849 city directory listed him as a marble cutter working at a small studio across the street from St. Louis Number 1. Employing his younger brother, Daniel, as an apprentice, Eugene produced funerary structures and their associated decor and sculptures by hand, using chisels and other traditional stone-working tools, as was the norm during the antebellum period.[41]

Daniel would practice the stonecutting art for the rest of his life, but Eugene, who studied, created, and exhibited sculpture as high art in addition to working on his cemetery commissions, had higher aspirations. In 1852, he took money from his cemetery work and also arranged to use proceeds from the sale of three of his deceased mother's slaves to help support his younger siblings and to finance his emigration to Europe. It was common for talented young Louisiana black Creoles to visit and sometimes relocate to France and other European countries, where they encountered less racial bigotry and more opportunities than they did at home. Eugene left for France to pursue a career as a sculptor.[42] Although today it may seem ironic that Eugene used money from the sale of slaves to escape the racial inequalities of Louisiana and find greater freedom for himself in Europe, during the antebellum period enslaved people were commonly viewed as financial assets.

In Paris, Eugene met John Young Mason, the US minister to France, who commissioned him to create a classical stone bust of himself. After spending some time working in France, Eugene traveled to Belgium and then to England, where he met the duchess of Sutherland, a philanthropist and abolitionist, who commissioned him to do a series of reliefs depicting scenes from *Uncle Tom's Cabin*.[43] After returning to France and spending over four years in that country as an art student and artist, he set out for Italy in 1857. Describing Eugene's travels, the *Daily Picayune* reported: "We have here a mulatto sculptor from New Orleans who brings commendation from Mr. Soulé [an influential family friend], Mrs. Stowe [Harriet Beecher Stowe] and the Duchess of Sutherland, who gives us some promise of respectable attainments in the profession."[44] Unfortunately, Eugene was never able to reach the artistic heights that his talents warranted. He died in Rome of a sickness in 1859 at age thirty-three.[45]

His younger brother Daniel, now in his twenties, continued to work in marble at his studio on St. Louis and Basin streets in New Orleans, where he lived with his father until his father died in 1860. Examples of his signed work from the 1850s to the 1910s, both closure tablets and whole tombs, can be found in most of the older New Orleans cemeteries, especially in St. Louis Cemeteries Numbers 1 and 2. His tombs include those of Anne Emile Mioton (1852), Marie Lucrecia (1853), Daniel Rivoil (1853), Charles Mony (1860), Rosse Marceline LeMarois (1861), and A. Sainville Casbergus (1863).[46] He also designed and carved the 1904 Holcombe-Aiken column in Metairie Cemetery, a tall, unfluted Doric column resting on a plinth and wrapped with a twisting morning glory vine (fig. 3.9).[47]

In later years, Daniel's son, Daniel Warburg Jr., followed in his father's footsteps and became a marble cutter who worked on funerary architecture and sculpture. If built during the period when both men were active, a tomb bearing the signature "Daniel Warburg" may have been executed by either father or son. As mentioned earlier, by the 1870s, larger operations began to replace the small craft-based marble studios, such as the one the Warburgs operated. Daniel Warburg Jr. closed his shop in 1871 and went to work for Florville Foy at his marble yard for a year. Daniel then changed jobs and was employed at the large marble yard of Kursheedt and Bienvenu for many years. He eventually found a position working at the yard of Albert Weiblen (see below), from which he retired around 1905.[48]

Aside from Foy and the Warburgs, most of the well-known New Orleans stonecutters came to the city from other countries or from distant areas of the United States. James Hagan (1833–1891), an Irish immigrant, traveled to the United States with members of his family to escape the devastating Irish potato famine of 1845–52. Although poor when he arrived, he made

FIG. 3.9. The artistic Holcombe-Aiken column (1904), crafted by Daniel Warburg, Metairie Cemetery. Photo by author, 2015.

his way working as a stonecutter and speculating in real estate with his brother-in-law. He later climbed the ranks of society to serve as a Democratic state senator.[49]

After the Civil War, Hagan became the sexton of Lafayette Cemetery Number 1 and Lafayette Number 2. Many New Orleans stonecutters, including P. H. Monsseaux, served as sextons. Sextons managed individual cemeteries and kept watch over them to ensure regular maintenance, to keep out vandals, and to enforce city ordinances related to burial and burial certificates. Tomb owners paid sextons set burial fees for opening and closing tombs and vaults. Their work was particularly difficult during epidemics, when cemeteries became so flooded with bodies that a sexton sometimes could not offer any available vaults.[50] During the epidemic of 1853, the *Daily Picayune* commented:

From the numerous complaints made this morning of the careless manner in which coffins containing dead bodies are left at the Fourth District cemeteries, it would appear that there are not enough hands employed there to bury the dead. . . . It is a sad enough necessity that we should live in the midst of an unsparing epidemic, but that in a city like this the victims of the disease should be allowed to rot and fester for hours, unattended, ere the sexton or his assistants are able to place them in their last resting place.[51]

Despite the challenges of the office, holding the position of sexton offered advantages for tomb builders. Being in charge of a cemetery kept them aware of the changing styles for new tombs and allowed them to offer their services for work in the cemetery for which they were responsible.

In addition to being a sexton, by 1869 Hagan operated two marble works, one of which was located in the Garden District near Lafayette Cemetery Number 1. Although he did much of his work in what is now Uptown New Orleans, he built elaborate tombs in cemeteries all over the city, many of which were clad in marble and executed in the eclectic revival styles that were popular at the time. A number of these were inspired by the designs of de Pouilly. While Monsseaux, Foy, and the Warburgs designed primarily for the French-speaking community, Hagan counted English-speaking Americans and economically successful immigrants from places such as Ireland and Germany among his clients.[52]

Another newcomer from abroad, Charles A. Orleans (1839–1923), arrived in New Orleans in 1878 from Canada. He had been involved in construction projects in Chicago, New York, and Paris, and had reportedly made and lost two fortunes by the time he came to Louisiana. Like so many outsiders before and since, he went to New Orleans to start his life anew. Orleans hired architect Theodore Brune and succeeded in creating a thriving tomb design and construction business. His operation was of the large-scale industrial variety that took business away from craftspeople like Foy and the Warburgs.

In 1894, Orleans claimed to have built "three fourths of all the principal granite vaults and monuments in New Orleans" during the previous sixteen years.[53] He brought much of the granite used to build his tombs from the Hinsdale-Doyle Granite Company in New York and from Hallowell, Maine, ushering in the period when the more expensive tombs in New Orleans were built of granite rather than marble.[54] The hardest stone aside from diamonds, granite is difficult to cut but resists damage and erosion far better than marble. In earlier times, working granite had been arduous; however, new technologies such as power saws and pneumatic tools had brought the costs down by the late nineteenth century, making this stone the best option for construction of tombs and monuments.

Orleans built the Army of Northern Virginia monument and mausoleum in Metairie Cemetery. He also constructed the Howard mausoleum (see chapter 6) and the cathedral-like David McCann mausoleum in that same cemetery. He went on to build many of the monuments in Metairie Cemetery's so-called "Millionaire's Row." His business thrived through the 1890s, but late in his life he must have repeated some of the financial mistakes of his early years, because in 1923 he was reputed to have died a poor man.[55]

Tomb builder Albert Weiblen's career began essentially where Charles A. Orleans's left off. Weiblen (1857–1956) immigrated to New Orleans from Metzingen in Württemberg, Germany, in 1887. He had apprenticed as a stonecutter in Switzerland and Germany. Weiblen claimed to have arrived in New Orleans with two dollars in his pocket.[56] Soon after his arrival, he began working for Kursheedt and Bienvenu marble works. In 1888, he started a grave design and construction firm of his own that would eventually become one of the largest such enterprises in the South. His business prospered because it used industrial machinery and could offer grander and more durable tombs and monuments at lower prices than the smaller marble yards.[57]

One of Weiblen's first major commissions was the David C. Hennessy monument, erected in 1893 in Metairie Cemetery (fig. 3.10). A city police superintendent who had actively fought organized crime, Hennessy was gunned down in 1890 in an ambush supposedly carried out by members of the local Italian mafia. Although the police had little evidence to go on, the shooting triggered a mass roundup and arrest of Italian men, reflecting the prevailing atmosphere of mistrust and ethnic hatred toward the Sicilian community in the city. Of the nine suspects tried for the shooting in 1891, the court found six innocent and ruled a mistrial for three others due to lack of evidence. Even before the trial, city newspapers had declared the defendants guilty. Incensed by the trial's outcome and claiming the jury had been bribed, a large yet organized mob stormed the parish prison, forced its way inside, and killed eleven prisoners, including five who had not even

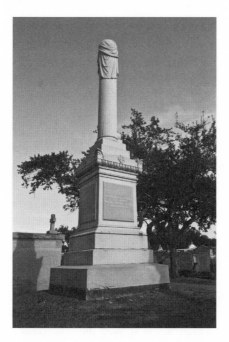

Fig. 3.10. The David C. Hennessy monument (1893), designed and built by Albert Weiblen, Metairie Cemetery. Photo by author, 2015.

been part of the trial.[58] This mass lynching made national news and initiated a diplomatic crisis between the United States and Italy. The impressive Hennessy monument, which stands in relative obscurity today, recalls not only the untimely death of David C. Hennessy but also the vigilantism and tragic violence that followed.

Defeating Charles Orleans among others, Weiblen's firm won a design competition for Hennessy's marker. The winning entry, designed by Weiblen himself, consisted of a granite column draped with a carved stone pall resting atop an intricate granite pedestal. The extravagant monument, which cost $3,300 (equivalent to around $85,000 2016 dollars), reflects the significance its promoters ascribed to Hennessy's memory.[59] Weiblen's name on such a high-profile funerary structure gave him the recognition he needed to establish his reputation and grow his business.

Some years later, in 1911, Weiblen built another significant funerary landmark, the Elks' Tomb in Greenwood Cemetery. Designed by local architect Thomas Sully and commissioned by the local Grand Lodge of Elks, the tomb, which cost around $10,000 (approximately $250,000 2016 dollars), took the conical tumulus form.[60] It has a granite, earth-sheltered entrance in the form of a Doric temple front, and the tomb is crowned by a nine-foot-tall bronze statue of an elk standing on a granite boulder.

In the early twentieth century, Weiblen opened a steam-powered plant on South Claiborne Avenue near the Illinois Central rail line. In this factory, Weiblen's employees used large-scale polishing and etching machines to dress stone shipped in from all over the United States.[61] Much of the granite came from a quarry the Albert Weiblen Marble & Granite Company owned in Stone Mountain, Georgia, although the granite used in the Elks monument came from Alabama. Weiblen constructed a larger number of monuments in Metairie Cemetery than any other single builder, including many of his most significant commissions. In 1951, near the end of his life, Weiblen and his son and daughter-in-law purchased Metairie Cemetery itself. The family operated the cemetery until 1969, twelve years after Albert Weiblen's death.[62] Orleans and Weiblen represent a generation of tomb builders that transformed the cemeteries, particularly Metairie Cemetery, into the marble and granite showplaces they are today.

Every one of the prominent New Orleans stonecutters discussed in this chapter, except Newton Richards, immigrated to the United States or had at least one parent born in a another country. Other than Florville Foy and the Warburgs, all of the tomb builders came from somewhere other than New Orleans. It is interesting, and perhaps ironic, that the city's cemeteries, considered to be unique to New Orleans and indicative of its peculiar culture, were largely designed and constructed by newcomers. The people of the city, with their emphasis on extravagance, art, aesthetics, and the commemoration of the dead, had created a fertile environment in which creative artisans and businesspeople from other places could flourish.

The builders of the cemeteries overcame significant social barriers and economic challenges to succeed in their chosen occupation. Foy and the Warburgs dealt with racial discrimination, while immigrants such as Hagan and Orleans came to the city penniless and had to assimilate into a foreign society. The stories of the stonecutters and tomb builders are tales of people who faced adversity and used their talents and business skills to create prosperity for themselves and their families as they constructed the magnificent variety of artistic tombs and monuments found throughout the cemeteries of New Orleans.

PALACES OF THE DEAD

Society Tombs and Fraternal Cemeteries

In the middle of the nineteenth century, large, multivaulted tombs began to spring up in New Orleans cemeteries. Often sheathed in decorative marble veneer, these monumental mausoleums dwarfed the family tombs that surrounded them. Many had intricate, often symbolic ornament (figs. 4.1, 4.2). Built by social organizations called "friendly," "burial," or "benevolent" associations, society tombs provided a respectable, aboveground burial for individuals from a variety of ethnic and socioeconomic backgrounds who did not have access to a family tomb and could not afford their own private oven vault.

Benevolent societies came to Louisiana during the eighteenth century and proliferated in the nineteenth. These groups took three basic forms. The first type, the benevolent or mutual aid society, existed mainly for social and economic reasons and were usually open to members of both genders. They sometimes held colorful street parades that led to funerals or fanciful tomb dedication ceremonies in the cemeteries. The second type, the fraternal society, which included groups such as the Masons, Elks, and Odd Fellows, had distinct sets of symbols, performed elaborate rituals, and were usually all male or, in rare instances, all female. The third variety were essentially labor unions created by workers in specific occupations, such as dock workers, stenographers, or teamsters, that formed mainly to promote the labor rights of their members but also had an associated burial society or special union committee that did such things as arrange and pay for their deceased members' funerals and burials.[1] Although some included members from various ethnic groups, with very few exceptions all three types of burial societies were segregated by race. The benefits of member-

FIG. 4.1. The imposing society tomb of the United Slovenian Benevolent Association, St. Louis Cemetery Number 3. Photo by author, 2013.

ship in these organizations were so attractive that in 1888, the *New Orleans Medical and Surgical Journal* reported that about 80 percent of all New Orleanians belonged to a benevolent society of some kind.[2]

During the second half of the nineteenth century, New Orleans was the nation's second busiest port of entry (behind New York City) for immigrants. Thousands of newcomers flooded into the city from many parts of the world, especially Ireland, Germany, Italy, Spain, Portugal, Greece, Croatia, and the Philippines. A good number of these immigrants arrived with small families or no close relatives at all. Most had left their homelands due to economic hardship and did not have much disposable income. Many did not speak English well, if at all, and found securing a social safety net in New Orleans difficult. In nineteenth-century America, health and life insurance were not widely sold, and very few governmental social services

FIG. 4.2 The templelike society tomb of the Societa Italiana Madonna Del Monte Triona, Metairie Cemetery. Photo by author, 2013.

were available. This made the often economically disadvantaged immigrants particularly vulnerable to poverty and disease.

Members of various ethnicities, religions, and trades, both immigrants and native New Orleanians, created benevolent organizations to provide opportunities to socialize with people with similar backgrounds and interests, participate in charitable activities, and receive medical assistance and burial when the time came. One such group, the Ahavas Sholem, was formed in 1895 to assist Eastern European Orthodox Jewish immigrants by providing burial insurance and other benefits to its members.[3] Membership in a society could save a person from social isolation or poverty, or even save his or her life in case of an accident or serious illness, and prevented members and their loved ones from being cast into a watery grave with a minimal funeral or possibly none at all. Members paid small weekly or monthly dues, which were pooled and used to help individuals in times of crisis and to cover funeral and burial expenses.

The recurring epidemics of yellow fever, cholera, and other diseases that plagued the city in the nineteenth century increased the demand for burial societies and sometimes even prompted their creation. The epidemics also created a need for new cemeteries and helped spur the construction of tens of thousands of vaults that would be built in the city during the nineteenth century, many of which were within society tombs. In 1844, Edward H. Durell compared the cemetery he had visited (probably St. Louis Number 2) to a rapidly growing city: "The tombs have a freshness about them which betrays their newness—nothing seems of yesterday—the peculiarity of their structure, their close juxtaposition filling the plats like blocks of buildings, the well graveled paths between, the wall about the whole, with its numerous receptacles for the dead rising story above story."[4]

A person visiting or living in New Orleans during one of its frequent epidemics would have no difficulty understanding the grim reality behind all of the construction. A newspaper reporter in 1833 relates a typically terrible scene during a cholera outbreak: "I have heard much of the trenches and pits in which cholera victims were buried . . . bodies without coffins piled in masses around these pits."[5] The same disease had hit the city just a year earlier, conjuring up scenes such as this one described by a doctor working there at the time:

The unshrouded dead dumped at the gateway of the Girod Street Cemetery accumulated in such numbers that the entrance to its precincts was so obstructed that arriving bodies had to be deposited on the outside; no graves at this time could be dug; no coffins were procurable, for there were neither grave diggers to be had or undertakers to be found. The City Council were forced to order out the chain gang "prisoners" from the city jails, to dig a trench the whole length of the lower side of the cemetery. It was dug some twelve or fifteen feet wide, and as deep as the filtering water soil would permit. Into this receptacle the decomposing bodies were dragged by hooks from the fire companies, without the formality of precedence or order of any kind. As part of the trench was filled, the earth taken from it was heaped upon the remains of the rich and the poor, the aged and the young.[6]

However horrible cholera was, yellow fever, also known as the saffron scourge or yellow jack, was the most destructive. From 1817, when records began to be kept, until 1905, the year of the last yellow fever outbreak in the city, at least forty-one thousand individuals perished.[7] The fever hit hard in 1819, killing over two thousand people in that year with subsequent outbreaks in 1837 and 1841, and it did not stop there. Over seven thousand people died of yellow fever in 1853 alone, representing around 10 percent of the city's population.[8]

In that year, the *Daily Picayune* reported, "The hearses bringing them place the coffins at the gate of the cemetery, and there, it is stated numbers of them remain for hours, and in some cases all day and all night, the effluvia given forth reaching houses four and five squares off."[9] Another severe epidemic came only three years later in 1857, claiming almost five thousand additional lives. The large society tombs helped to speed the process of getting victims buried, although many of the less-affluent burial societies would run out of funds to pay for interments or would fill all of the spaces in their tombs during severe epidemics.

The city was at the mercy of outbreaks of yellow fever and other diseases throughout the nineteenth century (fig. 4.3). The effects of yellow fever were devastating. When its third and most toxic phase struck, a victim vomited blood; his or her skin turned yellow; and the eyes, nose, and mouth bled. Most died from liver, kidney, or multiple organ failure. The treatments doctors provided, such as bleeding, washing the victim's body, or giving them mercurous chloride (calomel), did nothing to save lives or relieve the suffering of patients.[10] The medical profession had no idea what caused cholera or yellow fever, the two biggest killers, until researchers discovered the cholera bacteria in 1883 and that yellow fever was transmitted by mosquitoes in 1900.

Most of the burial societies were established before the periodic yellow fever and cholera epidemics finally ended after 1905. After this time, the overall number of societies in the city slowly began to decrease, because the epidemics, a significant reason for their existence, had subsided. Near the end of the 1850s, a local newspaper reported that the New Lusitanos Benevolent Association, a Portuguese group, had been founded "at a time of epidemic and public distress. . . . The summer of 1858 will long be sadly remembered for their [*sic*] particularly destructive fever. . . . It was such an occasion that gave form and purpose to the already cherished design of

NIGHT BURIAL ON THE MISSISSIPPI.

FIG. 4.3. Yellow fever victims being buried in the river during an epidemic. Drawing from C. W. Kenworthy, *History of the Yellow Fever in New Orleans, during the Summer of 1853* . . . (Philadelphia and St. Louis: C. W. Kenworthy, 1854). Courtesy Louisiana Research Collection, Tulane University.

forming in New Orleans a New Lusitanos Benevolent Association."[11] An elderly benevolent society member recalled in the mid-1930s: "I joined it in the year of the yellow fever in seventy-eight. . . . A lot of those societies were organized to help the people fight the yellow fever."[12]

The benevolent societies held regular meetings and often developed unique social and ceremonial cultures. Pageantry has long been a significant aspect of the culture of New Orleans, and the societies held elaborate ceremonies, funerals, and parades, often with colorful regalia and speech making. In 1881, the mostly German Washington Benevolent Association put on an impressive spectacle to unveil the new statue it had erected to adorn its society tomb at the Louisa Street (St. Vincent de Paul) Cemetery. It began with a procession headed by a brass band that included its association members as well as participants from a number of other city burial societies. Once the procession had made its way through the streets and reached the cemetery, a salvo of thirteen cannon was fired, and the society's president, Captain Sambola, addressed the crowd: "This spacious tomb is truly fulfilling its mission . . . to remind you of the state to which we are all hastening, and of the rewards to which we have all been entitled by discharge of duty to God and our fellow men." After the ceremony, the society returned to its hall and had a banquet followed by a dance.[13]

The aforementioned New Lusitanos Benevolent Association constructed its elaborate templelike society tomb in the now-destroyed Girod Street Cemetery. In addition to its Portuguese members, the organization accepted German, English, Irish, and French applicants. The motto of the six-hundred-member society was, "We nurse the sick, bury the dead, and protect the widows and orphans."[14] The New Lusitanos mausoleum, which J. N. B. de Pouilly designed, had a Greek temple-front portico with marble Doric columns and a central atrium lined with stacked burial vaults on both sides. A "massive iron gate" that closed off the interior to visitors when no members were present protected the vaults.[15]

In October 1859, when the tomb had just been completed, New Lusitanos members held a colorful opening ceremony, which illustrated the ritualistic practices of many of the burial societies. They met at their social hall wearing blue scarves and rosettes. Then they formed a colorful parade that included a band, the mayor of New Orleans, and the New Orleans city council, and marched through the streets to the cemetery flying American and French flags, and firing salutes several times along the way.[16] In later years, the association continued to parade on anniversaries and would decorate its tomb in the Girod Street Cemetery with flowers and black velvet draperies.

In addition to providing burials and other benefits to its members, the New Lusitanos Benevolent Association, like many other burial societies, also collected charity for orphans and other people in need. The *Daily Picayune* described the association's charitable activities on All Saints' Day in the Girod Street Cemetery in 1859. A reporter wrote, "The New Lusitanos Benevolent Society had taken their stand at the Girod Street Cemetery where they have built their tomb and also made a good collection for the relief of the orphans at the Camp Street Asylum."[17]

The Lusitanos survived the Civil War, Reconstruction, and the yellow fever epidemics of 1867 and 1878.[18] The group persevered until about 1920, after which it disbanded. Its elegant tomb fell into disrepair, was vandalized and looted, and was eventually demolished in 1957 along with the rest of the Girod Street Cemetery.

While the social, medical, and charitable benefits were important, ensuring a respectable burial was the key reason many of the societies existed.

FIG. 4.4. Society tomb of the Woodmen of the World, Palmetto Camp No. 2, Metairie Cemetery. Photo by author, 2009.

Because procuring a decent grave in a consecrated cemetery was more expensive in New Orleans than in most other American cities, a large segment of the population could not afford to keep their remains aboveground and dry unless they belonged to a burial society. In the 1890s, a simple funeral and interment in a society tomb in New Orleans cost about $100 (about $2,700 in 2015), a significant sum for most working-class people of the period to pay out all at once.[19] Without the benefit of membership in a burial society, a low-income person would most likely end up in one of the city's crude potter's fields. In 1867, a newspaper reporter wrote of a conversation with a New Orleans gravedigger: "He informed us that they were generally poor people who were buried in the ground—those who did not have the money to pay for building a tomb above ground."[20]

To make some of their members and their families avoided this unpleasant fate, the burial societies in New Orleans built the large mausoleums

FIG. 4.5. The deteriorated Cazadores de Orleans society tomb (ca. 1834), St. Louis Cemetery Number 2. Photo by author, 2015.

with multiple vaults for which they are known. Most family tombs contained between one and four individual vaults, while society tombs often had twenty or more (figs. 4.4, 4.5). Because the vaults in society tombs were reusable, over decades of service these beehive-like structures provided multiple burials at an affordable price to the societies, allowing them to survive on the modest dues paid by their members. A tomb with ten or more vaults could end up being the final resting place for hundreds of individuals over a number of decades.

The society tombs are indicative of the communal nature of New Orleans culture in the nineteenth century. The fact that many citizens of New Orleans paid dues to be buried in communal society tombs reflects the culture of a city that often valued the institutions of church, community, and society over private individuality and identity. Although burial societies existed in other parts of the United States, most people in other regions, even

FIG. 4.6. A columbarium, or ancient Roman society tomb, in Pompeii (ca. AD 70). Photo by author, 2012.

those belonging to burial societies, preferred individually marked graves in a cemetery plot or, in rare cases, permanent interment within a tomb. In New Orleans, a respectable burial meant a temporary resting place in a cell, sometimes one not even marked with a name, where others had probably lain previously and additional occupants probably would again.

Many society tombs did not bear the names of those laid to rest within, something visitors from other regions of the country sometimes found unacceptable. Some people in New Orleans found burial in society tombs unacceptable. A reporter for the *New Orleans Republican* wrote in 1867: "One does not like the thought of being offensive after he dies—of rotting away upon a stone shelf, broiling in heat, generating poisonous gasses and filling the air with odors not as fragrant as the zephyrs that sweep from Araby the blest. But if you don't like that, you had better not die in New Orleans, especially if you are unfortunate enough to belong to one of the benevolent societies who build there [*sic*] mausoleums and pack away their deceased brethren in them like so many sardines in a tin box—"[21]

Despite their strangeness in the eyes of many, as with the oven tombs, society tombs had deep roots in Western culture that dated back at least

FIG. 4.7. The Young Men's Progress Benevolent Association tomb (1885), Lafayette Cemetery Number 2. Photo by author, 2015.

to ancient Greece and Rome. In Rome, benevolent organizations called *collegia*, which were similar to the burial societies of New Orleans, built aboveground columbaria. In ancient times, each of the many niches of these communal tombs held an urn of a member's ashes until the rise of Christianity, when inhumation became the norm (figs. 4.6, 4.7).

As in New Orleans many centuries later, membership in an ancient Roman benevolent society ensured a respectable burial.[22] Also, as in New Orleans, the individual vaults in columbaria were reused. Ancient Roman benevolent societies were cooperative organizations made up of individuals who belonged to the same worker's guild or who otherwise practiced the same occupation. Sometimes the societies were made up of slaves or freed slaves who wanted the economic and social benefits of belonging to such a group while alive and also the privilege of being able to avoid being thrown in a pauper's grave. Such graves were bleak in ancient Rome, such as the large, uncovered hole in the eastern part of the Esquiline Hill near the city dump, which served as the final resting place for thousands.[23]

Potter's fields in nineteenth-century New Orleans were not much better. In 1835 the Rev. Joseph H. Ingram observed: "I came suddenly upon a desolate area, without a tomb to relieve its dark and muddy surface dotted with countless mounds where the bones of the moneyless, friendless stranger lay buried. . . . Fragments of coffins were scattered around, and new-made graves [were] half filled with water."[24] After the fall of Rome, European medieval trade guilds provided some of the benefits that the Roman burial societies had until the benevolent or "friendly" society was revived sometime in the 1600s.

Along with European immigrants and other white New Orleanians, African Americans and Creoles of color formed many burial societies in nineteenth-century New Orleans. African American benevolent societies sprung up early in the city's history. Members of the free black community founded the Perseverance Benevolence and Mutual Aid Association of New Orleans in 1783. Similar societies existed in other American cities at around the same time, such as the Free Dark Men of Color in Charleston (1790s), the Free African Society of Philadelphia (1787), and the Male African Benevolent Society in Philadelphia (1811).[25] Additional African American benevolent societies, some of which had existed in secret during the time of slavery, appeared all over the South after emancipation.

While they may have been at least partly inspired by the European traditions of the white benevolent societies, the black organizations also had roots in the West African cultures of their members' ancestors. The slave trade persisted in sending enslaved Africans to the United States into the 1800s, legally until 1808 and illegally afterward, and many of the founders of the early benevolent societies were first- or second-generation African Americans. Following deeply rooted African traditions, the black benevolent societies usually involved more ritual, symbolism, and religion, and they had a greater economic function than similar groups made up of members of different ethnicities.[26]

The West African democratic and patriotic societies that existed during the time of the slave trade, such as the Poro in Sierra Leone, controlled many aspects of their members' lives. The Ibo of Nigeria focused on mutual aid for its members and on enforcing their moral rectitude, while the Gbe society of Dahomey was primarily designed to cover its members' burial expenses.[27] Elaborate funerals and a proper burial were important in West African cultures, and this translated to the New World, paving the way for the African American benevolent associations of New Orleans. Africans believed that a respectable method of burial and an extravagant, well-planned funeral helped settle the spirits of the dead so they would reach the worlds beyond rather than becoming trapped on earth as ghosts, where they might cause harm to the living.[28] These ancient beliefs formed the cultural background for Christian funeral rights as many African Americans practiced them.

Similar to the organizations in Africa, the primary purposes of the American benevolent societies were guaranteeing a measure of financial security, providing healthcare, and ensuring a respectable funeral, preferably one with some pomp and panache—a proper, well-attended send-off for the deceased. Also like their African predecessors, the American groups encouraged and expected good moral conduct in their members.[29] Intricate ceremony was a key aspect of the culture of all burial societies, especially that of the fraternal orders. The popularity of the benevolent societies among African Americans reflected the ritualistic, moral, and communal nature of the West African cultures of their forebears.[30]

Healthcare concerns and the threat of disease provided additional incentives for African Americans in the nineteenth century to join benevolent societies. According to a Louisiana Board of Health report from 1883–84, between 1864 and 1880 the annual death rate for blacks fluctuated between 32 per 1,000 and 82 per 1,000, while the death rate for whites ranged between 5 per 1,000 and 32 per 1,000 during the same period.[31] The public health situation for African Americans in Louisiana did not improve by the turn of the twentieth century. In 1903, at the height of Jim Crow, members of the Louisiana Medical Society were told, in a manner that reflected the prevalent racism of the times, that, if unchecked, pneumonia and tuberculosis would undoubtedly "solve the negro problem."[32]

Although Louisiana's charity hospitals were established long before this time, medical services for African Americans remained inferior to those for whites. Between 1860 and 1880, the life expectancy for black males was thirty-six years, compared to forty-six years for white males.[33] This disparity gave added impetus for blacks to form benevolent societies, primarily to provide affordable healthcare, but also to provide burial in society tombs. Records from the Girod Street Cemetery and St. Louis Number 2 show that by about 1900, around two hundred African American benevolent societies had built tombs in those two cemeteries alone.[34] Another source reports

FIG. 4.8. The Coachmen Benevolent Association tomb (1890), Lafayette Cemetery Number 2. Note the iconic horseshoe motif in the tympanum. This historic tomb is decaying because the organization that built it is long defunct, and the city, which owns the cemetery, has created no means by which to restore or maintain its historic tombs. Photo by author, 2015.

that at least seventy-four such societies were organized in New Orleans before 1900, but given the number of African American society tombs, that number was certainly much higher.[35]

In addition to health insurance and burials, prior to emancipation free blacks created a number of benevolent societies for the express purpose of raising money to buy the freedom of their enslaved brethren.[36] And some African American societies were formed for the same reasons as other benevolent societies. In 1873, the mission of one such society, the Benevolent Daughters of Louisiana, was described thus: "The society is organized for works of charity and benevolence, including deeds of kindness toward their fellow beings in sickness and in suffering, even unto the grave. They have a very fine vault in the Greenwood Cemetery, wherein they bury their dead."[37]

Some African American benevolent societies grew out of social clubs. Others were associations formed among members of a certain occupation or craft, such as fruit handlers, longshoremen, and bricklayers; these associations had the qualities of labor unions. One black Creole benevolent society, Les Jeunes Amis, was organized by cigar makers. Black craftsmen formed the Société des Artisans Bienfaisance et D'Assistance Mutuelle, in 1834.[38] As the names imply, many of the meetings of the benevolent societies created by Creoles of color were conducted in French, especially before the Civil War. The Coachmen Benevolent Association, an African American brotherhood of coach and wagon teamsters, built its society tomb at Lafayette Cemetery Number 2 in 1890 (fig. 4.8).

Even prior to emancipation, tomb building appears to have been a priority of black benevolent societies. According to nineteenth-century writer C. W. Kenworthy, large numbers of African Americans, enslaved or otherwise, were buried in society tombs in the Girod Street Cemetery before emancipation. He wrote in 1854:

The largest and finest tombs in the Protestant cemetery (public or society tombs) are those *owned and built by slaves* [italics in original]. . . . The "ovens" contain a large number of slaves; for any one who has money enough to pay for an oven can be deposited in this cemetery, whether black or white, bond or free. The cost of a burial in the "ovens" or in the vaults of the society tombs, is about twenty dollars [around $520 in 2014]. This is sometimes paid for by the slave, and very frequently by the master. . . .

The slaves have, however, by means of the principle of the association, erected fine monuments and tombs as above named. They were owned by the following societies of slaves, viz: "The first African Baptist Association of New Orleans"; the "John Wesley Colored Society"; the "Colored Home Ministry Benevolent Society"; and the "Colored Benevolent Lutheran Society." This last Society has a tomb containing upwards of seventy large vaults—a very elegant and costly edifice entirely above ground.[39]

While Girod Street Cemetery records indicate that both slaves and free blacks were buried in society tombs, it is unlikely that slaves alone pooled enough money to build elaborate tombs such as those Kenworthy describes.[40] Although slaves did organize benevolent societies of their own, and slaves and free blacks did often belong to the same lodges, he seems to exaggerate this idea in order to make an argument that slaves were not mistreated in New Orleans, and by extension, that the institution might be justified as a whole. He clearly expresses his support of slavery later in his account when, after reiterating that slaves had constructed the society tombs in Girod, he writes: "This is a fact which should be taken notice of by Mrs. Stowe in her next edition of her 'Key.'"[41] He was referring to Harriet Beecher Stowe's recently published book *A Key to Uncle Tom's Cabin: Facts and Documents Upon Which the Story is Founded* (1853), which she wrote in response to criticism of her condemnation of slavery in her novel *Uncle Tom's Cabin*, which had been published the previous year. Kenworthy may have not been aware that New Orleans had a large and prosperous community of free people of color that had created most of the burial societies and financed the construction of most, if not all, of the society tombs he observed.

In the early twentieth century, black burial associations helped create the jazz funeral, for which New Orleans is known. Burial societies, both black and white, often incorporated processions with band music into their funerary observances. By ensuring their members a significant and well-attended funeral, the societies opened up opportunities for musicians to play at them.[42] When, during the Jim Crow era, white band members began refusing to perform at black funerals and funeral processions, black musicians stepped in. This provided opportunity for African American workers, who often played band instruments after-hours for extra income. The funerals of black benevolent society members provided exposure to the musicians who helped pioneer the invention of early blues and ragtime music.[43] Once jazz became popular in the second decade of the twentieth century, the musicians substituted jazz for the traditional band music they had been playing at funerals for years.

Larger and grander than most family tombs, the society tombs altered the scale and spatial configuration of New Orleans cemeteries. Societies formed by most every race, ethnicity, and social or occupational group in the city built impressive, architectural sepultures often finished with marble and decorated with sculpture, relief, and iron elements. The decoration was meant to elevate the status of the society and its members in the eyes of the members themselves and the public. Society tombs tower over most

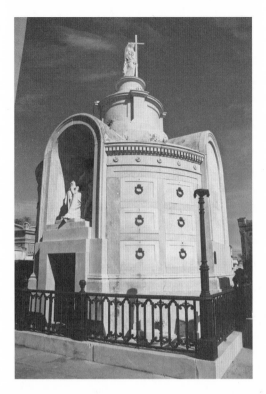

FIG. 4.9. The stylish New Orleans Italian Mutual Benevolent Society mausoleum (1856), designed by Italian artist Pietro Gualdi, St. Louis Cemetery Number 1. The design traditions and aesthetics of its Italian promoters are particularly evident in this tomb. Photo by author, 2013.

other tombs found in the cemeteries, like apartment blocks in a neighborhood of houses.

The design of some society tombs reflects the architectural heritage of the ethnic group that built them. The New Orleans Italian Mutual Benevolent Society mausoleum, designed by Italian artist Pietro Gualdi and erected in St. Louis Number 1 in 1856, is such a tomb (fig. 4.9). Its circular form resembles a classical rotunda. The tower above suggests a geometrically simplified version of the towers of Francesco Borromini's baroque churches in Rome. With rounded niches, classical statuary, and decorative rosettes, dentils, and the anthemion motif, the tomb reflects Italian Renaissance and baroque precedents.

Gualdi came to New Orleans from Mexico City, where he had been working since 1838, and he remained in New Orleans for the rest of his life.[44] The impressive mausoleum, which cost $40,000 to build (around $1 million in 2016 dollars), features two statues—one of a woman wearing an ancient Roman gown, who represents Italia; and the other, a woman sheltering two children, who represents America. The structure has twenty-four burial vaults and a receptacle for the bones of occupants displaced by later burials beneath an iron door in the floor of a corridor that extends the entire width of the tomb at its base.[45] Upon his death in 1857, Gualdi was buried in the tomb he had designed, the first of hundreds of society members interred during the decades it was in use.[46]

The Chinese tomb at Cypress Grove Cemetery is another example of a society tomb that reflects the culture of the group that built it. The Soon On Tong Association, one of a number of benevolent societies formed in New Orleans by Chinese immigrants around the turn of the twentieth century, constructed its society tomb in Cypress Grove in 1904 (fig. 4.10). By this time, the Chinese had an established "Chinatown" in New Orleans, centered near the intersection of Tulane and Loyola avenues. The structure, which contains fifty-two vaults, incorporates both Chinese and New Orleans burial traditions.[47] It faces east toward the rising sun, which is considered an auspicious orientation in traditional Chinese architecture. Like many other New Orleans society tombs, the Chinese tomb was built with a central barrel vault that serves as the roof above its primary interior space; however, unlike other tombs, it contained a funerary burner for the combustion of traditional Chinese funerary offerings such as "joss paper" and "hell banknotes." The interior also housed a "spirit tablet," where mourners burnt incense, and an altar where they left food offerings for the dead.[48] The association used the tomb to inter members temporarily until their bodies could be shipped to China for permanent burial. This practice continued until the 1930s, when Chinese families began entombing their dead permanently in the United States.[49] Because New Orleans lost its first Chinatown in 1937 when many merchants there lost their leases and a subsequent Chinese commercial area on Bourbon Street had mostly disappeared by the 1970s, the tomb is one of the last visible remnants of early Chinese settlement in the city.[50]

Along with ethnically based groups, associations identified with certain public services—such as firemen's associations, policemen's benevolent

FIG. 4.10. The Soon On Tong Association tomb (1904), Cypress Grove Cemetery. The Chinese influence on its architecture makes this tomb stand out from others in the cemetery. Photo by author, 2013.

societies, military groups, and sailors' and river pilots' associations—built distinctive society tombs. One such group, the Société Française de Bienfaisance et d'Assistance Mutuelle, commonly known as the "French Hospital," was organized in 1843 as a benevolent society to shelter French sailors while they were in port at New Orleans. It built a society tomb around 1849 in St. Louis Number 1 and later constructed an impressive ancient Roman–inspired tomb in Lafayette Cemetery Number 2 (fig. 4.11).[51] The decoration on some society tombs, such as depictions of fire engines, police hats and badges, marine cannon, and specialized machinery such as cotton scales, was related to the occupations of the deceased held within (fig. 4.12).

The New Orleans Typographical Union, a white group considered to be the first labor union in the city, was established in 1854. The group constructed its first society tomb in Greenwood Cemetery in 1855.[52] Hospitals and orphanages also sometimes constructed society tombs because of the low cost of burying large numbers of people within their walls compared to the expense of other respectable forms of burial. Other society tombs were constructed by purely fraternal organizations, such as the Masons, the Independent Order of Odd Fellows, and the Protective Order of Elks. The-

FIG. 4.11. The Société Française de Bienfaisance et d'Assistance Mutuelle tomb, Lafayette Cemetery Number 2. This tomb would not look out of place along the Appian Way outside Rome. Photo by author, 2015.

Fig. 4.12. Work-tool imagery in the pediment of the tomb built by the Cotton Yard Men, an African American labor group, in Lafayette Cemetery Number 2. Photo by author, 2015.

Fig. 4.13. The tomb of a Masonic lodge, St. Louis Cemetery Number 3. Note Masonic symbol in pediment. Photo by author, 2013.

matic decoration and mystical icons often adorned these fraternal tombs (fig. 4.13).

Occupational and fraternal societies went as far as to open entire cemeteries. Cypress Grove, also known as the Fireman's Cemetery, located near Bayou Metairie at the end of Canal Street, dates from 1840 when the large and well-endowed Firemen's Charitable and Benevolent Association opened it. The Firemen's Association dedicated its new cemetery to Irad Ferry, a fireman who had died in 1837 fighting a fire on Camp Street. The association erected an impressive, dignified memorial to the famous firefighting hero near the entrance to the cemetery. Designed by de Pouilly like so many other significant New Orleans tombs of the mid-nineteenth century, the marble structure consists of a monumental broken Doric column supported by a sarcophagus-like pedestal decorated with a relief depicting an 1830s fire engine. De Pouilly modeled the design on a similar monument he had documented in Père Lachaise in his sketchbook before coming to New Orleans (fig. 4.14).

Fig. 4.14. The Firemen's Charitable and Benevolent Association monument to Irad Ferry (1840), Cypress Grove Cemetery, designed by de Pouilly. Photo by author, 2013.

Frederick Wilkinson (1812–1841) designed Cypress Grove's grand entrance in the Egyptian revival style (see fig. 2.12), giving it the most impressive gateway of any New Orleans cemetery. Adding to its grandeur, the cemetery has a number of picturesque society tombs near its main entrance, many of them built by the various firemen's associations that existed in the city.

In 1841, not long after the cemetery opened, the Firemen's Charitable and Benevolent Association moved the remains of a number of firemen who had been buried elsewhere to Cypress Grove, including those of Irad Ferry. The ceremony had all of the elements of an elaborate nineteenth-century funerary spectacle. "The silken banners of the various companies hung drooping from the galleries. . . . Upon the communion table were the urns representing the ashes of those to be deposited in a new resting place, also covered with mourning drapery. . . . The fire companies in their picturesque uniforms, each man with his token of sorrow upon the arm, by their presence gave forcible identity to the occasion."[53]

Cypress Grove was New Orleans's first step toward realizing the rural garden cemetery that had been introduced in the Northeast a decade earlier (see chapter 6). Although it possessed greater urban density than true garden cemeteries, Cypress Grove had more open space and trees than earlier cemeteries in New Orleans. The grounds were formally arranged, with its main avenue acting as a central axis. The plan had three wide, parallel streets that ran its entire length, and the long sidewalls of the cemetery were lined with hundreds of oven tombs, which are currently in very deteriorated condition. Cypress Grove's location, which was outside of town at the time it opened, earned praise in the press: "Its location is in every way desirable, not only from its distance from the rude encroachment of a growing city but from its admirable position at one of the choicest points in the neighborhood of New Orleans."[54]

Cypress Grove represents what historian Dell Upton calls "reform cemeteries," those designed to lessen the morbidity of churchyard burial grounds and old urban cemeteries, such as St. Louis Number 1, by providing open space for lawns and trees and adding picturesque elements such as the aforementioned memorial to Ferry and the Egyptian revival main entrance. Despite this, reform cemeteries like Cypress Grove did not achieve the spacious, peaceful, parklike atmosphere of rural garden cemeteries such as Boston's Mount Auburn or Philadelphia's Laurel Hill.[55] Regardless, some contemporary observers saw Cypress Grove as an improvement over New Orleans's earlier cemeteries. When it first opened, the *Daily Picayune* described it as a "beautiful and admirably adapted place of sepulture."[56] Another reporter went so far as to elevate Cypress Grove to the level of the eastern garden cemeteries: "It is pleasant to observe in various sections of the country, a growing disposition to deprive grave yards of their gloom and to render them what they ought to be, beautiful and pleasant retreats from the turmoil of our daily existence. Mount Auburn, near Boston, sweet and lovely spot! The cemetery near Philadelphia, our own Cypress Grove Cemetery, are noble evidences of this feeling."[57]

The Firemen's Charitable and Benevolent Association posted many advertisements in local periodicals informing the public that the cemetery was open to everyone, not just firemen. Many Protestants elected to be buried at Cypress Grove as the Girod Street Cemetery became increasingly dilapidated after the Civil War. The cemetery was so popular that in 1852 the same association built Greenwood Cemetery across the street from Cypress Grove as a larger, more densely laid out, and less expensive version of their original cemetery.

In 1847, seven years after Cypress Grove opened, the Grand Lodge of the Independent Order of Odd Fellows established Odd Fellows Rest, another fraternal cemetery, not far from Cypress Grove. The Odd Fellows are an international benevolent society that started in England with the stated goals to "visit the sick, relieve the distressed, bury the dead and educate the orphans"—goals strikingly similar to those of most other New Orleans benevolent societies.[58] The Odd Fellows purchased the property where Canal Street and City Park Avenue intersect for the modest sum of $700 (around $20,000 in 2016 dollars) and created a cemetery designed to accommodate its members and their families.[59] Like the Firemen's Charitable and Benevolent Association, the Odd Fellows opened their cemetery with an impressive ceremony. They made a procession bearing the remains of sixteen deceased Odd Fellows members transferred from other cemeteries to mark the cemetery's official opening. "The procession with its bands of music, the showy regalia of the members, and the splendid funeral car, drawn by six white horses, with black housings . . . to the sound of solemn music through the principal streets of the city formed a scene picturesque and beautiful in the extreme."[60]

Just over twenty years later, in 1868, the Masons opened a cemetery not far from Odd Fellows Rest, and they did it with such pomp and grandeur as to even outdo their showy predecessors. "The procession headed by an escort of the Knights Templars on horseback, carrying the Beauseant, and in regalia, consisting of black chapeau, with two black and one white ostrich plumes, scarlet sword belts . . . white scarf crossing from the right shoulder. . . . A splendid band of music followed next. . . . The procession upon entering the cemetery formed an oblong square."[61] Processions such as this bear a striking resemblance to Mardi Gras parades. The Mistick Krewe of Comus, the first Mardi Gras parading organization, was founded in 1857. Additional krewes—the Twelfth Night Revelers, Rex, and Momus—formed in the early 1870s, a time when extravagant funeral parades staged by burial societies and fraternal organizations were still very common. Many of the same people must have participated in both the early Mardi Gras parades and the funeral processions. The Fat Tuesday parades we see today are survivors of an era when festive street demonstrations were associated not just with joyful holidays, but also with death.

In the late 1800s, hundreds of benevolent societies operated in New Orleans; however, by the turn of the twentieth century their numbers were beginning to decrease, particularly in the white community.[62] A small number survived into the mid-twentieth century, but by then, most of the magnificent society tombs scattered throughout the historic cemeteries of the city had fallen into disuse and disrepair. The societies began to lose their relevance as the New Deal programs of the 1930s provided workers with a better social safety net, family incomes generally increased, and medical and life insurance became available to a greater percentage of the population. The impact the benevolent associations had on the city and the lives of its citizens is evident in the many impressive and interesting tombs that they constructed, which can still be found throughout its historic cemeteries. These tombs represent an extinct social phenomenon, which, while not unique to New Orleans, was a significant aspect of its history, and one which has largely been forgotten.

SAINTS, VOODOO,
AND RACISM

Although the cemeteries are quiet places today, their history reveals the vital role they have played in the religious and social life of New Orleans. The cemeteries not only chronicle how the city's people have re-membered and honored their dead but also offer insights into its religious practices and its class and racial biases as well. During the nineteenth century and beyond, people socialized, celebrated, collected alms, mourned, and cast spells in the cemeteries of New Orleans.

The annual celebration of All Saints' Day on November 1 has focused the attention of New Orleanians on the graves of their ancestors since the early Catholic French and Spanish colonists brought the holiday with them from the Old World in the eighteenth century. All Saints' Day celebrates the legacy of the Catholic saints, especially those who do not have a specific holiday dedicated to them. All Souls' Day, which falls on November 2, has traditionally memorialized the immortal souls of deceased people of a less saintly nature.

All Saints' Day and the previous night, Halloween, have a history that goes back to pre-Christian cultures. The ancient Celts observed their New Year's Day, Samhain, on the night of October 31, when they lit fires to ward off the coming darkness of winter and to illuminate the night of the year when they believed the barrier between the spirit realm and the human world became least distinct. As the Catholic Church worked to convert the Celts to Christianity during the early Middle Ages, rather than trying to stamp out their traditional holidays, it replaced ancient religious obser-vances such as Samhain with Christianized versions that occurred at or close to the same time of the year. Despite efforts by the Church to completely transform the holidays, some of the older traditions persisted and became aspects of the new celebrations.[1] Even with the passage of time and a change of religion, the rationale behind both Samhain and Halloween remained strikingly similar.

All Saints' and All Souls' days also have roots in the ancient Roman Feast of the Lemures, which took place every May 13. On this day, the father of every ancient Roman household woke up at midnight, washed his hands, and then tossed black beans behind him as he recited prayers to placate the roaming spirits of the malevolent dead. In AD 610, centuries after Christianity had been declared the official religion of Rome, Pope Boniface IV consecrated the Pantheon in Rome, once a temple dedicated to all of the pagan gods, to the Virgin Mary and all of the Christian martyrs. He held a feast there to celebrate the conversion of the historic temple to a Christian cathedral; it became an annual event. In 837, Pope Gregory IV dedicated this celebration to "all of the saints" and changed the date to November 1, possibly to coincide with Samhain in order to create a holy day to follow the preceding unholy night.

By the early Middle Ages, most people in continental Europe celebrated All Saints' Day, which is known as La Toussaint in France.[2] When colonizing Europeans brought the celebration to the New World, transfer of the European focus on visiting cemeteries was mostly confined to southern Louisiana. As with Samhain, All Saints' Day in New Orleans involved lighting up the night with fire. A visitor to the city in the nineteenth century observed, "In addition to their trimming with flowers, the tombs on All Saints' Day are studded with burning candles, tastefully arranged on their fronts."[3] In 1853, the *New Orleans Crescent* reported this fantastic scene: "Not before midnight were the decorations complete. It was then that thousand [*sic*] tapers and waxen lights everywhere covering the tombs were lit up, and a light flashed over the scene, imparting to it an almost magical brilliancy."[4]

All Souls' Day, known in France as La Fête des Morts (The Feast of the Dead), was traditionally celebrated on the day following All Saints' Day, when the prayers of the faithful aided the souls of the deceased.[5] On this day, Christians would visit, refurbish, decorate, and sometimes eat food at family graves, following similar traditions of the pagan Romans before them.[6] Catholics visited and prayed at the graves of their ancestors more regularly than Protestants, because of the belief that prayer helps deceased individuals detained in purgatory to transcend into heaven more quickly. For Catholic New Orleanians in the nineteenth and early twentieth centuries, visiting the graves of loved ones was not just an expression of mourning, but also a means of promoting the redemption of their souls. Although this particular link between the living and the dead did not exist among Protestants, over time the city's Protestants adopted the tradition and started visiting and decorating the tombs and graves of their ancestors on All Saints' Day in much the same way as the Catholics. They also readily adopted other Catholic celebrations, such as Mardi Gras.

Although in Europe All Souls' Day was the time to visit graves and pray for the souls of the dead, the people of New Orleans visited the tombs of their ancestors on All Saints' Day instead. This may be because New Orleanians were celebrating the eve of the feast day of All Souls' by visiting and lighting candles at graves the night before, much as Christmas Eve is celebrated.[7] Europeans came to celebrate the holiday in a similar manner, and by 1878 visiting cemeteries on All Saints' Day was as popular in Paris as it was in New Orleans. A newspaper reported that in Paris "the crowd in the cemeteries was greater than ever on All Saints' Day. After 1 P.M. it was impossible to enter any cemetery in Paris so dense was the crowd."[8] In New Orleans, the day was of such importance that it was a legal holiday with schools, banks, and public offices closed. Each November 2 from the early 1800s well into the twentieth century, local newspapers published accounts describing and praising the event. The reports range from brief columns with cursive descriptions of the day's happenings to elaborate, full-page features, sometimes illustrated, that outline the specific activities that had taken place on the previous day at each of the major cemeteries, all of which were swarming with people.

In the days leading up to All Saints', families would go to work restoring, cleaning, and whitewashing tombs and often continued these activities into the day itself (fig. 5.1). When he visited St. Louis Number 1 on All Saints' Day in the early 1840s, G. E. Pugh, a traveler from the North, observed, "Parts of the cemetery were thronged with workmen repairing the plaster upon the tombs from the ravages of time and weather—some painting them again, or furbishing up the inscriptions."[9] The holiday required a great deal of effort and expense. "For weeks beforehand," writes a traveler in 1851, "the preparations are in progress. . . . Servants [pass] at all hours of the day laden with baskets, from which bouquets and garlands of paper,

FIG. 5.1. *All Saints' Day in New Orleans—Decorating the Tombs in One of the City Cemeteries*, a wood engraving drawn by John Durkin and published in *Harper's Weekly*, November 1885.

muslin, or wax—flower pots, containing living flowers, and tapers in silver candlesticks, richly trimmed with cut paper—peep forth."[10] A writer for the Federal Writers' Project described preparations as they were still being practiced in the 1930s. "During the week preceding November 1, Negroes can be seen hard at work cleaning and whitewashing tombs. Gilt paint is sometimes used to make more legible the inscriptions on the tombs and on the blocks of marble used as bases for flower containers."[11]

On the day itself, the people of the city festooned the graves of their ancestors and other lost loved ones with elaborate decorations and sophisticated flower arrangements in a festive atmosphere. In 1847, J. D. B. De Bow, editor of the *Commercial Review of the South and West*, described All Saints' Day in St. Louis Cemetery Number 2: "A thousand tombs and vaults are covered with flowers and garlands. Beautiful flowers load the breezes with odours and perfumery. . . . Strains of music, too, float over the tombs, and amidst them and around them solemn marches of priests chant at night-fall their requiems and mutter their prayers for the souls of the dead. . . . All day long, thousands and ten thousands have been visiting the habitations of the dead. . . . Gorgeous ornaments are here for gorgeous tombs, candlesticks, and crucifixes of gold and silver, rich vases and costly odours." Despite the inherently solemn nature of the occasion, it truly was celebrated as a holiday. De Bow continues: "The last traces of the daylight are lingering faintly on the scene—the waxen candles are lit up—throngs of visitors are growing gayer—music is wafting its lively notes—the laugh of merriment, and noise of cannon are heard."[12]

A newspaper reporter observed at All Saints' Day in 1905: "The majority of visitors who throng the cemeteries do not strike a stranger as mourners. They go cheerful bedecked in their best bib and tuckers, and the conversation that floats from the various groups seems to bear out the earlier significance of the day, that the dead have returned."[13] Pugh describes the All Saints' Day he witnessed at St. Louis Number 2: "There were . . . troops of quadroon girls and ancient negresses, arranging wreaths and long trailing festoons of flowers, and hanging over the epitaphs beautiful lace veils."[14] In 1851, A. Oakey Hall, a traveler from New York City, wrote of All Saints' Day: "The St. Louis Cemetery is thronged with pious devotees of all ages and sexes,—principally females—. . . bringing tapers, and incense, and flowers to put before them. It is not a little startling to jostle among the crowds."[15]

Like Mardi Gras, All Saints' Day brought the entire city together, functioning not only as a day of communion between the living and the dead but also as one between the living and the living. "All the graveyards are thronged with visitors. They pour through each, successively, in such multitudes that the vastness of the crowd resembles that often seen elsewhere at a public fair or popular exhibition: and it is composed of all ages, in every rank, color or condition—the gates being open alike to rich and poor, white and negro, citizen and stranger," writes a traveler from around 1850.[16] In 1869 the *Daily Picayune* expressed a similar sentiment as if describing a Dickensian Christmas: "It is a day . . . confined to no sect, race, condition or color, but a time when man is bound to his fellows by ties that religion sanctifies and humanity applauds."[17] In 1905, a reporter described the continuing "democratic nature" of the holiday: "Side by side with the rich, drudge the poor, each carrying his own offering to show that he has 'not forgotten.' The coachman in his gorgeous livery, driving his 'quality white folks,' jostled against the Sicilian in his fruit wagon packed in with his wife and the dozen of babies. Rich and poor meet together, and the Lord is the maker of them all."[18]

The holiday transformed the cemeteries into places of celebration and also of charity. An 1885 guidebook observes: "At each of the many gates of the very many graveyards of New Orleans on All Saints' Day sits a silent nun or sister of charity in her snowy habit of purity, with little orphans at her side. These are her flowers; their fathers, mothers, are up the avenue, further on, resting with the dead. A little plate sits by, and each person as he enters the cemetery drops something into it."[19] In addition to the charity of the nuns, throughout the era many of the benevolent societies with a tomb in a given cemetery set up tables there, collecting alms for the numerous children left as orphans by the periodic epidemics that ravaged the city throughout the period. Other city charities not associated with burial societies or tombs would collect donations at the gates of cemeteries as well. Until around 1912, groups of orphans themselves would congregate around the gates of many cemeteries to advertise their presence in the city.[20]

The day left a lasting mark on the cemeteries themselves. Not only were many tombs repaired with new stucco and recoated with lime-based wash, but the decorations and flowers lingered for days and even weeks afterward. The journal of John H. B. Latrobe (the son of Benjamin H. Latrobe) describes the aftermath of All Saints' Day in 1834 in St. Louis Number 1:

> Besides the mementos of decay of the tombs themselves, there were hanging about them faded garlands, and withered bouquets of green leaves and flowers, which on "All Saint's Day," that has just passed, had been there. . . . There were marks too, in long lines of smoke upon the white plaster, where candles had been stuck at the same time against the sides of the tombs. The flowers had decayed and the candles had burnt & the traces which they left spoke as audibly as the graves themselves of the uncertainty of the tenure of mortality.[21]

For over two centuries, the observance of All Saints' Day kept the diverse peoples of New Orleans focused on their cemeteries. Although originally a purely religious event, the holiday, like Mardi Gras, became a festive annual celebration that helped define and unify the city. All Saints' maintained a perennial link between the living and the dead, between the city's present and its history. This connection, along with the repair work performed on tombs on an annual basis, helped the preservation of New Orleans cemeteries into the twentieth century.

Catholics celebrating All Saints' Day are not the only people who have practiced their religion in the cemeteries. Since at least the early twentieth century, offerings of coins, cigarettes, food, alcohol, and other items have been found on historic tombs in the city, particularly on the last resting place of the celebrated nineteenth-century Voodoo "queen," Marie Laveau, located in St. Louis Number 1, and also on the so-called "Wishing Tomb" in St. Louis Number 2. Mysterious X's also mark these and other tombs. Such practices, although often imitated by tourists and tour guides, are expressions of Voodoo.

New Orleans was an ethnically diverse city from the beginning. When it was founded in 1718, the settlement consisted of French settlers and Native Americans; however, within two years enslaved Africans began to arrive. The number of people of African descent in New Orleans increased throughout the eighteenth century, and by 1810, African Americans and people of mixed race comprised a majority of the city's population. This is partly because of the more than ten thousand refugees fleeing the Haitian Revolution that had arrived in the city. Around two-thirds of these refugees had African ancestry. The influx doubled the city's population, and whites did not regain a majority in the city until the 1830s, after large numbers of immigrants from Europe began to arrive.[22]

The Voodoo religion came to south Louisiana with the Haitian refugees, although some aspects of West African religions were already being practiced in Louisiana prior to that time. The term "Voodoo" is an Americanized spelling of the Haitian term "Vodou," which, in turn, came from *vodu*, meaning "god" and "gods" in the Dahomean language.[23] Many Fon people, who came from Dahomey, an independent kingdom in West Africa that traded large numbers of slaves to the Europeans in the eighteenth and early nineteenth centuries, ended up enslaved in New Orleans as well as in other French and Spanish colonies in the Caribbean and in other areas of the American South.[24]

Voodoo is an amalgamation of the traditional religious beliefs and practices of the Ewe, Yoruba, and Fon cultures of West Africa combined with the Catholic faith, which the Church impressed on slaves after they arrived in the New World.[25] Rather than adopting Catholicism as their European masters interpreted it, enslaved Africans in Haiti and other Caribbean colonies, and also in Louisiana, incorporated Catholic imagery and mythology into their existing belief systems. Voodoo combines the worship of traditional African deities and Roman Catholic saints with ancestor worship.[26] In Louisiana, Voodoo practitioners work with fewer deities than their counterparts in Africa or Haiti. They worship a number of Catholic saints and a central god known as Li Grande Zombi, and they also summon the spirits of the dead.[27]

Voodoo is sometimes confused with "Hoodoo," and the two terms are often used interchangeably in early twentieth-century sources, such as the Works Progress Administration (WPA) narratives. Voodoo came from Haiti and remained mostly confined to the lower Mississippi valley. Hoodoo, on the other hand, is a system of folk magic also influenced by traditional West African religions, but mixed with Native American practices and, to some degree, with those of Christianity. Hoodoo spread throughout the English-speaking South and to areas in the North where its practitioners migrated. Hoodoo does not have the strong Catholic influence Voodoo has and, unlike Voodoo, it does not have a distinct set of deities or a religious doctrine. The two practices did influence each other, however, and many of their spells and rituals are similar.[28]

Like many religions, Voodoo supposes a pantheon of gods and a belief in spirits. Adherents work to develop close, magical relationships with supernatural entities: deities, saints, and spirits. They accomplish this through the use of charms and spells, and by performing magical ceremonies. Voodoo is a practical religion that presents ways of coping with and possibly controlling real-life situations, such as sickness, betrayal, a broken heart, poverty, and death, using a complicated system of mostly sympathetic forms of magic. In sympathetic magic, the magician works to influence a target individual or group positively or negatively by using objects or activities that have similarities or a clear relationship with those whom he or she intends to impact. An example is the well-known Voodoo doll. The Voodoo doll acts as a stand-in for the object of a spell who is supposed to suffer whatever punishments the practitioner subjects the doll to. Voodoo dolls probably evolved from a number of "artistic motifs" that originated in the Congo, Benin, Togo, and other cultures in Central Africa.[29]

Between 1928 and 1930, the African American anthropologist and novelist Zora Neale Hurston interviewed Voodoo practitioners in New Orleans, seeking their knowledge. Hurston observed symbolic spell ingredients, including nails or pins used to "pin down" the target of a spell, black thread to tie him up, and hot or pungent materials to quicken and strengthen the spell.[30] Rather than having a rigid ethical doctrine like conventional Christianity and many other faiths, Voodoo has few moral absolutes or strict mores. Its standards are relative and mold to different situations.[31]

Because of its moral and doctrinal ambiguities, and its potential to empower the slave and free black population, the French, Spanish, and later, the American authorities in Louisiana sought to suppress Voodoo. Before the Civil War, white slaveholders feared the religion as a possible means by which slaves could harm them directly through the magic itself or indirectly by providing slaves with a sense of purpose and confidence they feared could incite slave rebellions. In 1773, several New Orleans slaves were accused of conspiring with a new arrival from Africa to kill their master using a Voodoo charm known as "gris-gris" (also known as *"grigri"*). The Spanish authorities responded in 1777 by passing a revised "black code" that prohibited African rites. The code also further restricted African burial practices.[32]

Voodoo was widely misunderstood in the nineteenth century and often confused with other religions and magical practices. Because the Spanish ruled New Orleans for over three decades, and because the city had a close relationship with the Caribbean and Latin America, particularly Cuba, some Louisiana magicians were exposed to, and practiced, Santeria, another Afro-Caribbean religion. While the practice of Santeria is usually benign, it has a malevolent branch called Palo Mayombe (also known by several other names and sometimes just as Palo) that focuses less on the relatively benevolent gods of Santeria and more on engaging and manipulating the spirits of the dead. Palo Mayombe practitioners are known to use human remains in their spells and rituals, which naturally attracts them to cemeteries.[33] Many nefarious activities that have been blamed on Voodoo, such as breaking into graves to steal human remains and vandalizing tombs, were likely perpetrated by people performing Palo Mayombe spells rather than those of Santeria or Voodoo.

After New Orleans became part of the United States, the authorities continued to suppress Voodoo practices. In 1850, the police arrested a group of woman who were "slaves, free colored persons, and white persons assembled and dancing Voudou." The biracial quality of these meetings alarmed the authorities at least as much as the Voodoo itself. Louisiana law prohibited slaves, free blacks, and whites from assembling together, and slaves from assembling at all.[34] A significant number of women were

SUPERSTITION, DEPRAVITY AND LUST LOCKED ARMS.
CORRECT PICTURE OF THE VOU-DOU DANCE DOWN TOWN ON TUESDAY!

FIG. 5.2. Illustration from the *New Orleans Mascot,* 1889. This demeaning depiction of a Voodoo ceremony in the press demonstrates the prevailing intolerance and misunderstanding of the religion during the late nineteenth century.

arrested for practicing Voodoo in New Orleans in the years between 1850 and the beginning of the Civil War.[35] The repression of Voodoo forced the religion underground, making it seem even more mysterious and threatening, but also fascinating and alluring to many whites and others who did not understand it (fig. 5.2).

A factor that led both to suspicion and to the romanticizing of Voodoo was its presence in the cemeteries. Although Voodoo practitioners are not as prone to use human remains as a source of magical power as magicians in Palo Mayombe and other forms of black magic, Voodoo does regard cemeteries as magical venues. Voodoo practitioners have used dirt from on top of or adjacent to graves, sometimes referred to as "goofer" or "goopher dust," in spells and as an ingredient in charms, along with other exotic ingredients, such as frog bones and flakes of snake skin.[36] The dirt from the grave of a moral, upstanding person was generally used to cast beneficial spells, while the dirt from the grave of an immoral, disreputable individual was employed to do harm. Benevolent spells usually included goopher dust from the graves of children, whom Voodoo magicians saw as innocent and less threatening to the living than the ghosts of adults.[37]

Many Voodoo spells intended to kill or do harm made use of cemeteries. A spell described by Ruth Mason, "a well-known hoodoo [Voodoo] doctor of New Orleans," designed to kill had the following instructions: "Take one yard of a new black calico and tie [a] steak and all in it like a bundle. Knot it nine times. Take it to a cemetery and throw it in a broken grave with either a bottle of whisky uncorked or fifteen cents, and ask the spirit in there to follow them for you. Say, 'I am paying you to follow that person.'"[38] Zora Hurston characterized Samuel Thompson as a "Catholic hoodoo doctor of New Orleans" who claimed to be a grandnephew of Marie Laveau. He was in his seventies in 1928 when she interviewed him and was old enough to have remembered Laveau as an adult. Describing a spell "to gain all power," Thompson directed a magician to "Go to the graveyard at the night of All Saints at twelve o'clock. All of the blessed are gone from the cemetery at that time and only the damned are left. Go to a sinner's grave and get nine hairs from his head and give the spirit there a drink of whiskey. (They'll do anything for a drink of whiskey). Just leave a pint of liquor in there with the stopper out. Go home and burn nine red candles, and the spirit will do anything you want."[39]

Voodoo practice has been evident in New Orleans cemeteries for a long time. In 1868, the body of Edward Forrest was reportedly brought to St. Louis Number 1 and "laid out" with "the face downward and (as was said) an egg in the mouth and a small coin in the hand, in accordance with the Voudou religion."[40] In 1914, neighbors of François Pierre, an African American gravedigger caught illegally exhuming a body from a cemetery, accused him of being a "Voodoo doctor" who intended to use the head of the body to "concoct his potions."[41] A local newspaper reported in 1931 that relatives of a woman buried in St. Roch Cemetery found a black candle and a mound of excavated dirt on her grave. "Digging with their fingers, they found a tin can containing the photograph of a man, a pack of needles, and tobacco inside."[42] A 1938 article in the *Times-Picayune* relates, "On St. John's Eve—the most important night on the voodoo calendar—negroes visit Marie Laveau's tomb. They leave pennies in the dirt nearby, and mark with red brick crosses on the tomb. They whisper their desires to Marie Laveau, and some say they are answered."[43] Around 1940, the sexton of St. Roch Cemetery told a Louisiana Writers' Project (LWP) interviewer, "We've found plenty of stuff in this place. . . . I've found them burying tongues all stuck up with needles and pins and wrapped around with black thread."[44] And finally, author Eleanor Early wrote in 1947 that visitors could find "black candles such as those used in Voodoo" in St. Louis Number 1 and the St. Roch Cemetery.[45] The belief that spirits inhabited cemeteries and could be summoned to do one's bidding created a religious and cultural link between the city of the living and the cities of the dead, adding to the connection made by All Saints' Day.

The local press likely misinterpreted incidents of grave robbing or pure vandalism as being related to Voodoo in the nineteenth and early twentieth centuries. In 1864, the *Daily Picayune* reported that a cemetery in old Algiers (an area of New Orleans on the West Bank of the Mississippi across from the French Quarter) had been raided and pieces of bodies strewn about with parts missing. The newspaper attributed the crime to Voodoo without citing any solid evidence. With emancipation just having occurred in the city, the paper reflected the prevailing fear and racism among whites: "There is no doubt now but that this is the work of negroes; of such have as yet never lost the barbarous tastes of their ancestors, nor forsaken their heathenish rites. . . . Bones and integuments, human flesh, skin and hair, the human fat are all ingredients of these voudou spells."[46] In a similar case, on Halloween night of 1906, during the height of Jim Crow, J. T. Brown Sr. the sexton of the Girod Street Cemetery, blamed an incidence of vandalism where tombs were broken into and skeletons exposed in that cemetery on "superstitious Negroes" or "Halloween jokers." Without offering any evidence, the reporter writing the story chose to blame Voodoo practitioners: "Mr. Brown's conclusion regarding the negroes is doubtless the correct one. Halloween night, according to legend is the ghost night, and on ghost nights the voodoos gather their medicine for charms and spells. Dead man's bones and shrouds are good medicine from the voodoo view, and the desecrators were doubtless in search of that good medicine."[47]

Spells involving goopher dust or throwing various kinds of gris-gris into open graves seldom left an enduring mark on the cemeteries, but other practices have, such as the Voodoo altars maintained at what some believe to be the tombs of powerful Voodoo practitioners. Marie Laveau's tomb in St. Louis Number 1, which has become a major focus of Voodoo practice and lore, is probably the most frequented monument in all of the cemeteries of New Orleans. From the time the religion arrived in Louisiana, Voodoo has had a succession of significant female priests in New Orleans. Marie Laveau is the best-known of them.[48]

Marie Laveau (1801–1881) is reputed to have reigned as the queen of Voodoo in New Orleans for several decades. Legend has it that her father was a wealthy white planter and a member of the state legislature and that her mother was a woman of mixed race who was also a Voodoo priestess. She was supposedly a hairdresser who began a career in Voodoo in the 1830s and used her position cutting hair to gain the trust of the elite of the city and learn its secrets. She used the confessions and gossip she heard while cutting hair to sell her clients potions and spells designed to help them solve problems and overcome obstacles in their lives. Stories found in nineteenth-century periodicals and newspapers purported that she participated in Voodoo ceremonies, dances, and even orgies in a house on Lake Pontchartrain on special Voodoo holy days, particularly St. John's Eve. Laveau supposedly lived to be age ninety-eight. She allegedly had a daughter, sometimes referred to as "Marie II," who took over as Voodoo queen after the original Marie died, and who claimed she was the same "Marie Laveau" as her mother, who had never actually died.[49]

Few of these stories can be verified, and some have been disproven, such as her father's having been a rich planter and her having lived to be ninety-eight. Most are the product of embellishments and downright fiction crafted by late nineteenth- and early twentieth-century newspaper reporters and authors such as Lafcadio Hearn and Herbert Ashbury. All that is really known about her life and activities comes from sparse historical records and reports in local newspapers from the 1850s through the 1880s. In the first known reference to Laveau as a Voodoo priestess, the *Daily Picayune* dubbed her "head of the Voudou women" in 1850. Newspapers reported that she ministered to condemned prisoners in 1871, after having reportedly "retired" as the reigning voodoo queen in 1869.[50]

The newspaper reports make clear that Laveau did practice Voodoo and was likely the head of a group of practitioners. She also may have participated in the St. John's Eve celebrations on the shores of Lake Pontchartrain as the newspapers claimed; however, they were probably not the sensational, licentious events the papers described. In 1870, the *Times* reported that "Marie Lavou" observed St. John's Eve by Lake Pontchartrain with "Eliza Nicaux, and Euphraise," all in their "queenly glories." It is possible that in her old age she renounced Voodoo and returned to Catholicism, the religion of her youth, as a *Daily Picayune* reporter who visited her at her house on St. Ann Street in 1875 claimed.[51] Given that she had been baptized a Catholic, was married in the Church, and had her children baptized, she had actually never truly left the faith in the first place.[52] Despite the popular story that a daughter by the same name succeeded her as Voodoo queen and was buried in an oven vault in St. Louis Number 2, there is no evidence she ever had a daughter who practiced Voodoo. Regardless of the scarcity of historical evidence, the legend of Marie Laveau as the powerful and influential "queen of the Voodoos" is imprinted on the lore of the city and the sensationalistic stories that surround her are often taken as fact.

Most legends emerge from a combination of fact and fancy, and regardless of what the actual Marie Laveau may or may have not accomplished during her lifetime, she has come to represent Voodoo and spirituality generally in New Orleans. Her grave is a shrine and a popular tourist attraction. Historian Carolyn Morrow Long has established that Marie was indeed interned in the "Widow Paris" tomb in the heart of St. Louis Number I in 1881.[53] It has long been a tradition to leave offerings at this particular tomb in order to honor Laveau and to elicit her spiritual power. In 1940, a Voodoo practitioner named Lela told LWP writer Maude Wallace, "I love Marie Laveau. I go an' put flowers on her grave an' she help me too."[54] Lela, who claimed to have known Laveau as a child, also told Wallace, "I say a prayer to Marie Laveau—I say Marie, yo' de greatest—yo help me do my work. . . . She heard me, an' already dat white woman, she be getting' what she want—what I'm working for. Dat's why I go to Marie Laveau's grave—she help me—yes."[55] A witness reported to the LWP in 1940 that "for years after [Marie Laveau died] people used to go put money (silver) on her grave. . . . Up until now some people goes there and puts their hand on her grave and makes a wish . . . and their wish is granted."[56] Another ca. 1940 Maude Wallace interviewee, Ayola Cruz, who had been sexton of St. Louis Number 1 since the early 1920s, told her that people of different races "come almost daily to make offerings to Marie's spirit. They make crosses with red brick, charcoal, and sharp rocks. . . . Devotees knock three times on the marble slab . . . and put their ears to a crack, listening for an answer from the Voodoo queen . . . [and] they used to burn tapers."[57]

For quite some time, people have been making X's on Marie Laveau's tomb and on other sepulchers believed to be inhabited by deceased Voodoo priests or priestesses. One such tomb is an oven vault known as the "Wishing Vault," which some have contended was the actual final resting place of Marie Laveau. In 1921, the *Times-Picayune* devoted an article to this tomb located in St. Louis Number 2. The newspaper quoted the cemetery's sexton,

They come slipping through the gate and looking around so carefully to see that nobody is watching. . . . They go down an aisle, you see, and before every tomb they pause and tap three times with the tips of the fingers while they whisper the wish they want to come true. They then come to the Voudou tomb at the end of the aisle, and with a piece of shell from the walk they make a cross on the bricks and repeat the wish out loud. See all the scratches they have made.

The same sexton also reported that people had left charms at the tomb, such as "a rabbit's foot, a small onion pierced by a goose feather, bits of hair mixed with pepper or salt, or large thorns stuck to each other to form strange designs."[58] Another newspaper article describes practices at the wishing vault in 1938, "A cross mark on the door as a wish is made and a coin slipped behind the loose brick will work a certain charm."[59] In 1946, author Robert Tallant wrote about the Wishing Vault: "Its slab is always covered with literally hundreds of crosses made with red brick. Until recently there was a crack in the slab, and into this devotees would drop coins and make a wish. There was a particular belief here that any girl wishing a husband could be certain of having her desire fulfilled."[60]

Referring to the same tomb in 1936, an LWP interviewee states, "We came to a wall vault filled with red brick crosses with a piece of red brick on it. Grandma called this tomb 'La Beau Comptesse.' . . . Grandma said that the spirit in this tomb never fails to grant the requested favor. This vault is the one mistaken for the burial place of Marie Laveau."[61] The interviewee believed the wishing vault was the tomb of an early Voodoo queen named Marie Comtesse known as La Beau Comtesse (the beautiful countess). She may have been correct. Records indicate that a woman named Labeau or Zabeau Comtesse, who was born in Africa and died in 1834, was buried in St. Louis Number 2.[62] Unfortunately, no evidence has been found that she practiced Voodoo or was buried in this particular oven vault.

In recent years, the practice of drawing X's on historic tombs has usually been the work of tourists and others not actually practicing Voodoo. In 1997, a practicing Voodoo priestess said, "Marie Laveau does not like those X's being scratched on her tomb. Her spirit is there, but those X's chase it away."[63] Despite this sentiment, the X's do have roots in Haitian Voudou. According to Carolyn Morrow Long, the crosses stem from an African tradition that symbolizes the point where the living world intersects with the spirit world. This practice was transferred to the New World, and Voudou practitioners in Haiti draw crosses called *kwasiyen* to establish contact with spirits (*lwa*) and to summon the souls of the dead.

The practice of drawing X's on Laveau's tomb in St. Louis Number 1 dates back to at least 1930. Writing for the September 2, 1930, edition of the *New Orleanian,* historian Leonard Huber notes, "That vault is where Marie La Veau, Voodoo Queen lies buried, and the hundreds of little red crosses were put there by superstitious Negroes for good luck" (figs. 5.3, 5.4).[64] This practice has apparently been repeated ever since. In 1936, the *Baton Rouge Morning Advocate* stated, "Last night was St. John's Eve, the favorite night of the voodoos. . . . Cemetery workers today found a myriad of voodoo crosses scratched across the face of the sepulcher where tradition says the ashes of Marie are housed."[65] Twenty-two years later, a 1958 photograph of the tomb's front shows many X's marking it.[66]

Many of the popular beliefs about Voodoo are based on racist assumptions that the religion is inherently primitive. As in New Orleans as a whole, the history of race relations and segregation in the cemeteries is ambiguous and complicated. Unlike many cities in the South, even during Jim Crow (1877–1960s), New Orleans has always been a patchwork of interlocking neighborhoods where blacks, whites, and Creoles of color live in reasonably close proximity. They spend eternity in similar configurations. While some of the cemeteries had black and white sections at some point in their history, none were fully segregated despite stringent efforts made by whites during the Jim Crow era. This does not mean that there was racial equality in the cemeteries, any more than there was in the city itself.

In the 1700s, as we have seen, most high-status people were buried in the church, and the Ursuline nuns had their own graveyard, but before 1789, when St. Louis Number 1 opened, most everyone else ended up in the St. Peter's Street Cemetery, regardless of their race. An excavation done in the 1980s by anthropologist Douglas W. Owsley and colleagues exhumed twenty-nine skeletons from the St. Peter's Street Cemetery ground. Of the eighteen burials for which the racial background could be identified, two were white, thirteen black, one of possible combined white and Indian ancestry, and two of mixed race (African and Caucasian). Based on examinations of their bones, the researchers determined that most of the African Americans they identified had been enslaved.[67]

Historians believe that burial in St. Louis Number 1 was also integrated.

FIG. 5.3. Tomb of Marie Laveau in St. Louis Cemetery Number 1, its front covered with X marks. Photo by author, 2013.

FIG. 5.4. Close-up of the X's. Although the tradition of drawing or scratching an X on Laveau's tomb and making a wish has origins in Voodoo, the practice is now the domain of tourists and tour guides. Photo by author, 2013.

This is certainly true to some extent. A number of black Creole families, such as the family of Marie Laveau and that of civil rights leader Homer Plessy, owned family tombs. In addition, newspaper reports of burials from the nineteenth century show that slaves were buried in "the Catholic Cemetery." Two newspaper reports from February and March of 1823 state that of twenty-one people buried in St. Louis Number 1 between February 18 and March 10 of that year, seven were slaves, two were free people of color, and the rest were white.[68] Many of the people interred in St. Louis Number 1 in its early years were buried in the ground as opposed as being placed in a tomb or an oven vault, and it is likely slaves such as those reported to have been buried in St. Louis Number 1 by the *Courier* newspaper found damp graves there.

Some slaves, most likely a very limited number, were buried in family tombs. Timothy Flint, a visitor from Massachusetts, claims in his memoir to have seen the tomb of a slave in St. Louis Number 1 in around 1825: "The inscription of another plain but respectable monument was to me affecting. It purports to be erected as a grateful record of the long, faithful, and affectionate services of a black slave. The whole inscription wears a delightful simplicity, and honors the master that erected it as much as the slave."[69] Although his observation of the tomb itself was probably accurate, Flint uses it as an opportunity to sentimentalize slavery, an issue that would tear the country apart later in the century.

After the Civil War, an 1885 tourist guidebook expressed a similar sentiment about a tomb of a slave seen in the Girod Street Cemetery: "Many colored societies have large and well constructed receptacles for the dead, but an item of more than ordinary interest is recorded on a marble tablet of a slave, an old family servant. It reads as follows: 'Mammy, aged 84, a faithful servant. She lived and died a Christian.'"[70] Despite these rare examples, it appears that most African Americans of the nineteenth century, even those of mixed race, were buried in less elegant ways.

When it opened in 1823, St. Louis Number 2 was at least partially segregated. Square Number 3, the block closest to Canal Street, was designated for Catholic African Americans and Creoles of mixed race from the beginning. Although some whites were also buried in Square 3, by the mid-1820s, the influence of strict Anglo-American racial mores was beginning to take hold in the city. In 1824, the Church segregated the first sets of oven wall tombs built in St. Louis Number 2: three were designated for whites and three for nonwhites.[71] An article about the history of the cemeteries published in the *Daily Picayune* from 1859 states: "The St. Louis [Number 2] Cemetery extends from St. Louis to Customhouse Street, between Robinson and Claiborne, occupying thus three squares. It is divided into three cemeteries: the upper one between Bienville and Customhouse, being specially designed for free people of color."[72] Another nineteenth-century cemetery, Lafayette Cemetery Number 2, established in 1865 on a site seven blocks toward Lake Pontchartrain from Lafayette Number 1, may have had a defined area along Sixth Street that was designated for blacks only.[73]

By the Jim Crow period, segregation had come to most of the cemeteries, at least in theory. Some whites resisted integration not only in life but in death as well. In 1912, a white woman bought a vault and buried her "faithful Negro mammy" in the Odd Fellows Rest, ignoring a rule against African Americans being buried there. Shortly thereafter, the cemetery authorities removed the body and took it to another cemetery, to an area which was designated for blacks, without the vault owner's consent. The vault owner sued Odd Fellows Rest. Once the story appeared in the press, the managers of many of the cemeteries of the city tightened their procedures to enforce segregation.[74]

Despite such efforts, racial segregation of the dead was never truly implemented in New Orleans. Twelve years later in 1924, a white citizen complained bitterly in the *Times-Picayune:* "It is greatly to be deplored that the law of segregation recently enforced in theaters, cars, restaurants, and residential sections . . . was not extended to the old cemeteries where it is badly needed."[75] In the following decade, the 1938 *WPA Guide to New Orleans* told its readers, "Many of these cemeteries are controlled by church congregations, and several are city property. Almost every one now has a section for Negroes; and there are no exclusively Negro cemeteries."[76] It was not until the 1960s that people of different races could be legally interred in the same areas of cemeteries as they had been a hundred years earlier. Oddly, despite the existence of slavery, Reconstruction, and the first decades of Jim Crow, the practice of segregation in New Orleans cemeteries had not been a significant issue during most of the nineteenth century, a period when one's economic status was the greatest determiner of where and how one would be buried.

Much of the city's history and culture are expressed in its cemeteries. The enduring celebration of All Saints' Day demonstrates a reverence for tradition and sentiment in New Orleans that goes back to the ancient world. Voodoo altars and offerings at tombs express the presence of enduring African and Caribbean culture and religious beliefs in the city. The haphazard racial integration and largely unsuccessful efforts at segregation in cemeteries before and during Jim Crow recall the racial complexity and ambiguity of the antebellum period, the blatant racism and bigotry of the Jim Crow era, and the resulting medley of names from all over the world that can be found etched on closure tablets and on the cornices of tombs throughout New Orleans.

SUBURBS OF THE DEAD

The Victorian Garden Cemetery in New Orleans

I n May 1872, the *New Orleans Republican* heralded the creation of a new and different cemetery for the city of New Orleans:

> Although the city has many cemeteries located in different sections, and some of them in objectionable places, yet there is not a single one above the ordinary in point of rural beauty or artistic worth. Other large cities are provided with splendid cemeteries and some of them are world-wide in reputation. Greenwood in New York is one of the finest known; Rochester, Philadelphia, Detroit, St. Louis, Boston, Baltimore, Cincinnati and Louisville are provided with finely laid out grounds improved by art and nature. . . . We are pleased to inform our readers that an association of reliable gentlemen have purchased the old Metairie race course ground, for the purpose of converting it into an extensive cemetery.[1]

Metairie Cemetery was the first in New Orleans to be designed without the traditional French and Spanish Creole influences that had guided cemetery planning and building in the city since the eighteenth century. Instead, the design of Metairie Cemetery was based on the picturesque rural garden cemetery created in New England around 1830.

The first true rural garden cemetery in the United States, Mount Auburn in Cambridge, Massachusetts, opened in 1831. Although its creators had found much of their inspiration in the parklike character of Père Lachaise during its first decades, they laid out Mount Auburn to better resemble a naturalistic park than its Parisian forebear did, with scenic ponds, generous numbers of trees, and expansive areas of open space. The concept of creating a large suburban cemetery while combining the disciplines of horticulture and landscape design with burial was new. In the 1820s, Jacob Bigelow, founder of the Massachusetts Horticulture Society, promoted the idea of establishing a new cemetery to replace Boston's traditional crowded, ill-kept, and sometimes unsanitary urban graveyards.

Boston's rapidly rising population, which nearly doubled between 1820 and 1840, had pushed the city's urban graveyards to overflowing. Acting to carry out their plan, Bigelow and his partners purchased a seventy-two-acre parcel in Cambridge, four miles west of Boston. Using principles of European garden design, they laid out the cemetery, which would look and function more like a public park than any cemetery had up to that time. They spread Mount Auburn over seven rolling hills (fig. 6.1). Because it was such a radical departure from the tradition in New England of burying the dead in urban graveyards and churchyards (fig. 6.2), the enterprise posed a

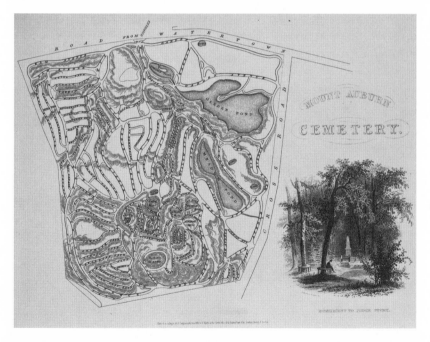

FIG. 6.1. Plan of Mount Auburn Cemetery, Cambridge, Massachusetts, and a drawing of the Judge Story monument in its pastoral surroundings. Compared to Mount Auburn, with its hills, lakes, and open fields, Père Lachaise looked urban. Engraving from James Smillie, *Mount Auburn Illustrated* (New York: Martin and Johnson, 1848).

FIG. 6.2 Old Swede's Church, Philadelphia, 1901. This was the familiar form of burial in the eastern United States at the time Mount Auburn was established. Postcard, author's collection.

FIG. 6.3. Egyptian revival main gate of Mount Auburn Cemetery (1843), designed by architect Jacob Bigelow. This stone gate replaced an earlier one of similar design constructed out of wood. The use of the exotic and romantic Egyptian style added to the cemetery's picturesque allure. Historic American Buildings Survey photo.

FIG. 6.4. Laurel Hill Cemetery in Philadelphia, established in 1836. Garden cemeteries such as this expressed a new pastoral view of death and memory. Photo by author, 2013.

financial risk for its promoters. But with the rise of American romanticism and Victorian sentimentality, which favored picturesque settings and encouraged the expression of melancholy, the cemetery quickly became popular, prestigious, and eventually famous (fig. 6.3).

Other American cities soon followed Boston's lead. Philadelphia established Laurel Hill Cemetery in 1836, Baltimore opened Green Mount Cemetery in 1838, and New York City created Green-Wood Cemetery in Brooklyn in 1839. By the Civil War, sixty-one American cities had established a rural garden cemetery of some kind, and these had usually become their most desirable burial ground (fig. 6.4).[2]

The rural cemetery movement reflected a changing view of death from the morbid image expressed by weathered and leaning tombstones, decaying crypts, and literal funerary imagery like the carved sculls and skeletons often found on tombstones prior to the 1830s. The garden cemeteries offered a more abstract and calming concept of deceased loved ones at slumber, recumbent under picturesque monuments shaded by weeping willows and adorned with angels and urns in a beautiful parklike setting.[3] By the 1850s, the word "cemetery," a term that had been used in New Orleans

Fig. 6.5. Mount Auburn grave in a pastoral setting. Image from Wilson Flagg, *Mount Auburn: Its Scenes, Its Beauties, and Its Lessons* (Boston: James Munroe and Co., 1861).

since the 1700s, came into common parlance throughout the United States to replace "graveyard," "burial ground," or "churchyard."

Garden cemeteries took on a significant role in the daily lives of ordinary people that is difficult to identify with now. This is partly because of the Victorian fixation on death. Victorians in the East and in most English-speaking countries added visiting the local garden cemetery to a long list of elaborate death customs, such as the wearing of black by widows for up to two years, the stopping of a household clock at the time of a family member's death, and the dressing of the dead in strictly prescribed ways prior to burial. The garden cemeteries represented a more pastoral and comforting side of death that attracted the living (fig. 6.5). Bostonians and tourists described Mount Auburn as a "pleasure garden" and "a place of general resort and interest." An English visitor to Boston wrote in the early 1850s that "cemeteries here are all the 'rage,' people lounge in them and use them (as their tastes are inclined) for walking, making love, weeping, sentimentalizing, and everything in short."[4]

The new cemeteries became popular places to spend a leisurely afternoon. Between April and December of 1848, Laurel Hill Cemetery near

FIG. 6.6. Victorian-era view of Laurel Hill Cemetery, by John Notman. Image from *Guide to Laurel Hill Cemetery, near Philadelphia, with numerous illustrations* (Philadelphia: C. Sherman, 1844).

Philadelphia received over 30,000 tourists.[5] Cincinnati's Spring Grove Cemetery (1844) received between 86,000 and 160,000 visitors a year in the 1860s and 1870s.[6] Green-Wood Cemetery in Brooklyn sold admission tickets. It also produced and sold a tour book, which included a guided carriage tour. Victorian rural cemetery guidebooks often listed rules of etiquette for recreational visitors, designed to ensure their demeanor showed respect for the dead and for those who had come to the cemetery to mourn them.[7] Cemetery tourism became a national phenomenon. Families would spend an entire Sunday afternoon picnicking among the graves of their ancestors (fig. 6.6).

It is little wonder garden cemeteries became so popular. As the nineteenth century progressed, they evolved into sculpture gardens filled with carefully placed and artfully created monuments and art set within pastoral, designed landscapes. Lost loved ones were either memorialized in a designated family plot, often surrounded by flowers, grass, and shrubbery, and marked with a carved monolith, column, or obelisk, or placed in a stylish family tomb. The wealthy built fantastic monuments that towered over the landscape and tombs that looked like model temples or cathedrals. These cemeteries represented mortality, resurrection, history, and sublime nature all at once. With their spaciousness, trees, and lawns, and well-defined plots, garden cemeteries were truly posh "suburbs of the dead."

Despite the national fascination with rural cemeteries from the 1830s on, cemeteries in New Orleans remained compact and urban until Metairie Cemetery opened, long after most American cities had established one or more garden cemeteries. Cypress Grove, designed in 1840, had some of the parklike characteristics of a Mount Auburn or a Green-Wood; however, like Père Lachaise before it, the cemetery soon filled with tombs, making it more closely resemble its crowded predecessors.

Many northern visitors writing in the 1830s–60s compared and contrasted the historic cemeteries they found in New Orleans with the new garden cemeteries they were familiar with up north and often found them wanting. After touring St. Louis Number 2 around 1834, Joseph Ingraham wrote: "The citizens of the United States will not certainly acknowledge themselves second to any nation in point of refinement. But look at their cemeteries. Most crown some bleak hill, or occupy the ill-fenced corners of some barren and treeless common. . . . Our neglect of the dead is both a reproach and a proverb."[8] The garden cemetery was just being developed in the United States at the time Ingraham was writing, and he welcomed it: "The Bostonians, in possession of their lonely and romantic Mount Auburn, have redeemed their character from the almost universal charge of apathy and indifference by their fellow countrymen upon this subject."[9] At least one contemporary resident of New Orleans agreed. In 1833, a reporter for the *New Orleans Commercial Bulletin* complained: "Mount Auburn [is] situated a few miles outside of Boston, on a romantic site; it is a beautiful garden, adorned by splendid specimens of 'Monumental Marble.' . . . Cannot such a thing be done here?"[10] Some years later, Fredricka Bremer, a visitor in the early 1850s, wrote of the "French burial ground" (probably St. Louis Number 1), apparently comparing it with rural cemeteries: "It is really a 'city of the dead' whole streets and squares of tombs and graves . . . and among these no trees, no grass plots, nothing green. . . . All was dead; all stony all desolate. . . . Wherever we walked, we walked between graves and tombs; wherever we turned, the eye encountered tombs and bare walls with nothing over them."[11]

As the rural cemetery movement, with its emphasis on peaceful contemplation and preserving the memory of dead individuals in perpetual serenity, became increasingly popular in the rest of the United States, New Orleanians continued to find their inspiration in historic Spanish and French models of a densely packed necropolis filled with reusable family and society tombs that emphasized family and community over individualism. This approach, of a collective, temporary, and often anonymous method of burial, perplexed many American and English travelers and added to their sense of the exotic otherness of Creole New Orleans, its climate, culture, and architecture.

Despite such deeply ingrained local traditions, in 1872, over forty years after Mount Auburn had opened, the garden cemetery had finally arrived in New Orleans. In May of that year, a charter was granted to the Metairie Cemetery Association to plan and construct a large new garden cemetery on the site of the Metairie Race Course, a former horse-racing venue. The racecourse was located on the Metairie Ridge, an ancient bank of the Mississippi River, a natural levee that had created high ground (at least for New Orleans) about halfway between where the river is today and Lake Pontchartrain. The racetrack had opened in 1838 and soon became famous throughout the country. It operated successfully until the Civil War. After the war, its owners attempted to keep the track open, but the operation had gone bankrupt by 1872.[12]

Local businessman Charles T. Howard, who had amassed a fortune running the Louisiana State Lottery Company, bought the 108-acre property with a group of partners with the intention of creating a rural garden cemetery there.[13] According to a popular story, Howard had been refused membership in the Metairie Jockey Club, which had operated the Metairie Race Course, because he was "new money." Of course this angered him, and once the track became insolvent, he decided to buy the land with a portion of that new money and turn their former playground into a cemetery, eclipsing their happy memories forever. While this tale has not been verified, it is true that the tomb in which his body was interred in 1885 is located at the very center of the cemetery and features a Greco-Roman–style statue of an old man with a finger to his lips, perhaps to encourage eternal silence at the site that had once seen such noisy excitement and intractable snobbery (fig. 6.7).

FIG. 6.7. Statue inside the tomb of Charles T. Howard, the businessman who created Metairie Cemetery. Photo by author, 2015.

Howard and his partners held a competition for the design of the new cemetery, but none of the entries impressed them. Rather than choosing a design from the contest, the cemetery's board of directors hired architect Benjamin Morgan Harrod to design the cemetery.[14] A Confederate veteran and Harvard graduate, Harrod was familiar with many of the board members.[15] He would go on to design the Confederate monument in Greenwood Cemetery (1874). In addition to being an architect who participated in the design of many of the buildings on the Tulane University campus dating from the 1890s and including Gibson Hall, he also engineered a number of large-scale water drainage projects and dams later in his career. He developed such a reputation that in 1905 President Theodore Roosevelt appointed him to the Panama Canal Commission.[16] In his plan for the cemetery, Harrod incorporated the original oval track into its layout.[17] The alignment of the track can still be seen when viewing the original part of the cemetery from the air. Like the rural garden cemeteries of the East,

FIG. 6.8. "Millionaire's Row," Metairie Cemetery. Photo by author, 2015.

Metairie Cemetery was laid out with a system of curving roads and water features in a parklike environment, setting it apart from any cemetery that existed in New Orleans at the time (fig. 6.8).

The 1872 *New Orleans Republican* article quoted at the beginning of this chapter described what the new cemetery would soon become: "Roadways, paths and divisions will be laid out, beds of rare flowers and choice shrubberies planted, and the stately magnolia and mournful cypress will be given a place. One important feature will be especially attended to, namely, that of planning the roads so that carriages can drive into the yard."[18] In 1873, the Metairie Cemetery Association advertised, "It is the purpose of the Association to so improve and ornament this cemetery as to make it equal, in point of beauty to any in the country."[19] Others agreed. In 1877, a reporter for the *Daily Picayune* wrote: "Undoubtedly the Metairie Cemetery is destined to be the great Necropolis of the South. As far as its location, ornaments, care and poetry are concerned, we say that this great city of the dead is unrivaled."[20]

When Metairie Cemetery opened, the rural garden cemetery was still a novelty in New Orleans. Although most of the older cemeteries remained in operation, people who could afford to do so flocked to Metairie Cemetery, and before long, hundreds of stone tombs and monuments, many of them large, opulent, and ornate, had appeared among the live oaks and

Fig. 6.9. Avenue of tombs in Metairie Cemetery. Photo by author, 2010.

cypress trees in the pastoral settings promised by the *New Orleans Republican* and the Metairie Cemetery Association. In the mid-1890s, an engineer named George H. Grandjean enhanced the pastoral quality of the cemetery when he reworked its drainage system, adding three artificial lakes and a decorative bridge.[21] Grandjean had made similar improvements to New Orleans's City Park.[22]

Although in other regions of the country, Victorian-era rural cemeteries mostly had underground burials, with only a limited number of impressive mausoleums built by the very rich, in Metairie Cemetery aboveground burial in tombs and mausoleums became the norm (fig. 6.9). Rather than functioning only as an efficient method of burying the dead in order to keep their bodies aboveground and dry, the tombs at Metairie acted primarily as monuments to social status, especially given the fact that it was possible to excavate deep subterranean graves without them filling with water in many parts of the cemetery because of its relatively high elevation. From the very beginning, the majority of burials there were aboveground, demonstrating that the tradition of tomb building had become an integral aspect of the culture of the city by the late 1800s. "Many bury in the ground today—particularly the poor," wrote historian Leonard Huber in 1930, "but the strong-rooted custom of tomb burial defies time and improvements; Orleanians who can afford it for the most part still erect tombs."[23]

Despite early similarities in design, the prevalence of tomb building resulted in the cemetery developing differently than garden cemeteries in the rest of the United States. Although Metairie does not have the density of Père Lachaise, fanciful tombs lining formal avenues characterize both cemeteries. Whereas most garden cemeteries are parklike landscapes punctuated by monuments, Metairie has a more architectural character, embodying a unique combination of the traditional New Orleans and rural garden cemetery types.

The grand cemetery gradually filled with substantial structures designed in a myriad of architectural styles using decorative motifs taken from throughout history. Tombs and monuments suggesting ancient Egypt, ancient Greece and Rome, the Middle Ages, the Italian Renaissance, and traditional Islamic architecture, as well as modernistic styles such as art deco, eventually crowded the cemetery. These tombs took on spectacular forms: temples and pyramids, chapels, shrines, churches, columns, and stone sarcophagi (fig. 6.10). A number of Italian burial societies con-

FIG. 6.10. The Mayer sarcophagus tomb (1907), Metairie Cemetery. Monuments such as this were a grand departure from the brick and stucco tombs introduced to the city a century earlier. Photo by author, 2011.

FIG. 6.11. The Minerva Benevolent Association tomb, Metairie Cemetery. In need of restoration, this society tomb would not appear out of place in the Italian countryside. Photo by author, 2012.

structed impressive society tombs there, some of which resemble Renaissance chapels (fig. 6.11).

The Brunswig tomb, ca. 1892, is essentially a copy of the pyramidal tomb of Francesco Bruni, who died in 1876, in Cimitero Monumentale, Milan, Italy. The Bruni tomb's architect was Angelo Colla and its sculptor, Giulio Monteverde. The Brunswig tomb also closely resembles the pyramidal Schoenhofen tomb in Graceland Cemetery, Chicago, as well as a tomb in the General Cemetery in Santiago, Chile. All of these monuments take the form of a steep-sided, Nubian-style pyramid resting on a plinth. A sphinx and the statue of a woman who looks more Greco-Roman than Egyptian flank the Brunswig tomb's key entrance, which has a lintel featuring a cavetto cornice and a winged solar disc (fig. 6.12).

Another highly distinctive tomb in Metairie Cemetery is the Beauregard-Larendon tomb, built about 1890. Made of Belgian limestone, it has scalloped arches and a squared onion dome topped by an Eastern Orthodox triple cross. Islamic arabesque relief covers the outside walls in the col-

FIG. 6.12. The Brunswig tomb (ca. 1892), showing Egyptian influences, Metairie Cemetery. Photo by author, 2012.

umned section. One of its most striking features is its circular stained-glass window (fig. 6.13).

The design of one of the most monumental tombs in the cemetery, the Lacosst tomb, is based on the architecture of ancient Rome. In 1918, Albert Weiblen built this mausoleum using costly select white Alabama marble, and he located it conspicuously in sight of Metairie Road. The tomb takes the form of a triumphal arch with a coffered half dome sheltering an ornately carved sarcophagus (fig. 6.14). It is possible that Eugene Lacosst believed he needed to outdo other members of the well-to-do who built their tombs nearby, because he was a hairdresser who somehow made a fortune in the stock market.[24]

Representing the gothic revival style, the eccentric Egan tomb mimics the gothic ruin of a medieval abbey in Ireland owned by ancestors of

FIG. 6.13. The Beauregard-Larendon tomb (ca. 1890), Metairie Cemetery. Its style, based on traditional Islamic design, is sometimes referred to as Moorish exotic revival. Photo by author, 2010.

the Egan family.[25] The structure, which reflects the prevailing nineteenth-century Romantic affection for the Middle Ages, has false cracks in its walls and floor and a seemingly collapsed roof that make the monument appear to be in a ruined condition (figs. 6.15, 6.16). The floor of the diminutive abbey has a tablet bearing the names of the deceased family members buried beneath it. The tablet also has faux cracks running through it to make it appear to be broken.

Many of the larger monuments in Metairie Cemetery memorialize political and military figures, particularly those associated with the Confederacy. Many Confederate veterans held influential positions during the period in which the Metairie Cemetery was being developed. Adding to this, in the late nineteenth century the myth of the Lost Cause became very popular. This nostalgic doctrine attempted to justify the Confederate ideology and

FIG. 6.14. The Lacosst tomb (1918), designed and built by Albert Weiblen, Metairie Cemetery. Photo by author, 2015.

create complimentary explanations of why the South had lost the Civil War. It sought to vindicate the white South after it had suffered defeat and to perpetuate a romanticized memory of the antebellum period while celebrating state's rights and liberty as a Southern principle, as well as advocating racial segregation.[26] Prevalent in New Orleans, this ideology had many advocates among whites all over the South and even the nation as a whole in the late nineteenth and early twentieth centuries.

One of the key ways to express the Lost Cause version of history was to glorify former Confederate military leaders, especially Stonewall Jackson and Robert E. Lee. One manner in which Confederate veterans and their allies sought to memorialize the Confederate forces was to erect extravagant funerary monuments in cemeteries, and New Orleans has a number of significant examples. Expressing the spirit of the Lost Cause, a 1910 tourist guide praised the Confederate monument in Greenwood Cemetery that Benjamin Morgan Harrod had designed in the 1870s: "The beautiful and artistic monument dedicated to the Confederate dead, under which sleep near five hundred soldiers of the Lost Cause, and over which a marble sentinel ever keeps watch, is one of the finest tombs in the country."[27]

FIG. 6.15. The gothic revival Egan tomb (1884), Metairie Cemetery. Photo by author, 2015.

The 1900 *Standard History of New Orleans, Louisiana* praises the Civil War monuments in Metairie Cemetery without mentioning any of the cemetery's other impressive structures: "In this cemetery are many beautiful and interesting monuments, conspicuous among them are the tomb of the Army of Northern Virginia, surmounted by a column bearing a statue of Stonewall Jackson; the tomb of the Washington Artillery, crowned by a statue of their old commander Colonel J. B. Walton; and the Gothic vault of the Army of Tennessee, upon whose grassy summit is posed a bronze equestrian statue of Albert Sidney Johnston."[28]

Positioned on a mound in a circle at the very heart of the cemetery, the tomb of the Army of Northern Virginia is one of the most conspicuous landmarks at Metairie (fig. 6.17). Monuments such as this were inaugurated with much fanfare. On May 10, 1881, the eighteenth anniversary of Stonewall Jackson's death, a crowd of ten thousand people attended the dedication of the monument. Honored guests included Jackson's widow

FIG. 6.16. Entrance to the Egan tomb. Photo by author, 2015.

and Jefferson Davis, former president of the Confederacy, who would be buried in the same tomb eight years later. The plinth beneath the monument's thirty-two-foot-tall gray granite column depicts crossed Confederate battle flags. Underneath, 2,500 Confederate veterans are buried.[29]

Another significant Civil War memorial in the cemetery, the vault of the Army of Tennessee, was dedicated in 1887 (fig. 6.18). Built in the form of a tumulus mound, an ancient conical tomb type often used for royalty that dates back to prehistoric times, it was designed to hold multiple bodies like a society tomb; however, its primary purpose was to honor the Southern forces at a time when Lost Cause nostalgia was at its height. A statue of a Confederate sergeant calling roll stands in front of the tomb. His face was modeled after the photograph of an actual soldier from Louisiana who fell in action in 1864.

In addition to these grandiose monuments, Metairie Cemetery contains a number of extraordinarily flamboyant and storied tombs and funerary

FIG. 6.17. The tomb of the Army of Northern Virginia (1881), Metairie Cemetery: half grave marker, half monument to the Lost Cause. Photo by author, 2015.

markers. One of the most conspicuous of these is the mammoth Moriarty monument, erected near the tomb of the Army of Tennessee close to the original cemetery entrance. The Moriarty monument cost an astounding $85,000 (approximately $2.2 million in 2016 dollars) to build. A special railroad spur was constructed to deliver massive granite components to its site in the cemetery (fig. 6.19). Daniel Moriarty, a nouveau riche businessman of Irish descent, erected the monument to the memory of his wife around 1905. She had died nearly two decades earlier, in 1887. A story relates that, as with the cemetery's founder, Charles T. Howard, New Orleans high society never accepted Moriarty despite his wealth. He supposedly built the colossal monument so tall that it would look down on the final resting places of members of the city's old-money elite forever.

According to another story, the comely female statues that surround the base of the monument's obelisk represent the "four Graces"—Faith, Hope,

FIG. 6.18. The tomb of the Army of Tennessee (1887), with the historic Metairie Cemetery gate in background. Library of Congress, Prints and Photographs Division.

Charity, and Moriarty's wife (fig. 6.20). According to the 1938 *WPA Guide to New Orleans,* however, "the four statues were simply stock female sculptures placed on the monument for effect by the builder."[30]

In 1914, Albert Weiblen designed and built the lavish and notorious Morales mausoleum for Josie Arlington, a rich madam who operated a brothel in the Storyville district (fig. 6.21). Storyville, at the time usually referred to simply as "the district," occupied an area roughly between St. Louis Number 1 and St. Louis Number 2 cemeteries, bounded by North Robertson, Iberville, Basin, and St. Louis streets. In order to contain rampant prostitution, the city government declared prostitution "not illegal" in this rundown section of town from 1897 until 1917, when the Department of the Navy closed the district because of its proximity to a naval base. The once-thriving area was demolished in the 1930s to make way for the Iberville Public Housing Project, the majority of which has since been razed to make way for another housing scheme. The district contained hundreds of shabby brothels, or "cribs," but was also home to a small number of

FIG. 6.19. The spectacular Moriarty monument (1905), Metairie Cemetery. This giant monument dwarfs other tombs and grave markers in the cemetery. Photo by author, 2015.

FIG. 6.20. The "four Graces," Moriarty monument. Photo by author, 2015.

FIG. 6.21. The Morales tomb (1914), designed and built by Albert Weiblen for notorious brothel madam Josie Arlington. Note that the Morales name has been incised into a recess in the granite where Arlington's name was ground off. Photo by author, 2015.

high-class establishments arrayed along Basin Street, including the one owned by Arlington.

Josie Arlington's stylish tomb features a bronze statue of a young woman rumored to be a virgin who would never gain entry. Sometime after 1914, the polished pink granite tomb became a public attraction because someone noticed it emitted a mysterious red glow at night, perhaps mystically reflecting the unwholesome career of the woman entombed within. The tomb drew nightly crowds until it was discovered that the source of the strange light was a traffic signal just outside the cemetery. At some point prior to 1930, Arlington's heirs sold the tomb to the family of José Morales. The madam's remains were removed and taken to another tomb in the cemetery, which the cemetery's managers kept secret to avoid Arlington's second resting place becoming a tourist attraction like the first.[31]

With its scenic grounds and lavish tombs, Metairie Cemetery embodies the power and the myths of the city's elite of the late nineteenth century and beyond. The cemetery received the greatest number of elite burials

FIG. 6.22. Historic entrance to Metairie Cemetery. This gatehouse, built in 1883, was removed in 1954 to make way for an interstate overpass. Postcard, author's collection.

FIG. 6.23. Former lagoon at Metairie Cemetery. This lake is now filled in and is beneath an interstate overpass. Library of Congress, Prints and Photographs Division.

of any cemetery in New Orleans from its inception in 1872 until well into the twentieth century. It remains one of the most visited and active New Orleans burial grounds to this day. Although the cemetery is still largely intact, in 1954 the historic 1883 gatehouse and one of its lakes were removed to make way for the Interstate 10 overpass at City Park Avenue and Pontchartrain Boulevard (figs. 6.22, 6.23).[32]

An ornamental showplace unique to New Orleans, Metairie Cemetery was the first and last of its kind in the city. By the time any significant new cemeteries were created in the New Orleans area, the Victorian garden cemetery had become obsolete. Newer burial grounds took the form of the memorial park that came about in the early twentieth century. Hubert Easton opened the first such cemetery in 1917 in Glendale, California, and the idea spread rapidly across the nation. Easton designed the memorial park to make the business of death more pleasant, efficient, and profitable.[33] Like garden cemeteries, the new variety was parklike, as the name suggests. However, the picturesque family monuments and tombs disappeared. The once-distinctive Victorian gravestones morphed into simple, nondescript grave markers, significantly reducing their presence in the landscape. As with the earlier garden cemeteries, they feature lawns, ponds, shade trees, statues, and fountains; however, at first glance, a visitor to some memorial parks might not even realize he or she has entered a cemetery. Some have no tombstones, instead requiring each grave be marked with a horizontal stone block or metal plate low enough to the ground to be easily mowed over.

Memorial parks offer the illusion of bland equality; deceased occupants are lined up with geometric precision in visual anonymity with only their names and dates of birth and death and perhaps a vase of plastic flowers to differentiate them from their neighbors. Some families of the deceased have attempted to create a lasting identity for their lost loved ones by having photographs of them etched on ceramic plates or printed on plastic disks and adhering them to their humble grave markers, although many memorial parks forbid this.

In recent decades, the open quality of some memorial parks has been altered as the corporations that usually own them have constructed mourning chapels and massive multivaulted mausoleums. These modern structures are reminiscent of the old New Orleans wall tombs, but are more uniform and industrial in appearance (fig. 6.24). Their vaults are not re-

Fig. 6.24. Modern mausoleums, Lake Lawn Memorial Park. Warehouse-like funerary structures of this type can be found all over the nation, and in many other parts of the world as well. Photo by author, 2015.

used, however, making it necessary for the complexes to be very large, with periodic additions to increase capacity and maximize profits. Some have sheltered areas or indoor corridors furnished like the lobbies of middling hotels or suburban living rooms. In this way, death is organized, sanitized, and brought under a false sense of control.

Woodlawn Memorial Park, established in 1939 adjacent to Metairie Cemetery just over the Jefferson Parish line, was, with the exception of a few potter's fields, the first cemetery with entirely belowground burials to be created in the New Orleans metropolitan region after 1789.[34] At first, the new memorial park had no architectural or artistic features particular to Louisiana, but the tradition of tomb building in New Orleans is so well entrenched that a portion of its grounds has since been built over with granite family tombs indistinguishable from the twentieth-century tombs constructed in nearby Metairie Cemetery (fig. 6.25). In 1939, Woodlawn was renamed Lake Lawn Memorial Park, and in addition to the family tombs, many massive communal mausoleums have been constructed there. Although memorial parks dominate burial in most cities in the United States today, they have never displaced older cemeteries such as Metairie and the

Fig. 6.25. Recent yet traditional New Orleans–style tombs at Lake Lawn Memorial Park. Photo by author, 2015.

earlier walled cemeteries in New Orleans, most of which continue to receive interments, and which still help to define the concept of burial in the city.

Metairie Cemetery represented a fundamental shift in the burial traditions of New Orleans. It brought the city more in line with other parts of the country. The transition was never complete, however, because aboveground burial in family and society tombs continued at Metairie as it did in cemeteries all over the city, even though conventional burial was possible in most parts of the metro area after the turn of the twentieth century, when massive pumps drained the wetlands and lowered the water table. Although it began as a garden cemetery, Metairie resembles Paris's Père Lachaise more than it does Boston's Mount Auburn or Brooklyn's Green-Wood. Even its modern neighbor, Lake Lawn Memorial Park, could not maintain its mainstream appearance in the context of the ingrained burial traditions of New Orleans.

SLUMS OF THE DEAD
Decay and Cemetery Preservation

I n New Orleans, maintaining almost any building, structure, lawn, or garden is a challenging task. Cemeteries are no exception. Tombs tilt and sink into the city's spongy soils. Tree roots tear at walls. Vines invade roofs. Rainwater erodes stucco, brick, and even stone. Nature, fueled by ample rain, frequent floods, and a humid, semitropical climate, seeks to return the city to a brambled riverbank surrounded by swamps. Adding to the many threats caused by natural forces, human activity also endangers the historic cemeteries. Although tourism can act as a motivating factor for cemetery preservation, it can also be detrimental unless managed in a manner that protects cemeteries from vandalism and looting on the one hand, but prevents them from being transformed into Disneyfied tourist sites on the other.

Throughout their history, the cemeteries of New Orleans have been neglected, demolished, vandalized, and looted. In 1835, a reporter for the *New Orleans Commercial Bulletin* commented, "A cultivated taste would find ample field for improvement in all our burial grounds in the city—and mostly in the Protestant Cemetery, which we cannot but deem to be in a more neglected condition than either of the Catholic grounds."[1] In 1835, the Girod Street Cemetery was only thirteen years old and already showing signs of wear. In 1845, a time when St. Louis Number 1 was less than sixty years old, a visitor's description makes that cemetery seem ancient: "Part of the cemetery contained some very old tombs with quaint French inscriptions. . . . These were mostly moldering into piles of rubbish, and soon would be indistinguishable from the dust around."[2] In 1851, another observer echoed these sentiments about the tombs in St. Louis Number 1:

"Many are old and crumbling, and dyed green with moisture."[3] St. Louis Number 2 had even more serious early preservation issues. In 1844, a New Orleans reporter scolded: "Our attention has been called to the dilapidated state of a portion of the vaults in the Catholic cemetery on Claiborne street. . . . We were astonished—nay shocked—at witnessing the manner in which the northern wall of the cemetery has been suffered to crumble and fall down without apparently an effort on the part of those whose duty it is to have it repaired. There are several coffins exposed to the gaze of every passer-by."[4]

Throughout the nineteenth and twentieth centuries, the care of tombs was inconsistent, with some being meticulously maintained and others left shamefully neglected. The family or organization owning a tomb has always been responsible for its maintenance. The reasons a family might neglect a tomb are numerous. Some families died out, while the descendants of others moved away or lost the economic resources that had allowed their ancestors to build a family tomb. After about 1950, the Archdiocese of New Orleans started offering perpetual care contracts, but apparently few bought them. To make matters worse, the maintenance performed under these contracts has not always been sensitive or respectful to the historic character of the tombs.[5]

Although many crumbled, some tombs remained in good condition for decades and perhaps centuries. A visitor in 1851 observed: "The freeness of . . . these graveyards from the settlings of dust, and the numberless other defacing marks of time, is worthy of observation. This is attributed to the constant washings to which the tombs are subjected. By undergoing that process continually, they appear ever new."[6] In 1883, Mark Twain commented, "Many of the cemeteries are beautiful and are kept in perfect order."[7] New Orleans historian Leonard Huber, writing in 1930, explained: "The forgotten tomb, neglected, no flowers, not whitewashed, stands alone, deserted—a silent deserted spectacle. . . . There are not many neglected tombs, however, those which perhaps belonged to families which were wiped out by one of the numerous epidemics."[8]

Despite these observations, by the late nineteenth century a good number of tombs in the older cemeteries, especially in St. Louis Number 2 and the Girod Street Cemetery, had fallen into ruin. As once-distinct cultures assimilated and neighborhoods shifted, many families lost touch with the graves of their ancestors and stopped maintaining them. In the late nineteenth and early twentieth centuries, burials in the older cemeteries decreased, as did visitation, and some family tombs became abandoned.[9] The historic cemeteries fell out of favor, with the elite increasingly migrating to newer burial grounds, particularly Metairie Cemetery. In addition, at the turn of the twentieth century, many of the burial societies disbanded or built new tombs at Metairie Cemetery. Without the support of the benevolent societies that had built them, society tombs fell into disuse and were left to the elements, vandals, and looters.

Along with neglect, some cemeteries were willfully destroyed. In 1822, shockingly early in its history, the Protestant section of St. Louis Number 1 was partially demolished to make way for road construction. In the following decades, large swaths of historic tombs, the supposedly sacred resting places of people's ancestors, were razed. In 1839, the *Daily Picayune* reported that upon visiting St. Louis Number 1, one of its reporters was dismayed to see that sections of the cemetery's walls had been taken down and stakes for a new road had been planted through the cemetery itself.[10] An 1859 newspaper article recounts the partial destruction of St. Louis Number 1: "St. Louis Cemetery . . . extended several squares in length, and was divided on the opening of Tremé and other streets some fifteen years ago. The greater parts of the remains taken from the tombs broken up, were removed to other tombs in the new cemetery."[11] So much of the cemetery fell to road construction and was paved over that the pyramidal Varney tomb, which is now close to the cemetery's entrance, was once near its center. What visitors to St. Louis Number 1 see today is but a remnant of what was once a much grander necropolis.

When they were not wantonly demolished, many tombs in the older cemeteries were simply left to the mercy of the elements. In 1880, writer, humorist, and New Orleans resident Lafcadio Hearn quipped: "They are hideous Golgothas, these old intermural cemeteries of ours. In other cities cemeteries are beautiful with all that the art of the gardener and sculptor can give. . . . There the horror is masked. Here it glares at us with empty sockets. The tombs are fissured, or have caved in, or have crumbled down into shapeless bricks and mortar . . . [and] crawfish undermine the walls to feast upon what is hidden within."[12] In 1885, a tourist guide to New Orleans echoed Hearn's sentiments: "The older cemeteries, such as St. Louis . . . are now at the heart of the most populous parts of the city, and every consideration of public sanitation demands that they be closed. . . . In this cemetery many of the oldest tombs are so dilapidated that they cannot be identified and some are missing altogether."[13]

In that same year, Hearn complained in his own New Orleans guide-book: "Girod Cemetery is old and dilapidated. It does not bear the marks of constant attention seen elsewhere."[14] The *Standard History of New Orleans, Louisiana,* published in 1900, states, "Many of the old tombs are empty and falling to pieces, the tablets gone, or so worn by winter's storms and summer's heats that the inscriptions are no longer legible."[15] The decay continued into the twentieth century. In 1906 a newspaper article about vandalism in the Girod Street Cemetery relates, "There are vaults and tombs so far decayed and rotten that the passer-by can look within and see iron caskets that have been resting there for perhaps half a decade."[16] And in 1910, a New Orleans tour book otherwise designed to promote tourism in the city describes St. Louis Number 1 thus, apparently plagiarizing the 1885 tourist guide cited above: "Many of the oldest tombs are so dilapidated that they cannot be identified, and some are missing all together."[17]

Because of the deplorable state of many tombs, in 1923 a group of activists led by the well-known New Orleans author Grace King formed the Society for the Preservation of Ancient Tombs. In that year, the *Times-Picayune* reported: "The society was recently organized to save for future generations the historic tombs of New Orleans' old cemeteries, many of which are without headstones and are rapidly crumbling away."[18] Its 150 original members undertook a research project to identify and document the tombs of individuals with the greatest historical significance and to create a plan for their restoration. The society's main objective appears to have been the identification and restoration of the tombs of key figures in New Orleans history in order to celebrate their memory with a "patriotic purpose."[19] The society used its "limited resources" to restore tombs of influential elite individuals in the old St. Louis cemeteries and made efforts to find the descendants of such people and urge them to restore the tombs of their ancestors.[20] How historically accurate these restorations were is difficult to gauge.

By the late 1940s, St. Louis Number 1 began to attract increasing numbers of tourists. Many of these visitors enjoyed the picturesque quality created by the continuing decay of some of its tombs. In his 1948 history of St. Louis Number 1, Joseph Carey cites deterioration as an aspect of its attractiveness: "Those who are interested in the past will find much of ab-

FIG. 7.1. Early, somewhat deteriorated and picturesque tombs, St. Louis Cemetery Number 1 (ca. 1900). Even this early, some tombs had fallen into ruin. Postcard, author's collection.

sorbing interest in this venerable old Cemetery. The peculiar architecture of some of the tombs, the historic associations of many buried here, the crumbling remains of what once were beautiful burial places" (fig. 7.1).[21]

The decision whether to repair and renew historic structures or to pursue a passive approach in order to appreciate quaintness, wear, and decay over time has been debated at least since the nineteenth century. French historian and architect Eugène Emmanuel Viollet-le-Duc (1814–1879), who specialized in the restoration of medieval buildings, argued that historic structures should be aggressively renovated rather than being left to molder in their original state.[22] He restored a number of gothic churches and cathedrals, including Notre Dame in Paris, in the belief that "to restore a building is not to preserve it, to repair, or rebuild it; it is to reinstate it in a condition of completeness which could never have existed at any given time."[23] Viollet-le-Duc took this to mean that in some of his restoration work, he could add significant elements of his own design, which inevitably diminished the authenticity of the historic building he had altered.

One of his contemporaries took an opposing view. English artist, writer, and founding member of the Society for the Preservation of Ancient Buildings, John Ruskin (1819–1900), argued that historic structures should be left in their original condition with minimal intervention to rehabilitate them. He believed that full restoration, even without altering the original design as Viollet-le-Duc sometimes did, decreased their authenticity and historical value. In *The Seven Lamps of Architecture*, Ruskin wrote: "Neither by the public, nor by those who have the care of public monuments, is the true meaning of the word *restoration* understood. It means the most total destruction which a building can suffer. . . . It is impossible, as impossible as to raise the dead, to restore anything that has ever been great or beautiful in architecture."[24]

Both of these philosophies on how to treat historic structures have been applied in New Orleans cemeteries, although not always with the conscious understanding expressed by Viollet-le-Duc or Ruskin. Many historic tombs have been heavily restored using inappropriate modern materials to the point where they do not even appear historic anymore, while others have been left to erode away completely. Neither of these extremes represents good preservation.

Mostly left to decay, perhaps as Ruskin would have preferred, St. Louis Number 2 and the Girod Street Cemetery continued to sink into ruin at a significantly faster rate than St. Louis Number 1 and most other cemeteries in the city. A writer for the 1938 *WPA Guide to New Orleans* describes Girod Street Cemetery in the late 1930s: "It has not been used much in recent years, and the luxuriant vines and shrubs with which it is overgrown give it a haunted appearance. Gnarled fig trees push their way through the bulging sides of the old tombs, and the wall 'ovens' are damp and green with maidenhair fern."[25] No preservation strategy would ever be pursued at Girod, which would eventually be replaced by the parking garage of the Louisiana (Mercedes-Benz) Superdome and an urban shopping center.

Because of the loss and neglect of historic cemeteries in the state, in 1974 the Louisiana legislature began to pass laws forbidding the demolition of cemeteries. By this time, two prominent New Orleans cemeteries had already been lost: the Girod Street Cemetery and the Gates of Mercy Cemetery, the first Jewish burial ground in the city. Both were demolished in 1957. The 1974 law essentially dictates that once "human remains have been interred in a piece of property, that property is forever dedicated as a cemetery."[26]

Late in 1974, apparently ignorant of the recently passed state law or perhaps ignoring it, the Archdiocese of New Orleans announced plans to demolish many of the wall vaults of St. Louis Number 2. In a *Times-Picayune* article dated December 4, 1974, entitled, "Slums of the Dead: Archdiocesan Director Reveals Plans to Demolish St. Louis No. 2 Cemetery," reporter Joyce Davis claimed that the Archdiocese intended to demolish the entire cemetery and argued that the 151-year-old burial ground was decrepit and doomed. Throwing aside any pretense of impartiality, she writes: "Now the sun only reveals dingy, crumbling cells of bones and dust. Now its fate is inevitable. They're going to demolish it."

She continues her unflattering eulogy of the historic necropolis: "Some cemeteries in New Orleans are no longer places of sanctity. These once spiritual cities are now slums—slums of the dead."[27] The article, which reveals an indifference to preservation that was all too prevalent in the 1970s, mentioned nothing about the recently passed state law forbidding the demolition of cemeteries or the views of anyone wanting to preserve the cemetery, only stating that some tomb owners had protested the impending loss of the resting places of their ancestors while adding that the Catholic Church did not have the money needed to renovate the cemetery. The caption of a picture embedded in the article, depicting a severely eroded tomb, reads, "This tomb in St. Louis No. 2 is an example of how bad some of the areas of this 151-year-old cemetery have become. The state board of health says tombs such as this are a health hazard and should be either renovated or destroyed."[28] Apparently, the reporter had misinterpreted the plan to demolish the vaults as a plan to demolish the entire cemetery and had no problem with the prospect of its loss.

In that same year, New Orleans preservationist Mary Louise Christovich spearheaded the creation of Save Our Cemeteries (SOC), an organization with the stated mission of increasing public awareness of the plight of the city's historic cemeteries and to raise funds for cemetery restoration. The new organization was formed, in part, specifically to prevent the demolition of the St. Louis Number 2 oven tombs. The SOC organization developed a broader vision than the Society for the Preservation of Ancient Tombs had, as is indicated in its mission statement: "Save Our Cemeteries is dedicated to the preservation, promotion, and protection of New Orleans' historic cemeteries through restoration, education, and advocacy."[29]

In 2001, SOC and the Archdiocese of New Orleans received a $150,000 grant from the now-defunct federal historic preservation program Save America's Treasures to study and restore St. Louis Number 1. Phase 1 of the project, which was funded with state, local, and private matching funds, documented the cemetery's history and development using historical documents including "surveys, drawings, plans, maps, paintings, watercolors, family histories, and photographs."[30] During this phase, the Graduate Program in Historic Preservation at the Graduate School of Fine Arts, University of Pennsylvania, created guidelines for the proper restoration of the cemetery's historic tombs. Phase 2, funded by Save America's Treasures, involved detailed study of the tombs themselves and resulted in the actual restoration of about eighty-five tombs.[31] Today, SOC funds a very limited amount of cemetery restoration, maintaining its focus primarily on education, offering cemetery tours, and advocacy for the city's historic cemeteries.[32]

Save Our Cemeteries listed St. Louis Number 1 and St. Louis Number 2 in the National Register of Historic places in 1975. Lafayette Number 1 had already been listed in 1972. Odd Fellows Rest was added to the National Register in 1980, and Metairie Cemetery in 1991. The National Register of Historic Places is the official list and record of historic properties in the United States. It was created in 1966 by the federal Historic Preservation Act and contains tens of thousands of historic districts, sites, buildings, structures, and objects. The National Register is a comprehensive database of historic properties deemed worthy of preservation through the application of a set of specific criteria and standards.

Although cemeteries are normally excluded from listing in the National Register, if a cemetery is particularly historically significant for the design of its monuments or for a direct association with notable people in history or with historic events, it may be eligible for inclusion. Since cemeteries cannot be listed solely based on the historical importance of the people buried there, historic New Orleans cemeteries are generally easier to list in the National Register than are cemeteries elsewhere because of their unique architecture and special significance to the culture of the city. Many of the other historic cemeteries in New Orleans are most likely eligible to be listed and should be.

Listing in the National Register is worth pursuing, because it helps protect cemeteries and other historic properties in significant, if limited, ways. Listing provides formal recognition to the public, corporations, nonprofits, and governments that a cemetery is indeed historic and has been deemed worthy of preserving based on national standards. Listing also provides some specific protections. It makes tombs and other cemetery structures eligible for certain federal grants for preservation planning and physical rehabilitation. Also, listing ensures that if federally funded or licensed construction projects, such as road widening or levee construction, which have the potential to affect a historic cemetery are proposed, the project has to go through a systematic review process. Before construction of such projects can go forward, any possible adverse effects that the project may have on the historic cemetery must be assessed by the state historic preservation office and possibly the federal Advisory Council on Historic Preservation using federal preservation guidelines. These reviews, referred to as the "Section 106" process, have slowed many projects down enough to allow for considerations of historic places to be implemented before any damage is done.

Despite the legal protections provided by tools such as the National Register and Louisiana's ban on the wholesale destruction of cemeteries, individual tombs, markers, and other cemetery structures continue to be threatened by a number of forces. Some of these threats are natural, while others are caused by human activity. It is important to understand that the cemeteries and their monuments and tombs are a fragile resource in need of protection and periodic maintenance and repair. The primary reason for the decay of family tombs is neglect and abandonment by the families that own them. The owners of cemeteries are under no obligation to maintain the tombs and monuments within them. Many people may not be aware that they even own or have responsibility for the maintenance of the tombs of their ancestors.

An effective cemetery preservation project would be to organize and execute a sustained effort to identify the rightful owners of historic tombs and to encourage these families to take an active interest in restoring and maintaining them. In addition, such a project could offer financial incentives to families to assist them in completing any required work where the need exists, and it could provide professional consultation on correct restoration and preservation methods. It could also create a referral service to identify and contact available craftspeople qualified to work on historic tombs.

FIG. 7.2. A leaning tomb, St. Louis Cemetery Number 2. Settling exposes a tomb to additional erosion from rainfall and, if left uncorrected, will lead to collapse of the structure. Photo by author, 2013.

The natural threats to neglected tombs and monuments stem from the city's spongy soils and wet climate, while the types of destruction caused by humans are usually an issue not only in New Orleans but in historic cemeteries in other places around the world as well. The natural phenomena that threaten cemeteries in New Orleans are numerous. To begin with, the city is built over layer upon layer of loamy silt, at least a hundred feet thick and devoid of bedrock. This silt expands when wet and contracts when dry, causing settling, shifting, and cracking in masonry funerary structures that usually have little in the way of sound foundations or engineered footings (fig. 7.2). Early brick tombs are particularly vulnerable to this and other environmental threats. The bricks they were built with were soft, the stucco used to protect the bricks was made from sand and lime, and the construction methods employed to create them were not always of the highest quality.

In addition to settling, water intrusion can be a major problem. Most of the cemeteries were built on low ground, historically at the edges of the city, and are subject to flooding from frequent rainstorms and hurricanes. Virtually all of the cemeteries received floodwaters from Hurricane Katrina

FIG. 7.3. St. Louis Cemetery Number 2, partly submerged by floodwaters from Hurricane Katrina, September 4, 2005. Photo by FEMA employee Liz Roll.

in 2005, and many have been inundated by the tropical storms that have periodically hit the city before and since (fig. 7.3). While flooding of tombs in the city's levee system does not usually result in the kinds of catastrophic damage seen when storm surges hit cemeteries in low-lying areas outside the levee system, the flooding does weaken their structures by rusting iron elements and washing minerals out of bricks, mortar, and stucco, causing these historic building materials to be more vulnerable to damage from future floods and other environmental threats.

Tombs can also be damaged by water under normal circumstances. Roofs of historic tombs are often just brick covered in stucco or raw brick or stone blocks exposed to the elements and left to absorb water in one of the rainiest climates in North America. Excess water seepage into historic brick is inevitable unless tombs receive routine maintenance, such as having cracks repaired and their traditional lime-wash finishes replaced periodically by new coats of the same material, which consists of a mixture of slaked lime putty and water. Lime-wash creates a durable, paintlike coating that does not break down in sunlight when dry.[33] Any excess wetness absorbed by the masonry has to eventually dissipate and evaporate,

FIG. 7.4. Side of a stucco tomb damaged by water intrusion, St. Vincent de Paul Cemetery. The white corrosion, known as efflorescence, is evidence that minerals in the walls of the tomb are being washed away. The stucco seen here is an inappropriate Portland cement–based stucco. Photo by author, 2013.

sometimes leaving powdered minerals that were once part of the structure behind (fig. 7.4). This occurs most often when the tomb has been covered with inappropriate Portland cement–based stucco. The cement-based material does not allow moisture to escape as readily, causing it to build up within the structure and find a way out through cracks and fissures, often widening them in the process.

Vines, shrubs, and trees, which grow voraciously in New Orleans's wet climate, are another natural threat to tombs and monuments of all kinds. Since ancient times, people have planted ornamental greenery in cemeteries to improve the appearance of gravesites and tombs. Also, wild plants can grow most anywhere in New Orleans, even in tiny cracks in masonry. Typically, the harm comes when the roots of bushes and trees push up foundations, penetrate walls, and create or widen gaps in the stucco or stones that make up tomb bases, walls, and roofs (fig. 7.5). Trees and bushes can also grow on top of tombs and wall vaults, creating cracks and destabilizing them (fig. 7.6). In addition, fast-growing vines, such as cat's claw, English ivy, poison ivy, and Virginia creeper, can tear up the surface materials of tombs as they send out branches with roots that penetrate building materials. If left uncorrected, root intrusion from trees, bushes, and vines may eventually cause a structure to collapse.

FIG. 7.5. Tomb seriously damaged by the roots of a juniper tree, Cypress Grove Cemetery. Without remediation, this architecturally distinctive historic tomb will soon cease to exist. Photo by author, 2015.

FIG. 7.6. The Deutscher Handwerk Verlein society tomb (1868), damaged by neglect and the roots of shrubs and trees, Lafayette Cemetery Number 2. Sections of this unique society tomb are in danger of collapse. Photo by author, 2015.

FIG. 7.7. Portland stucco on a historic brick tomb, St. Louis Cemetery Number 2. As the stucco flakes off, it damages the brick and also leaves it exposed to erosion. Photo by author, 2015.

Along with natural threats, the activities of humans can pose significant danger to cemeteries. Improper repairs of tombs are commonplace. Portland cement, a hard material first manufactured in the United States in 1872, is a component of modern mortar and stucco. Using Portland cement–based stucco to replace the historic material covering nineteenth-century brickwork seems logical, because the material is denser and more weather resistant and seemingly should last longer than traditional lime-based stucco. However, this type of stucco does not expand and contract with changing humidity and temperatures like the historic porous brick structure behind it, and it will eventually crack and break off, often taking parts of the original structure with it (fig. 7.7). The use of Portland cement–based stucco on nineteenth-century tombs in New Orleans cemeteries poses a significant threat to their long-term viability. Unfortunately, many masons contracted by the Archdiocese, the city of New Orleans, and individual families continue to use this unsuitable material.

Another misguided activity often carried out by well-meaning people is harsh cleaning of brick, stucco, or stone. Sandblasting and using high-pressure water cause harm to historic building materials. Old brick is softer than today's brick, and high-pressure cleaning strips away its exterior

FIG. 7.8. Undermined brick on a severely deteriorated tomb in St. Louis Cemetery Number 2. When a tomb has decayed to this point, little can be done to bring it back. To do so would constitute reconstruction rather than restoration. Photo by author, 2015.

and pits the surface, which actually causes the latter to collect dirt more quickly than before. Harsh cleaning also washes out mortar between the bricks, weakening the structure (fig. 7.8).

Another common harmful practice is the use of bleach to clean and brighten marble elements of tombs, such as exterior sheathing, relief, sculpture, and closure tablets. Although bleaching initially makes the marble look bright and clean, the bleach damages the soft, porous stone, making it stain more easily and often causing it to turn yellow or orange. Bleach also makes marble erode more quickly.[34]

Vibrations created by trucks, buses, and trains pose another danger to historic cemeteries. The thickness of New Orleans's soils causes the ground to shake when heavy vehicles pass to a greater degree than in most other places. The vibrations act as tiny earthquakes that shake apart structures in historic cemeteries over time. Leonard Huber witnessed an example of this in the Girod Street Cemetery in the 1950s: "The tomb of the 'Sobriety Benevolent Ass'n, Founded 1854' was surmounted by a small obelisk which had assumed a wholly new position on its base due to the vibration of passing trains."[35] Given the location of some of the cemeteries, such as St. Louis Number 2, near major arteries and potential construction sites, this can prove a difficult problem to solve.

Some damage done to cemeteries is intentional. New Orleans newspapers have reported incidents of vandalism in its cemeteries since the 1800s. These include tombs broken into and human remains scattered in 1864 by possible cult members; tombs smashed open and skeletons exposed in the Girod Street Cemetery on Halloween night, 1906; the wanton destruction of tombs and vaults in 1912 by a group of young men after a drunken brawl; and tour guides encouraging tourists to crawl up on and take souvenir fragments from historic tombs in 1931.[36] More recently, Lafayette Cemetery Number 1 in the Garden District was vandalized repeatedly from the 1960s through the 1980s, with vaults broken into, a recently buried body decapitated, and entire tombs virtually demolished.[37] Destruction caused by vandals continues. In 2015, a number of tombs in Lafayette Cemetery Number 2 were left open, having been damaged by vandals over the preceding months or years.[38]

Although most cases of vandalism have no known rationale, one motivation for vandals opening tombs or digging at gravesites is to acquire human bones. In 2015, reports of people combing through Holt Cemetery in search of human remains caused the Louisiana Attorney General's office to investigate. In that year, New Orleans television station KSLA reported that a woman in New Orleans posted on Facebook that she went to scavenge human bones and teeth at Holt Cemetery for "curse work and spells" and was considering collecting more and selling them.[39] Unfortunately, an active black market for human bones exists.

Responding to incidents of vandalism, in 2015 the Archdiocese of New Orleans stipulated that all people visiting St. Louis Number 1 be accompanied by a registered tour guide. Unsupervised visitors had been damaging the cemetery by marking tombs and chipping at them for souvenirs. In a particularly destructive case in 2014, several men posing as tour guides broke into at least a dozen tombs in St. Louis Number 1 in order to pull out bones to show to tourists.

In the most notorious example of vandalism prompting the new rule, an unknown person slathered pink latex paint all over the tomb of Marie Laveau in December 2013. Removing the paint and restoring the tomb cost the Archdiocese and Save Our Cemeteries around $10,000.[40] Tourists

Fig. 7.9. The Grailhe tomb, 1850, with doors present. HABS photo from 1930, Library of Congress, Prints and Photographs Division.

continuing the longstanding tradition of scratching X's on the tomb's sides for good luck were also damaging the historic structure over time. Exacerbating the problem, they often made the marks using brick chips pulled from neighboring tombs.[41]

Potentially even more destructive is the looting of cemeteries for profit. Much of the statuary, wrought iron, and bronze doors recorded in historic photographs of the cemeteries from the early twentieth century have since been removed by looters and souvenir seekers. In one unfortunate case, the bronze doors of the 1850 Egyptian revival Grailhe tomb in St. Louis Number 2, designed by J. N. B. de Pouilly, were stolen sometime between 2003 and 2013 (figs. 7.9, 7.10).

At times, cemetery looting has occurred on a large scale. Two 1999 articles, one in *People* magazine and the other in the *Economist*, describe how during an investigation, police discovered over a million dollars' worth of New Orleans cemetery art that had been stolen by a single gang of tomb

Fig. 7.10. The Grailhe tomb today. The doors have been cut off and stolen. One can only speculate as to whether thieves sold the doors for scrap metal or they ended up on the black market and are now in someone's garden. Photo by author, 2013.

robbers. The gang had sold much of the stolen art to local merchants, and it was on display in antique stores along Royal Street in the French Quarter.[42] Although the police apprehended these particular thieves and returned at least some of the stolen statues and architectural elements to the cemeteries they had been taken from, this was just one instance that garnered media attention among many cases of cemetery theft that have gone largely unreported and uninvestigated. Looting for profit and for the taking of souvenirs by tourists remains a constant problem in the cemeteries, and one which is difficult to control, because of the difficulty of monitoring such a collection of diverse and often infrequently visited places.

As we have seen, even those attempting to save tombs and funerary monuments can do them harm. Inappropriate tomb restorations not only damage historic and aesthetic features but also threaten the survival of the tomb itself in the long run. For a restoration to be successful, a tomb

Fig. 7.11. This tomb in St. Louis Cemetery Number 1 is in poor repair. Many of its original features have eroded away or been removed, diminishing its historic integrity. Nevertheless, if proper documentation of its historic condition exists, a tomb in this condition can still be restored. Photo by author, 2015.

must retain its historic integrity once the work is complete, meaning that it appears similar to the way it did when constructed or at least the way it looked during the greater part of its history. It is possible for a tomb that has lost historic integrity to be carefully renovated in such a way that the structure regains its historic character; however, all changes made must be based on sound research to determine what its actual historic characteristics and appearance were (fig. 7.11).

Examples of measures that reduce or destroy the integrity of a tomb are removing its original closure tablet(s) and replacing them with new and dissimilar ones, removing historic iron features, covering historic brick or traditional lime-based stucco with Portland-based stucco or another unsuitable material, altering the overall shape or volume of the tomb, or removing historic decorations, such as sculpture, urns, vases, and stone relief (fig. 7.12).[43]

FIG. 7.12. This tomb in St. Louis Cemetery Number 2, dating from at least as early as 1862, was apparently redone at some point during the early twentieth century when a veneer of granite rubble held in place with Portland cement–based mortar was added to its walls. A case of tomb remodeling, the work destroyed most of its original features, diminishing its historic integrity and architectural significance. This treatment was quite common until around 1930, and some preservationists now argue that the granite rubble has itself become historic due to its age. Photo by author, 2015.

Retaining the historic integrity of the cemeteries is important because of their educational value; their distinctive architecture, art, and landscapes; their role as active burial grounds and memorials to those interred there; and their unique aesthetics. Because they have such a wide appeal, New Orleans cemeteries, especially St. Louis Number 1 and Lafayette Number 1, receive many thousands of visitors each year.

When it decided to restrict access to some of the historic cemeteries it owns, starting with St. Louis Number 1, the Archdiocese of New Orleans began to change the traditional role of the cemetery as an open public venue for burial and mourning to that of a tourist site, trading free and open access to a civic asset for increased security and presumably more effective preservation of the resource. The Archdiocese charges tour guides a significant fee to maintain the registration that allows them to bring paying tourists to the cemetery.[44] Shortly after announcing the decision to limit access in January 2015, Sherri Peppo, director of the Archdiocesan cemeteries office, said the income generated from the registration fees would be used to improve nighttime security and to pay additional staff to watch over the cemetery when visitors are present. She added that any funds left over would be spent on the restoration of damaged tombs.[45]

In addition to limiting its role as an active cemetery, which has been its primary purpose for well over two centuries, making St. Louis Number 1 more difficult to access by turning it into a paying tourist attraction erodes its other cultural functions, one of which is its use by local Voodoo practitioners who pray and leave offerings at the tomb of Marie Laveau and other tombs believed to be occupied by significant deceased Voodoo priests.

Despite these drawbacks, the cases of vandalism have been so destructive that closing the cemetery to unaccompanied visitors may have been the Archdiocese's only viable option to save it from continued subjection to significant damage. Also, the funds the Archdiocese generates by registering tour guides relieves the heavy financial burden associated with protecting the historic cemeteries. A possible less obtrusive and cumbersome alternative to requiring licensed tour guides might be for the Archdiocese to simply charge a modest admission fee to those visitors who are not tomb owners, and then use that money to pay for round-the-clock security.

Another way to safeguard a historic cemetery is to simply close it to all visitors, as the city did with the Odd Fellows Rest cemetery in the 2010s. In this case, however, rather than visitors posing a threat to the cemetery, the cemetery posed a threat to visitors. Some tombs were so deteriorated and unstable that the city had to confront the possibility of components of the cemetery's structures falling on people.[46] The city decided to prohibit public access. Although it promotes public safety, this solution bars the public and the descendants of people buried there from having any experience of the cemetery at all. Rather than closing them or requiring tour guides, an alternative strategy would be to encourage more visitation by making cemeteries especially inviting to tourists through intensive restoration and by adding museums, gift shops, and cafés. While this approach may seem

FIG. 7.13. Visitor's center and café, Glasnevin Cemetery, Dublin, Ireland. Photo by author, 2014.

inappropriate for a place of mourning and reflection, one cemetery where it has been successfully applied can be found in Ireland.

In the past decade or so, the Glasnevin Cemetery in Dublin, which was opened in 1832 as a nondenominational garden cemetery, has become one of the most popular tourist destinations in Ireland. Although the vast majority of interments there are belowground, the cemetery has a high density of artful monuments and markers, making it both impressive and picturesque.[47]

A nonprofit organization called the Glasnevin Trust runs the cemetery as an active burial ground and as a historic tourist attraction. The trust uses revenue from the sale of burial plots, souvenirs, and refreshments to operate and preserve the cemetery. To make the cemetery more inviting, the trust has redesigned the site to be both comfortable and informative. It has a glass-and-steel visitor's center in plain sight of the historic cemetery entrance, with a museum, an interactive databank of graves and genealogical information, a gift shop, and a café where one can sip tea while gazing out at rows of nineteenth-century tombstones through floor-to-ceiling plate-glass windows (fig. 7.13).

Glasnevin offers a variety of themed, guided tours that examine various aspects of its history and the lives of the people buried there. Visiting the cemetery makes for a pleasant and educational afternoon, but one cannot help but suspect that in packaging such a place so thoroughly, something may have been lost.

The Glasnevin approach guarantees protection and preservation in a dignified setting, but also reduces the sense of discovery and mystery that has drawn tourists to historic cemeteries across the world. When people visited St. Louis Number 1 before the Archdiocese limited access, they could wander alone among the ancient tombs of a sometimes vacant cemetery. Having discovered a sorrowful, fascinating, and beautiful place, the visitor might be left to experience the site slowly and authentically, free of the giggling, snap photography, and entertaining anecdotes of guided tourism. With access to the cemetery restricted to tour groups, visitors seeking to meander aimlessly among the tarnished houses of the dead of past centuries and to contemplate the tombs' subtle qualities on their own will have to find their way to St. Louis Number 2 or another of the lesser-known cemeteries, but how long will it be before access to additional historic cemeteries is restricted? The conflict between the urge to protect and possibly profit from fragile historic resources and the desire to maintain free and authentic access is a challenging one to resolve (fig. 7.14).

It is difficult to determine how visitors to New Orleans would view a proposal to locate a gift shop and café overlooking St. Louis Number 1, but such a plan would certainly reduce the historic integrity of the site and the historical quality of the visitor experience. So much in the French Quarter and other historic neighborhoods in the city has already been taken over or at least threatened by the tourist industry and heavy-handed developers that preserving not only the physical buildings and structures but also the essence of the city is of utmost importance.

Perhaps a museum similar to the one at Glasnevin, located not within or adjacent to the cemetery itself, but beyond its walls a distance away, might better serve both the visitors and the cemetery itself. Copying Glasnevin's idea of providing a tourist-friendly, on-site genealogical database of the people buried in New Orleans cemeteries for genealogists and the curious is intriguing, although the visual record of who was buried in St. Louis Number 1, with its nameless society tombs and worn tablets on eroded, often altered tombs, is not as clear as at Glasnevin, with its individually

FIG. 7.14. St. Louis Cemetery Number 1, ca. 1900. Solitude and contemplation are hallmarks of the authentic experience of visiting a historic cemetery. Library of Congress, Prints and Photographs Division.

marked gravestones and monuments. Any public genealogical project could certainly make use of the comprehensive survey of the graves in New Orleans cemeteries done by Save Our Cemeteries and the Historic New Orleans Collection in 1981.

Historically, physically, and functionally, Metairie Cemetery has more in common with Glasnevin than do the older walled cemeteries. Metairie was designed on a scale similar to Glasnevin's, and it possesses a similar grandeur. Perhaps a museum and café would meld better there with the setting, so long as it was located in a nonhistoric area of the grounds and did not impact the historic landscape significantly. It is not difficult to imagine tour buses pulling up and tourists eating jambalaya and drinking beer at the café as they pour over glossy brochures describing the cemetery's numerous stunning landmarks.

Perhaps the best preservation strategy would take the middle ground. The sprawling Victorian garden cemetery Laurel Hill in Philadelphia (1836) takes an approach to visitation somewhere between that of New Orleans cemeteries and Glasnevin. As with Glasnevin, a private entity, the Laurel Hill Cemetery Company, owns and manages the site as an active burial ground, generating revenue that helps fund the cemetery's preservation. Also like Glasnevin, Laurel Hill has a gift shop, but the modest store is discreetly housed in the historic gatehouse. The cemetery hosts programs for visitors, such as a "yoga in the cemetery" program; "Lunchbox Lectures" on aspects of the cemetery's history; and a series of monthly themed, guided tours; however, the physical adaptations made for the tours and other activities have had a minimal impact on the cemetery itself. In addition to participating in organized tours, visitors are also free to wander around unsupervised on the site, which does not look very different than it did in the 1800s.

Laurel Hill also has a nonprofit support group called the Friends of Laurel Hill, which assists in preserving the historic character of the burial ground and promoting it to the public. The Friends of Laurel Hill develops and implements educational programs at the cemetery, sponsors special events, and offers public and private tours of the site, often in collaboration with local schools, nonprofit groups, and historical organizations.[48] The group also carries out special preservation projects, such as the restoration of the "Silent Sentry," an 1883 bronze statue of a Union soldier that was stolen in the 1970s and later recovered. In 2013, the Friends raised around $40,000 in donations for its restoration and return to the cemetery. Like Glasnevin, Laurel Hill operates a genealogy archive that is open to the public. Overall, Laurel Hill serves as an example of a historic cemetery that serves tourists, the families of the deceased buried there, genealogists, and its neighbors, while also managing to remain in a relatively unspoiled state.

In another instructive example of historic cemetery preservation and management, the Savannah Department of Cemeteries operates five historic cemeteries owned by the city of Savannah, Georgia. The most visited and well known of these burial grounds is St. Bonaventure Cemetery, a rural garden cemetery opened in 1847. The Savannah Department of Cemeteries receives funds directly from the city budget, and one of its primary responsibilities is preserving the historical and cultural significance of the cemeteries in its care.[49]

To this end, the Department of Cemeteries employs qualified preservation specialists who perform repair and restoration work on historic grave markers and tombs located within the city-owned cemeteries. Under Georgia law, tombs and grave markers that have not been used or maintained by the families that own them for seventy-five or more years may be summarily restored. In its work, the department uses internationally accepted standards for the restoration of funerary monuments. This helps preserve many of the older monuments; however, grave and tomb owners who have not neglected or abandoned their plots have no restrictions placed on them as to how they repair or alter their historic markers. This means that contractors are able to, and often do, employ inappropriate methods, such as using bleach to clean stones and performing repairs on nineteenth-century tombs with Portland cement–based mortars.[50]

The City of New Orleans has a cemetery office within its Department of Property Management which, like the Savannah office, manages the cemeteries that the city owns (such as Lafayette Cemeteries Number 1 and Number 2 and the Carrollton Cemetery). The New Orleans cemetery office does not, however, employ preservation specialists to perform repairs or do historically appropriate restoration work, nor does it offer any kind of consultation on maintenance or restoration to tomb owners. If New Orleans were to follow Savannah's lead and better fund its cemetery office and then direct it to hire trained individuals to oversee repair and restoration work in the cemeteries the city owns, their overall condition and prospects would surely improve.[51]

Like Philadelphia's Laurel Hill, Savannah's St. Bonaventure Cemetery benefits from having a nonprofit that actively supports its preservation. Called the Bonaventure Historical Society, this group works in concert with the city to preserve the cemetery by providing guided tours, issuing tour maps, maintaining a burial-site database, and soliciting funding for restoration projects.[52] Having a nonprofit dedicated to its preservation benefits St. Bonaventure in a number of ways. It provides the city with a partner to acquire grants and motivate volunteers, generates public interest in the cemetery, and recruits members who help monitor it, aiding in the prevention of vandalism and looting. The preservation strategies employed at St. Bonaventure appear to be quite successful. In contrast with St. Bonaventure, Laurel Grove North, another historic cemetery in Savannah also owned by the city, has no nonprofit support group. Over the years,

Laurel Grove North has suffered from more vandalism, looting, and neglect than other cemeteries in the city, especially St. Bonaventure, which is fairly well preserved.[53]

Like St. Louis Number 1 and Lafayette Number 1, St. Bonaventure Cemetery is popular with tourists, hosting as many as five tour groups on a given Saturday or Sunday. Unlike Glasnevin, tourism has not reduced the historic integrity of St. Bonaventure. For the benefit of visitors, some cemetery plot and tomb owners have erected interpretive bronze plaques on poles describing the lives and historical significance of those buried there. This gives the burial ground the feel of a tourist attraction, but not nearly so much as would the addition of a modern visitors' center or a requirement that tour guides accompany everyone who enters.[54] Similar informational plaques have been attached to tombs in St. Louis Number 1 and other New Orleans cemeteries; however, most have been placed by the Archdiocese or the city rather than by tomb owners and appear to be uncontroversial.

The goal of successful cemetery preservation cannot be to freeze time, because change is inevitable. There is no neutral stance in the field of historic preservation. Doing nothing is a form of gradual demolition, and every other action will impact and alter a historic resource in some way. The best preservationists can do is to carefully manage and direct change with the goal of retaining the key features that make a place historic and special. Resisting change is a particular challenge in New Orleans, a city that was founded in a less-than-ideal location in order to meet immediate strategic and economic requirements, and which is prone to storms and flooding. Its cemeteries have always been subject to decay, damage, and mistreatment, sometimes by the very visitors who came to experience them. Preserving the forty-two historic burial grounds in the city is a difficult task. As some cemeteries or tombs are preserved, others fall into disrepair.

In 1998, Save Our Cemeteries received a grant to create a comprehensive cemetery preservation plan for the city. The plan was written but never implemented.[55] If the city, the Archdiocese of New Orleans, and the SOC worked together to develop a new comprehensive and well-conceived strategic preservation plan for the historic cemeteries and put it into practice, the cemeteries would surely benefit. Perhaps, among other things, such a plan would create a city cemetery preservation department similar to that of Savannah. Although New Orleans has the SOC to advocate for the city's cemeteries as a whole, some of its most historic cemeteries, particularly

St. Louis Cemeteries Numbers 1 and 2, Cypress Grove, and the Lafayette cemeteries, would receive better care if they had individual nonprofit historical friends' groups similar to those in Philadelphia and Savannah that would focus specifically on their preservation, restoration, promotion, and management. The cemeteries would also be better preserved if the city issued guidelines, preferably regulations, governing the preservation and restoration of tombs and other historic cemetery resources. It is to be hoped that new and innovative measures and programs with the ultimate goal of saving these fantastic cultural landmarks for future generations will be developed by the city, the Archdiocese, and concerned citizens.

CONCLUSION

New Orleans's sea-level location, combined with its rich blend of cultures, gave birth to the "cities of the dead." In the first decades of the nineteenth century, the city's largest cemetery, St. Louis Number 1, evolved from a dismal, muddy field into the walled "city" that has enchanted people ever since. Although almost everyone in New Orleans had been buried underground during the 1700s, greater prosperity, together with the high water table and the cultural roots of many of its inhabitants, precipitated the switch to aboveground burial. In addition, the city finally forbade all burials within St. Louis Cathedral by 1805, forcing the elite to find a respectable and dry alternative.

The city's rapid growth in the early 1800s consumed the area's buildable land, constraining the size of its early cemeteries and increasing their density. Before long, family tombs and oven vaults crowded the spaces within cemetery walls. The tombs took the forms they did because of ancient Greek, Roman, and medieval burial traditions, which the Spanish and French had modified and brought to the New World. In the 1830s, New Orleans's relatively simple cemetery architecture became more varied, fashionable, and intricate as revivalist architectural styles, particularly those brought from Europe by French architect J. N. B. de Pouilly, transformed the formerly boxy brick-and-stucco tombs into sophisticated architectural expressions resembling miniature Greco-Roman temples or medieval chapels, often finished in cut marble. As the cemeteries developed, craftspeople and designers from various parts of America and Europe came to the city to design and construct distinctive tombs and markers.

As the Victorian rural cemetery movement, with its emphasis on preserving the memory of individuals in perpetuity in a parklike setting, emerged in England and the eastern United States, New Orleanians, with their mostly Mediterranean and African roots, continued to find inspiration in the ancient models of reusable family, oven, and society tombs that emphasized family and community over individualism. Even in the grand Metairie Cemetery, New Orleans's only nineteenth-century garden cemetery, the traditional aboveground tombs of New Orleans continued to be built into the twenty-first century.

The thousands of family tombs speak of the importance of kinship in the city. The many oven tombs recall the necessity of respectable aboveground interment of the large number of victims of a consistently high death rate made worse by periodic epidemics. The monumental society tombs remind us of the city's benevolent associations that provided security and other benefits to their members, both black and white, native and immigrant, in an era that offered workers little in the way of a social safety net. Burial society members shared the pleasures and trials of life together and often found a dignified burial under the same roof.

In addition to housing the dead, the cemeteries have long played host to the living, especially during the annual All Saints' Day celebrations that brought people from all walks of life together to share a common respect for the dead and reverence for their final resting places in a surprisingly celebratory atmosphere. As an integral part of the life of the city, the cemeteries also drew practitioners of the shadowy religion of Voodoo, who used them as places of worship and centers of memory, power, and magic. The cemeteries also bear witness to the injustices of slavery and segregation in the nineteenth and twentieth centuries. To a greater degree than in most other places, the cemeteries of New Orleans have provided and continue to provide a point of contact between the past and the present, the living and the dead.

New Orleans is a city where everything changes yet little changes, where events and people come and go but the same essential spirit lives on. The friendliness and humor of its people have endured through the best and worst of times. The humid breeze still carries the smell of the river into the French Quarter as it did when the city was founded. A ship horn sounds in the distance as clouds above are taken across the sky by the brisk

Gulf wind. The old cemeteries embody this timeless quality. They offer an authentic glimpse into the past. Despite Hurricane Katrina and other storms and so much damage and neglect, the fundamental appearance and nineteenth-century character of the cemeteries have endured. As people wander the lonely avenues of these silent cities, they experience a past that has vanished amid crowds, noise, and commercialism almost everywhere else.

Although most of the cemeteries survive, many of the tombs and monuments in them, particularly those in the lesser-known grounds, such as Lafayette Number 2, suffer from neglect and vandalism and are in danger of being lost. Securing the long-term future for the cemeteries and the structures within can be achieved by implementing a number of preservation measures, such as encouraging and empowering families to restore the tombs of their ancestors, creating nonprofit advocacy groups for the preservation and active restoration of individual cemeteries, expanding the city's cemetery office by adding preservation specialists to restore and oversee the restoration of tombs, passing an ordinance enforcing guidelines to protect tombs and monuments from damaging repairs and destructive alterations, as well as creating guidelines to better regulate and control tourism so that it neither endangers the cemeteries by leaving them vulnerable to vandalism nor turns them into overly managed history theme parks. If the people of New Orleans choose to actively preserve their cemeteries through these and other measures, these amazing historic places will survive to enchant future generations.

APPENDIX A

Types and Styles of Tombs in New Orleans Cemeteries

TYPE AND STYLE

Type: For purposes of this list, a tomb's type defines its basic form and massing. Tombs that belong to a particular type have fundamental design features in common, such as their overall form, footprint, massing, and roof design. The concept of type used here is similar to that employed to define historic houses in New Orleans. These include Creole cottage, Creole townhouse, center hall cottage, single shotgun house, double shotgun house, camelback shotgun, and so on.[1] Structures that belong to the same house or tomb type can be rendered in various styles.

Style: Style derives primarily from the prevailing fashions and available building technologies during the period in which it is popular. Styles are classifications assigned to buildings and structures based on their distinctive decorative motifs, proportions, materials, methods of construction, and the historical periods they represent. Although buildings of a particular style often take on similar overall forms—such as Greek revival buildings, which usually have rectangular plans and low-pitched, gabled roofs—a building's decorative elements usually determine its style. A single style can be used in multiple structures representing different types.

TYPOLOGY OF NEW ORLEANS TOMBS

Box tomb, St. Louis Cemetery Number 2.

Box tomb. Box tombs were built as elongated cubes around a single coffin resting directly on the ground. These plain structures consist of four walls, a flat or nearly flat roof, and a dirt floor. They were constructed of soft, locally made brick, usually covered with a layer of lime-based stucco. Approximate dates: 1790–1850.

Step tomb, St. Louis Cemetery Number 2.

Step tomb. Like box tombs, step tombs normally contain just one burial; however, unlike box tombs, they have setbacks incorporated into their roofs. Today, one finds more step tombs than box tombs in the city's historic cemeteries. It is likely that many of the older box tombs have been lost or were added to or otherwise modified. A wide variety of step tombs exist, but their unifying features are their basic oblong cube form, their squatness, and a flat roof with stepping. Along with box tombs, they were among the earliest tombs built in New Orleans. Approximate dates: 1800–1870.

A wall of oven tombs, St. Louis Cemetery Number 2.

Oven tomb. Oven tombs were traditionally called *fours,* French for "ovens," because of their visual similarity to old-fashioned brick bread ovens. The burial vaults are incorporated into thick brick walls located at the perimeters of the earlier historic cemeteries. The ceilings of the individual burial chambers are composed of arched brick barrel vaults. The burial chambers are usually stacked three or four tiers high. Each vault contains a single body at any given time, but has always been reusable. Closure tablets mounted to the sealed opening normally relate the names and dates of any and all of the successive inhabitants of a particular cell; however, many of the vaults are unmarked today. Some individual chambers have small shelves, pedimented frames, or ornate tablets often made of marble, usually dating from the nineteenth or early twentieth century, attached to their fronts. Approximate dates: 1805–1860.

Wall vault tombs, St. Roch Cemetery Number 1.

Wall vault tomb. A later adaptation of the oven tomb, the individual chambers within wall vault tombs have flat ceilings that are stone slabs rather than the rounded brick barrel vaults found in oven tombs. Each burial chamber is an oblong cube that contains an individual coffin. Wall vault tombs were constructed in New Orleans cemeteries after the Civil War. Later examples have concrete structures. Like oven tombs, wall vault tombs were built in many cemeteries in Spain and Latin America, and the individual vaults are reusable. Approximate dates: 1860–1950.

Block vault tomb, Metairie Cemetery.

Block vault tomb. These are essentially the same as wall vault tombs except they do not encompass an entire cemetery wall. These large, rectangular structures of burial chambers were built both on the edges of cemeteries and also within them. Many functioned as benevolent society tombs or group tombs operated by charitable organizations, such as orphanages and hospitals. Approximate dates: 1850–1940.

Restored pediment tomb, St. Louis Cemetery Number 1.

Pediment tomb. A common early tomb type, pediment tombs are tall, free-standing family or society tombs containing two or more stacked vaults. They are shaped like miniature temples or houses with rectangular plans and low-pitch gable or stepped roofs. Pediment tombs have narrow fronts and are taller than they are wide. Their façades are crowned with a pediment sometimes surrounded by a decorative cornice. They were usually built of stucco-covered brick. Approximate dates: 1810–1890.

Parapet tomb, St. Louis Cemetery Number 1.

Parapet tomb. Parapet tombs are single- or multiple-vault structures with a high wall called a parapet wall on the façade that is taller than the roof behind. Their roofs can be vaulted, gabled, stepped, or flat. The parapet wall often supports a pediment, usually surrounded by a decorative cornice. They are normally constructed of brick that is stuccoed over. Approximate dates: 1810–1880.

Platform tomb, St. Louis Cemetery Number 1.

Platform tomb. Platform tombs are similar to pediment tombs except they are normally not as tall in relation to their width. Unlike box tombs, the coffin(s) within are elevated above the ground on a visible brick or stone pedestal. They can have a gabled or a flat roof. When seen today, many of the older examples of these tombs have sunk into the ground and were once taller than they are today. They are usually constructed of brick with a stucco coating. Approximate dates: 1810–1890.

Barrel-vaulted tomb, St. Louis Cemetery Number 2.

Barrel-vaulted tomb. Although similar to pediment tombs, barrel-vaulted tombs have a rounded roof, normally constructed of brick and covered with stucco. Some serve as family tombs, while others, built at a larger scale, were built as benevolent society mausoleums. They can possess from one up to a dozen or more burial chambers. Approximate dates: 1820–1920.

Sarcophagus tomb, St. Louis Cemetery Number 2.

Sarcophagus tomb. Sarcophagus tombs or graves (if the coffin is buried belowground) were designed to mimic classical sarcophagi (Greek for "flesh eaters"), the stone caskets in which the ancient Greeks and Romans buried high-status individuals. In New Orleans, the body was usually encased in a pedestal beneath the sarcophagus element, which functioned solely as a funerary monument. Sometimes the body was buried beneath the entire funerary structure. These tombs were built of brick and stucco, stone-faced brick, or ashlar stone. Approximate dates: 1830–1910.

Table grave, St. Louis Cemetery Number 1.

Table grave. Table graves consist of a flat stone slab elevated above the ground, supported by either partial walls or posts. The body is buried beneath. They usually have brick piers supporting a stone slab or stone columns holding up a stone slab. The slab or "table" sometimes supports a burial receptacle or marker, such as an urn or a vase to hold flowers. This style is found most often in the eastern United States and is rare in New Orleans. Approximate dates: 1800–1850.

Coping grave, Metairie Cemetery.

Coping grave. Coping graves are belowground burials where a coffin is buried within four short walls, which rise about one to three feet above grade. Used extensively in Jewish cemeteries in New Orleans, the purpose of the coping grave is to allow in-ground burial above the historically high New Orleans water table. The walls are usually brick or stone with the center filled in with earth. The grave is usually marked with a conventional gravestone. This grave type is very common in New Orleans cemeteries, particularly those established after the Civil War. Approximate dates: 1820s–present.

Fenced grave, Orange Grove Cemetery, Lake Charles, La.

Fenced grave. Fenced graves are tombs or tombstones enclosed by a fence, usually of cast or wrought iron. The fence ordinarily has a gate to allow access to the tomb or grave marker. In New Orleans, the fence usually surrounds an aboveground tomb or coping grave. Sometimes the fence was constructed of other materials, such as wood, which was commonly used for grave fences in cemeteries for lower-income individuals, such as in Cypress Grove Number 2 and Holt Cemetery. Unfortunately, many grave fences throughout New Orleans have been lost to vandals and looters. Approximate dates: 1820–present.

Society tomb of the Young Men of St. Michael's Benevolent Society (ca. 1910), St. Louis Cemetery Number 2.

Society tomb. These normally large tombs sprang up in the mid-nineteenth century. They were built by benevolent organizations, which individuals joined and to which they paid yearly dues to be ensured a respectable burial place (see chapter 4). The tombs themselves are larger than family tombs and are often more elaborate and stylistic in design. Their overall forms vary, but they always have multiple, reusable burial chambers, which often comprise a grid on the façade. They are sometimes constructed entirely of stone slabs or have brick walls usually faced with stone. Some earlier examples were constructed of brick covered with stucco. Approximate dates: 1840–1940.

Monument tomb, St. Louis Cemetery Number 2.
The monument shown here is an obelisk.

Monument tomb. This tomb type has any configuration of obelisks, columns, statuary, urns, or other funerary forms set atop a tomb with burial inside the structure. The base structure can mimic a variety of other tomb types, such as a stepped tomb or the battered form pictured here. Structural materials for the base can be of brick or stone, although the monument on top is usually solid stone. Approximate dates: 1830–1900.

Pedestal monument, St. Louis Cemetery Number 2.

Pedestal monument. These graves can have any configuration of obelisks, columns, statuary, urns, or other funerary forms set atop a pedestal or plinth with burial beneath the structure. Sometimes the pedestal at the bottom of the monument rests on a coping or was positioned at grade. In addition to being present in historic New Orleans cemeteries, these monuments are found across the United States in Victorian-era garden and rural cemeteries. They are almost always made of solid stone. Approximate dates: 1830–1920.

Twentieth-century veterans' headstones, Holt Cemetery.

Headstone. Headstones are the archetypal grave markers in Western material culture. They mark an underground burial and are incised with the occupant's name and dates and sometimes an epitaph. They also sometimes feature incised or chip decorative relief. They come in many varieties and styles, such as stelai, stone wedges, and freestanding crosses. They also come in a variety of stones, including slate, sandstone, marble, and granite. Some (such as the stones depicted above) are uniform stone markers designated for veterans. Most are made of a solid piece of stone, although wooden markers that emulate headstones are found in cemeteries used by low-income individuals. Approximate dates: 1810s–present (possibly earlier, although graves in New Orleans dating from before the early 1800s were reportedly marked with iron or wooden crosses).

Ledger stone, St. Louis Cemetery Number 2.

Ledger stone. A ledger stone is a stone tablet or gravestone that rests horizontally on the ground, often embedded in concrete where burials were made underground, normally beneath the tablet. Some of these may have been standing tombstones at one time that broke and fell and were later permanently laid flat on the ground. Approximate dates: 1810s (possibly earlier)–present.

Neoclassical tomb, St. Louis Cemetery Number 2.

Neoclassical or classic revival. This style is based on the forms and motifs of Greco-Roman and Italian Renaissance architecture and has classical features such as columns, arches, and pediments. These tombs often include classical decorative motifs such as dentils, fretwork, wreathes, and egg-and-dart moldings. Unlike Greek revival tombs, classical revival tombs sometimes feature arches and decorations derived from Renaissance and even baroque design. Monument and tomb types built in this style include pediment tombs, parapet tombs, monument tombs, society tombs, sarcophagus tombs, and pedestal monuments. Approximate dates in New Orleans cemeteries: 1830–1860s, with some early twentieth-century examples influenced by Beaux-Arts classical architecture mostly found in Metairie Cemetery. A few extravagant classic revival tombs reflecting postmodern design dating from the 1980s to the present can also be found in Metairie Cemetery.

Greek revival Lacoste family tomb (1849), St. Louis Cemetery Number 2.

Greek revival. This style mimics ancient Greek temple architecture. Sometimes tombs in this style, such as the 1923 Chapman H. Hyams tomb in Metairie Cemetery, are essentially scale copies of Greek temples with burial vaults inside. Common features are temple fronts; shallow-pitch, gable roofs; Doric, Ionic, or Corinthian columns; triglyphs and metopes; and steps leading up to the entrance. They are usually made of stone slabs or ashlar blocks. In addition to the Greek temple model, Greek revival tombs can take the form of cylindrical or octagonal towers or sarcophagi based on ancient Greek precedents. Approximate dates in New Orleans cemeteries: 1830–1930.

Egyptian revival Williams tomb (ca. 1920), Metairie Cemetery.

Egyptian revival. This style was inspired by ancient Egyptian temple architecture. Examples usually feature battered walls; a flat roof; thick lotus columns or pilasters; and winged solar discs, often located directly above the entrance or centered in a cavetto cornice. Some Egyptian revival tombs were inspired by ancient Egyptian pyramids. These unusual tombs form quadrangular pyramids often with steeper sides than most actual Egyptian pyramids. Although many cultures have used the pyramid form for tombs often based on Egyptian models, this tomb type is very rare in New Orleans. The Varney tomb, built around 1813 of brick covered with stucco in St. Louis Number 1, and the 1892 Brunswig tomb (discussed in chapter 6) are two prominent examples. Approximate dates in New Orleans cemeteries: 1840–1930s.

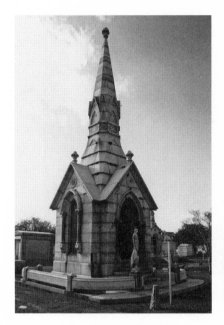

Gothic revival church tomb,
Metairie Cemetery.

Flat-roofed gothic revival tomb,
Metairie Cemetery.

Gothic revival. This style mimics late medieval gothic church architecture. Examples often have steep roofs; ogival, pointed arches; attached buttresses; stained-glass windows; and gothic-era decorative motifs, such as crosses, trefoils, quatrefoils, and crockets. Many are decorated with statuary. A number of the church-type gothic revival tombs have small chapels with altars located within. The majority were built of stone slabs or ashlar blocks or a combination thereof. Approximate dates in New Orleans cemeteries: 1840–1890s.

An ornate Romanesque revival tomb, Metairie Cemetery.

Romanesque revival. This style mimics early medieval, Romanesque church architecture. Examples often have rounded arches; squat columns with uniquely designed, carved stone capitals; rusticated stone walls; pitched roofs; statuary; turrets; and attached buttresses. Most were built of stone slabs, ashlar blocks, or a combination thereof. Approximate dates in New Orleans cemeteries: 1870–1920.

Renaissance revival tomb of Isaac Delgado, Metairie Cemetery.

Renaissance revival. Inspired by classical Italian Renaissance architecture of the 1420s–1500s, examples often have classical temple fronts; arches; elongated domes; classical columns or pilasters in one or more of the five orders used by the Romans (Tuscan, Doric, Ionic, Corinthian, and Composite); pediments; marble veneer; quoins; statuary; low-pitch roofs; sarcophagi; and urns. Many society tombs designed in this elegant style were built by burial societies founded by Italian immigrants and their descendants. Twentieth-century examples were often influenced by the Beaux-Arts style. Most were built of stone slabs, ashlar blocks, or a combination thereof. Approximate dates in New Orleans cemeteries: 1890–1930.

Byzantine revival Beauregard-Larendon tomb (ca. 1890), Metairie Cemetery.

Byzantine/Islamic revival. This style of tomb was inspired by Byzantine and traditional Islamic architecture. Examples can feature conventional domes or onion domes; rounded, horseshoe, or scalloped arches; columns with basket capitals; and arabesque relief. Most were built of stone slabs, ashlar blocks, or a combination thereof. Approximate dates in New Orleans cemeteries: 1880–1940.

APPENDIX B

Brief Histories of Selected New Orleans Cemeteries

ST. LOUIS CEMETERY NUMBER 1 (1789)
Basin Street and St. Louis Street, near Tremé Street
Catholic with Protestant section (1804)

In 1789, the Catholic Church, in cooperation with the Cabildo (the Spanish city council), founded St. Louis Cemetery (now referred to as St. Louis Cemetery Number 1) to replace the earlier St. Peter's Street Cemetery, which had become overcrowded and unsanitary. St. Louis Number 1 operated as the city's only public cemetery until the now-demolished Girod Street Cemetery opened in 1822 for Protestants. St. Louis Number 1 grew to occupy the equivalent of a number of city blocks; however, the city demolished significant parts of it by cutting roads through the Protestant section in 1822 and by destroying additional areas for more streets in 1839. Although fairly well preserved today, the current cemetery represents only a small portion of the historic cemetery. St. Louis Number 1 is the burial site of many historically significant individuals, including Voodoo "queen" Marie Laveau and civil rights activist Homer Plessy.

ST. LOUIS CEMETERY NUMBER 2 (1823)
Claiborne Avenue between St. Louis and Iberville streets
Catholic

Founded in 1823, St. Louis Number 2 was originally designed to replace St. Louis Number 1, although the earlier cemetery was never closed. The

Church laid out St. Louis Number 2 in a more formal manner than St. Louis Number 1, with a straight, central avenue running the entire length of the cemetery. Originally, the cemetery comprised an uninterrupted rectangle from Canal Street all the way to St. Louis Street; however, early in its history it was split into four separate blocks when Iberville, Bienville, and Conti streets were cut through it.[1] In 1846, the Archdiocese of New Orleans sold the block closest to Canal Street in the belief that operating a cemetery so close to the busy street posed a health hazard. St. Louis Number 2 is the first cemetery in the city known to have had specific areas designated exclusively for African Americans. Although many of its tombs have been neglected and are endangered, the cemetery itself remains relatively intact.

LAFAYETTE CEMETERY NUMBER 1 (1832)
Coliseum Street and Prytania Street, Garden District
Municipal

Lafayette Cemetery Number 1 started out as a municipal burial ground in the area now known as the Garden District. Originally, the site was located in the city of Lafayette (not to be confused with the present-day city of that name), which was established by Americans who moved into the area after the Louisiana Purchase. It was a section of the Livaudais plantation. The grounds have been used for burials since at least 1824. Benjamin Buisson, the city surveyor of Lafayette, laid out the plan for the cemetery by intersecting two roads that still divide the property into quadrants, which were lined with magnolia trees. The first known burial dates from August 3, 1843. The city of New Orleans annexed the city of Lafayette in 1852, and Lafayette became a city-owned cemetery, the first of seven public nondenominational cemeteries to be established in New Orleans. In 1858, the city enclosed the cemetery with brick walls, some with wall vaults incorporated into them. From its inception, the cemetery was not segregated by race.[2] The surrounding area became the home of many immigrants in the mid-nineteenth century; German and Irish names still mark numerous tombs. Many epitaphs are in German. The cemetery is quite well preserved and is popular among tourists. Because the Archdiocese forbade the filming of movies in its cemeteries after the unauthorized filming of *Easy Rider* in St. Louis Number 1 in 1969, many movies and television shows intending to portray a traditional New Orleans cemetery have been filmed in Lafayette Number 1.

CYPRESS GROVE CEMETERY (1840)
120 City Park Avenue
Fraternal

Cypress Grove, also known as the Fireman's Cemetery, is located near Bayou Metairie at the end of Canal Street, in an area originally on the outskirts of the city. In 1840, the Firemen's Charitable and Benevolent Association dedicated its new cemetery to Irad Ferry, a fireman who died in 1837. The association built a number of picturesque society tombs near the cemetery's Egyptian revival main entrance, representing various firemen's groups in the city. The grounds were formally arranged with three wide, parallel streets that ran its entire length and a main avenue acting as a central axis. The long side walls of the cemetery were lined with hundreds of wall tombs, which are currently in deteriorated condition. The cemetery helped establish the large cemetery district that grew up around it in subsequent decades. Although many of the tombs in Cypress Grove are in urgent need of repair, the cemetery has retained much of its historic character.

ST. PATRICK CEMETERIES NUMBERS 1, 2, AND 3 (1841)
143 City Park Avenue
Catholic

The Irish Catholic immigrant parishioners of St. Patrick Church on Camp Street founded the St. Patrick Cemeteries in 1841. St. Patrick Cemetery Number 1 came into intense use during the tragic yellow fever epidemics of 1853 and 1857, when thousands of Irish victims were hastily buried there.[3] Many early Irish settlers performed manual labor for low wages and ended up in unmarked graves in St. Patrick Number 1, especially during epidemics, when many were even buried in trenches. Unlike most early New Orleans cemeteries, St. Patrick Number 1 has a majority of belowground burials, many in coping graves. As the prosperity and the population of the Irish community increased, St. Patrick Church added St. Patrick Cemeteries Numbers 2 and 3. Although these cemeteries fell into disrepair in the early twentieth century, the Archdiocese of New Orleans took over management of them in 1966, and some restoration work was done in subsequent decades.

ST. VINCENT DE PAUL CEMETERIES NUMBERS 1, 2, AND 3
(1844: NUMBER 1)
1322 Louisa Street
Catholic

These cemeteries occupy three blocks in the St. Claude neighborhood of the city's Ninth Ward, downriver from the French Quarter and Faubourg Marigny. The three cemeteries probably started out as parish cemeteries for the Church of St. Vincent de Paul, also located in the Ninth Ward. An 1857 city directory states that St. Vincent De Paul Number 1 had been chartered in 1844, although it may have been opened as early as 1830.[4] In 1857, Don José "Pepe" Llulla, a well-known duelist and Spanish patriot, purchased the cemetery; he operated and developed it until his death in 1888.[5] Eventually, Albert L. Stewart purchased the grounds and expanded them into the full three blocks they occupy today. St. Vincent de Paul Cemetery Number 1 experienced large-scale commercial tomb development, with rows of uniform structures built along its walkways.[6] The cemetery, while fairly well preserved, has suffered from a number of historically insensitive tomb rehabilitations in recent years.

CHARITY HOSPITAL CEMETERY (1847)
5050 Canal Street
Nondenominational

The Charity Hospital burial ground, which is located near Cypress Grove and the St. Patrick Cemeteries, is the final resting place of the many thousands of indigent individuals who died in Charity Hospital beginning in September 1847, many of whom ended up in mass, unmarked graves. People who had donated their bodies to science were also buried there.[7] In 1937, when a new Charity Hospital was constructed, workers took earth excavated from its foundations and transported it to the cemetery, where it was used to raise the level of the ground by several feet to reduce flooding and help eliminate water-filled graves.[8] In 2007, the Katrina Memorial was built on the site of the old Charity Hospital nearby, giving the cemetery added significance.

ODD FELLOWS REST (1847)
5055 Canal Street
Fraternal

The Grand Lodge of the Independent Order of Odd Fellows established Odd Fellows Rest, not far from Cypress Grove Cemetery. The Odd Fellows, an international benevolent society that started in England, purchased the property where Canal Street and City Park Avenue intersect for the modest sum of $700 (around $20,000 in 2016 dollars) and created a cemetery designed to accommodate the burial needs of its members and their families.[9] One of the cemetery's most historically significant tombs is the society tomb of the Howards, a local service organization founded by John Howard, which was made up of young men and provided assistance to victims during the numerous yellow fever epidemics that plagued the city until 1905. The cemetery fell into disuse in the mid-twentieth century and was eventually closed to all visitors in the 2010s as a public safety measure, due to the deterioration and instability of some of the tombs.[10] Since the Odd Fellows no longer exist in New Orleans, ownership of and responsibility for the cemetery is uncertain.

ST. BARTHOLOMEW AND ST. MARY CEMETERIES (1848, 1861)
Newton, Diana, and Nunez streets
Catholic

St. Bartholomew Cemetery is the oldest cemetery in Algiers, located on the West Bank of the Mississippi River across from the French Quarter. The Duverje family deeded the land for this cemetery in 1848 on the condition that it would forever remain a burial site. As the only cemetery in Algiers, St. Bartholomew quickly became overcrowded, spurring the creation of St.

Mary Cemetery nearby in 1861. Like most nineteenth-century New Orleans cemeteries, both St. Bartholomew and St. Mary have a combination of coping graves, family tombs, and society tombs.[11] Originally a Catholic cemetery, St. Mary Cemetery was taken over by the city in 1921.

CARROLLTON CEMETERY (1849)
Adams Street between Hickory and Birch streets
Municipal

The City of Carrollton, then a suburb of New Orleans, established the Carrollton Cemetery on ground deemed high enough for belowground burial. In 1874, the City of New Orleans annexed Carrollton, and the cemetery became a municipal cemetery. In addition to in-ground burials, families and burial societies built a number of tombs there. The cemetery has been poorly maintained for much of its history.

ST. LOUIS CEMETERY NUMBER 3 (1854)
3421 Esplanade Avenue, Mid City
Catholic

St. Louis Cemetery Number 3, initially known as the Bayou Cemetery, is located on Esplanade Avenue on the Esplanade Ridge near Bayou St. John, on the site of a former leper colony. It opened in 1854, and it is the third Catholic cemetery established in the city still in existence. Immediately put to use to bury victims of the severe 1853–55 yellow fever outbreak, the cemetery is densely packed with orderly rows of tombs arranged along three broad avenues that run lengthwise through the entire site (a plan similar to that of Cypress Grove). While many of the tombs within its confines are nondescript, the area near the cemetery gates on Esplanade Avenue has a collection of distinctive monuments, such as the Gallier Cenotaph, designed by the well-known New Orleans architect James Gallier Jr. to honor his father in 1866, and the Dante Lodge Society Tomb. St. Louis Cemetery Number 3 was expanded in 1865 and much later in the 1980s.

ST. JOSEPH CEMETERIES NUMBERS 1 AND 2
(NUMBER 1: 1854; NUMBER 2: 1873)
2220 Washington Avenue
Catholic

Founded by German immigrants, the St. Joseph Cemeteries were created as a burial ground and a source of income for the Sisters of Notre Dame, who ran the St. Joseph German orphan asylum. After both cemeteries filled and began to become dilapidated, the order donated them to the Archdiocese of New Orleans. Each of the cemeteries still features a functional Catholic chapel built in the gothic revival style. Both cemeteries contain a majority of coping graves.

GREENWOOD CEMETERY (1852)
120 City Park Avenue
Fraternal, Nondenominational

Due to the astounding success of Cypress Grove Cemetery, opened in 1840, the Firemen's Charitable and Benevolent Association decided to create Greenwood Cemetery nearby a decade later. To make the cemetery especially profitable, the association designed it to contain the largest possible number of densely packed cemetery plots. The grounds themselves have few decorative features and little open land. The most significant monuments there include the Confederate monument, designed by Benjamin M. Harrod (1874); the tumulus-style Elks' society tomb, built by Albert Weiblen (1912); and the impressive gothic revival Firemen's Monument, designed and built by Charles A. Orleans (1887).

LAFAYETTE CEMETERY NUMBER 2 (1858)
Washington Avenue between Loyola Avenue and Saratoga Street
Nondenominational

A municipal cemetery, Lafayette Number 2 was formally surveyed by the city in 1865. The cemetery was segregated, at least partly, from its inception. In addition to having many family tombs and coping graves, Lafayette

Number 2 became the home of a large number of society tombs, mostly built by labor groups made up of members from a particular occupation. Both black and white associations constructed the impressive society tombs found here. Among the most interesting of these is the tomb of the Coachmen's Benevolent Association, an African American brotherhood of coach and wagon drivers built in 1890; the classic revival tomb of the Société Française de Bienfaisance et d'Assistance Mutuelle, or "French Hospital"; and the artistic Deutscher Handwerk Verlein society tomb built in 1868. Unfortunately, most structures in the cemetery, especially its society tombs, are in dire need of repair.

DISPERSED OF JUDAH AND GATES OF PRAYER (1846, 1864)
4901 Canal Street, 4800 Canal Street
Jewish

The first Jewish cemetery in New Orleans, called Gates of Mercy, was established in 1828 by the Gates of Mercy Congregation, made up mainly of Jews of German background.[12] The cemetery was closed to interments in 1866 and eventually demolished in 1957. The second Jewish cemetery in New Orleans, and the oldest still in existence, is the Dispersed of Judah, opened, on land donated by Judah P. Touro, in 1846 by the Congregation Nefuzoth Yehudah, mostly of Sephardic Spanish and Portuguese origin. The Dispersed of Judah Cemetery is located on Canal Street within the city's cemetery district.[13] During the nineteenth century, a section of the cemetery was reserved for suicides.[14] The Temmeme Derech Cemetery (renamed Gates of Prayer in 1939) was opened in 1864 by a Polish congregation in what was the city of Lafayette at the time. Jewish cemeteries, such as Dispersed of Judah and Gates of Prayer, have belowground burials. According to Jewish tradition, a grave should allow the body to reunite with the earth and should be restricted to a single corpse. Many Jewish graves in New Orleans have copings to elevate the level of the coffin buried within and keep the deceased's body dry. Both cemeteries are relatively well preserved.

HEBREW REST CEMETERIES NUMBERS 1 AND 2,
AHAVAS SHOLEM CEMETERY (1860, 1897)
4100 Elysian Fields Avenue, 4400 Elysian Fields Avenue
Jewish

Because of a desire for dry belowground burials, the Jewish community purchased land on the relatively high ground of the Gentilly Ridge to create Hebrew Rest Cemetery. In 1872, Congregation Shangarai Chassed (Gates of Mercy of the Dispersed of Judah) sold the cemetery to Congregation Temple Sinai, and construction began on a second section (Hebrew Rest Cemetery Number 2) in 1894.[15] The last remains of those who had been buried in the demolished Gates of Mercy Cemetery are buried at Hebrew Rest Number 1. Although many of the Jewish cemeteries of the city have artistic grave markers, Hebrew Rest Cemetery has the most impressive. The Ahavas Sholem Cemetery was opened in 1897 by a Jewish benevolent society of the same name that was formed to assist Eastern European Orthodox Jewish immigrants by providing burials for its members. The cemetery was open to any Orthodox Jew, regardless of his or her synagogue affiliation.[16]

MASONIC CEMETERY (1868)
400 City Park Avenue
Fraternal

Founded by the Grand Lodge of the State of Louisiana, Free and Accepted Masons, the Masonic Cemetery contains a large number of society tombs built by various local lodges. During its period of active use, all profits produced by the cemetery were dedicated to maintaining the cemetery itself. Burial in the cemetery was restricted to Masons, although the heirs of Masons could retain ownership of graves and tombs even if they were not Masons themselves.[17]

ST. JOHN CEMETERY (1867)
4800 Canal Street
Nondenominational

St. John Cemetery was first consecrated as a Lutheran cemetery by the First German Evangelical Lutheran Church shortly after the Civil War. After the city repaved Canal Street in 1929 and began charging property owners along the street higher city taxes, the Lutheran congregation decided to sell the property to Victor Huber, one of its members who owned a stone-cutting business that produced and sold grave makers and built tombs. In the early 1930s, Huber began to construct the large Hope Mausoleum, which came to dominate the cemetery and continues to do so today. Still active, the now nondenominational cemetery is managed by descendants of the Huber family.[18]

METAIRIE CEMETERY (1872)
5100 Pontchartrain Boulevard
Nondenominational

In 1872, the Metairie Cemetery Association began to construct a large new garden cemetery on the 108-acre former site of the Metairie Race Course, a horse-racing venue located on the Metairie Ridge, an ancient bank of the Mississippi River. Local businessman Charles T. Howard and his partners held a competition for the design of the new cemetery, but eventually hired local architect Benjamin Morgan Harrod to design it.[19] Harrod incorporated the original oval track into the cemetery's layout and, like the designers of rural garden cemeteries of the East, laid out Metairie Cemetery with a system of curving roads and water features in a parklike setting, unlike any other cemetery in New Orleans at the time. In the decades that followed, people who could afford it built stone tombs and monuments, many of them large, opulent, and ornate, in Metairie Cemetery. In the mid-1890s, an engineer named George H. Grandjean enhanced the pastoral quality of the cemetery by adding or enlarging three artificial lakes and building a decorative bridge.[20] The cemetery, which is still active today, is the site of a number of monumental Civil War tombs and a large collection of extravagant grave markers and tombs constructed by the city's elite.

ST. ROCH CEMETERIES NUMBERS 1 AND 2 (1874)
1725 St. Roch Avenue
Catholic

Among the more interesting burial grounds in New Orleans are the St. Roch Cemeteries, begun in 1874. Father Peter Leonard Thevis, a Catholic priest born in one of the German states, was pastor at Holy Trinity Catholic Church in an area of lower New Orleans known at the time as "Little Saxony" because of the large numbers of German immigrants living there. Shortly after Thevis arrived in 1868, a yellow fever epidemic struck the city. St. Roch was known as a healing saint, and during European epidemics, members of Thevis's congregation in Germany had prayed to him for assistance. Thevis had his congregation pray to the saint, and he promised that if the disease spared them, he would construct a chapel to St. Roch. His flock survived, and, as promised, he built the chapel, which he modeled on the Campo Santo dei Tedeschi in Rome, near St. Peter's Basilica. He then established a cemetery around it. The chapel became an active religious site where the faithful prayed to St. Roch for intervention to cure all manner of maladies. Those who believed St. Roch had healed them sometimes left gifts representing the part of the body that had been healed, in the tradition of many chapels of healing saints in Europe and the Americas. Many of those gifts remain and can be seen today in a small room adjacent to the main chapel.

HOLT CEMETERY (1879)
635 City Park Avenue
Nondenominational

Holt Cemetery, named after Joseph Holt, a city health official, and founded in 1879 in the area of New Orleans now known as Mid City, has been used to bury mostly low-income individuals ever since. Holt was created as an indigent cemetery to replace Locust Grove Cemeteries 1 and 2, because it was on higher ground and was farther from residential areas than Locust Grove.[21] However, research done in the 1990s indicates that early in its history, Holt was the site of burials of people from a wide variety of backgrounds. Some Protestants may have chosen Holt for religious rather than financial reasons due to a shortage of plots in non-Catholic cemeteries in the city.[22] By 1908, though, the *New Orleans Daily Picayune* described Holt as a "paupers' cemetery."[23]

NOTES

1. FROM MUD AND CRAWFISH TO CITIES OF THE DEAD

1. Ned Sublette, *The World That Made New Orleans: From Spanish Silver to Congo Square* (Chicago: Lawrence Hill Books, 2009), 38.

2. Joan B. Garvey and Mary Lou Widmer, *Louisiana: The First 300 Years* (New Orleans: Garmer Press, 2001).

3. Peter M Garber, "Famous First Bubbles," *Journal of Economic Perspectives* 4, no. 2 (Spring 1990): 41–46.

4. Rachel S. Watts, "Creole Bodies and Intersecting Lives and Oppressions: An Intertexual Dialogue between Kate Chopin and Alice Dunbar-Nelson" (master's thesis, University of Alabama, 2010), 11.

5. Katy Frances Morlas, "La Madame et la Mademoiselle: Creole Women in Louisiana, 1718–1865" (master's thesis, Louisiana State University, 2005), 19.

6. Sublette, *The World That Made New Orleans*, 52–53.

7. Douglas W. Owsley, Charles E. Orser Jr., Robert Montgomery, and Claudia C. Holland, "An Archaeological and Physical Anthropological Study of the First Cemetery in New Orleans" (Baton Rouge: Louisiana Division of Archaeology, 1985), 15–16.

8. New Orleans Cabildo, Session Minutes, March 14, 1800, bk. 4, vol. III.

9. "The City: Our Cemeteries and Their History," *New Orleans Daily Picayune*, October 10, 1859, 3.

10. Samuel Wilson Jr., "The First New Orleans Cemetery," *Save Our Cemeteries* (December 1982): 2.

11. Ibid., 3.

12. New Orleans Cabildo, Session Minutes, March 14, 1800, bk. 4, vol. III.

13. Owsley et al., "An Archaeological and Physical Anthropological Study," 19.

14. Jordan Andrea Krummel, "Holt Cemetery: An Anthropological Analysis of an Urban Potter's Field" (master's thesis, Tulane University, 2013), 7.

15. Anthony J. Stanonis, "Dead but Delightful: Tourism and Memory in New Orleans Cemeteries," in *Destination Dixie: Tourism and Southern History*, ed. Karen L. Cox (Gainesville: University Press of Florida, 2012), 248.

16. New Orleans Cabildo, Session Minutes, October 17, 1788, bk. 3, vol. II, 39.

17. Cindy Ermus, "The Good Friday Fire of 1788: Implications of a Disaster in Spanish Colonial New Orleans" (master's thesis, Florida State University, 2010), 36.

18. Ibid., 54.

19. Owsley et al., "An Archaeological and Physical Anthropological Study," 19.

20. New Orleans Cabildo, Session Minutes, October 17, 1788, bk. 3, vol. II, 39.

21. Katherine Smith, "Dialoging with the Urban Dead of Haiti," *Southern Quarterly* 47, no. 4 (Summer 2010): 61.

22. Harold Holloway, *The South Park Street Cemetery: Calcutta* (Calcutta: Statesman Commercial Press, 1978), 3.

23. New Orleans Cabildo, Session Minutes, November 14, 1800, bk. 4, vol. IV, 38.

24. Ibid., June 26, 1801, bk. 4, vol. IV, 101.

25. Ibid., Session Minutes, November 14, 1800, bk. 4, vol. IV, 38.

26. Owsley et al., "An Archaeological and Physical Anthropological Study," 21–24.

27. "Unearthing of Coffins: Mr. Cruzat Says Spot Was Former Old Cemetery," *New Orleans Daily Picayune*, October 10, 1910; Krummel, "Holt Cemetery," 7.

28. New Orleans City Council, Session Minutes, August 16, 1804, 154:110.

29. New Orleans Cabildo, Session Minutes, June 26, 1801, bk. 4, vol. IV, 101.

30. David Lee Sterling, ed., "New Orleans, 1801: An Account by John Pintard," *Louisiana Historical Quarterly* 34, no. 3 (July 1951): 230.

31. New Orleans Cabildo, Session Minutes, March 14, 1800, bk. 4, vol. III.

32. Doris Kent, "Figures from the Past Long Ago Seem to Greet the Visitor to the Old St. Louis Cemetery . . .," *New Orleans Times-Picayune*, February 1, 1920.

33. New Orleans City Council, Session Minutes, June 9, 1804, 86–87, 112–13.

34. Benjamin H. B. Latrobe, *Impressions Respecting New Orleans: Diary & Sketches, 1818-1820*, ed. Samuel Wilson Jr. (New York: Columbia University Press, 1951).

35. New Orleans City Council, Session Minutes, May 8, 1816, 209.

36. Ibid., December 8, 1804, 222–23.

37. Ibid.

38. New Orleans City Council, Session Minutes, July 31, 1805, 216.

39. Howard Colvin, *Architecture and the Afterlife* (New Haven: Yale University Press, 1991), 102–3.

40. James Stevens Curl, *A Celebration of Death: An Introduction to Some of the Buildings, Monuments, and Settings of Funerary Architecture in the Western European Tradition* (New York: Charles Scribner, 1980), 72–73.

41. Mary Gehman, *The Free People of Color of New Orleans: An Introduction* (New Orleans: Margaret Media, Inc., 1994), 9.

42. Charles E. Orser Jr., "The Archaeology of African-American Slave Religion in the Antebellum South," *Cambridge Archaeological Journal* 4, no. 1 (1994): 33–45.

43. Erik R. Seeman, *Death in the New World: Cross-Cultural Encounters, 1492–1800* (Philadelphia: University of Pennsylvania Press, 2011), 198.

44. Douglas W. Owsley et al., "Demography and Pathology of an Urban Slave Population from New Orleans," *American Journal of Physical Anthropology* 74, no. 2 (October 1987): 187.

45. Ross W. Jamieson, "Material Culture and Social Death: African-American Burial Practices," *Historical Archaeology* 29, no. 4 (1995): 52.

46. Richard A. Etlin, *The Architecture of Death: The Transformation of the Cemetery in Eighteenth-Century Paris* (Boston: MIT Press, 1984), 12.

47. Ibid., 33.

48. Ann M. Masson, "Père La Chaise and the New Orleans Cemeteries," *Southern Quarterly* 31, no. 2 (Winter 1993): 84.

49. Masha Stoyanova, "From Archaeology to Imitation: Pompeii in the Work of Alexander Briullov" (master's thesis, George Mason University, 2014), 1–2; Rachel Carly, *The Visual Dictionary of American Domestic Architecture* (New York: Henry Holt, 1994), 90.

50. Curl, *A Celebration of Death*, 41.

51. Colvin, *Architecture and the Afterlife*, 56–57.

52. Stahl, *The New Orleans Sketch Book: Library of Humorous American Works* (Philadelphia: A. Hart, Late Carey & Hart, 1853), 58.

53. Latrobe, *Impressions Respecting New Orleans*, 82.

54. Curl, *A Celebration of Death*, 44.

55. Latrobe, *Impressions Respecting New Orleans*, 84.

56. José Montero de Pedro, *The Spanish in New Orleans and Louisiana*, trans. Richard E. Chandler (Gretna, LA: Pelican Pub. Co., 2000), 237.

57. Katherine Lee Bates, *Spanish Highways and Byways* (New York: Macmillan, 1900), 250–51.

58. Historical marker, Comillas, Spain, July 2014. In 1648, the congregation of the medieval church that would eventually become the cemetery began the construction of the Church of San Cristobal, which would replace it.

59. Latrobe, *Impressions Respecting New Orleans*, 83.

60. Edward Henry Durell (H. Didimus), *New Orleans as I Found It* (New York: Harper, 1845).

61. C. W. Kenworthy, *History of Yellow Fever in New Orleans . . . Summer of 1853* (Philadelphia: C. W. Kenworthy, 1854), 50.

62. G. E. Pugh, *The Day of All Saints at New Orleans* (Cincinnati: Robert Clarke & Co., 1845), 13.

63. "A Walk among the Graves," *Louisiana Courier*, June 18, 1833, in Albert E. Fossier, *New Orleans: The Glamour Period, 1800–1840: A History of the Conflicts of Nationalities, Languages, Religion, Morals, Cultures, Laws, Politics, and Economics during the Formative Period of New Orleans* (1957; New Orleans: Pelican Pub. Co., 1999), 426.

64. "West Views of the South: Editorial Correspondence of the *Daily Wisconsin*," *New Orleans Daily Picayune*, March 6, 1864.

65. *Norman's New Orleans and Environs: Containing a Brief Historical Sketch of the Territory and State of Louisiana and the City of New Orleans* (New Orleans: B. M. Norman, 1845), 109.

66. Sublette, *The World That Made New Orleans*, 4–5.

67. Paul Barrett Niell, "Classical Architecture and the Cultural Politics of Cemetery Reform in Early Nineteenth-Century Havana, Cuba," *Latin Americanist* 55 no. 2 (June 2011): 57.

68. Ibid., 57.

69. "Hieroglyphics on Havana: Number XIV," *New Orleans Daily Picayune*, June, 23, 1843.

70. Narciso G. Menocal, "Etienne-Sulpice Hallet and the Espada Cemetery: A Note," *Journal of Decorative and Propaganda Arts,* Cuba Theme Issue, 22 (1996): 57.

71. Charles B. Reynolds, *Standard Guide to Cuba: A New and Complete Guide to the Island of Cuba, with Maps, Illustrations, Routes of Travel . . .* (Havana and New York: Foster & Reynolds, 1905).

72. Timothy Flint, *Recollections of the Last Ten Years, Passed in Occasional Residences and Journeyings in the Valley of the Mississippi . . .* (Boston: Cummings, Billiard & Co., 1826), 312.

73. Leonard V. Huber, "New Orleans Cemeteries: A Brief History," in Huber et al., *New Orleans Architecture, Volume III: The Cemeteries*, ed. Mary Louise Christovich (1974; New Orleans: Pelican Pub. Co., 1997), 10.

74. Ibid., 11.

75. Joseph H. Ingraham, *The South-west, by a Yankee* (New York: Harper & Brothers, 1835), 155.

76. Ibid., 157.

77. Ibid., 154.

78. Huber, "New Orleans Cemeteries: A Brief History," 19.

79. Liliane Crété, *Daily Life in Louisiana, 1815–1830*, trans. Patrick Gregory (Baton Rouge: Louisiana State University Press, 1981), 194.

80. New Orleans City Council, Session Minutes, September 14, 1819, 150:148.

81. Crété, *Daily Life in Louisiana, 1815–1830*, 199.

82. Flint, *Recollections of the Last Ten Years*, 313.

83. Ingraham, *The South-west, by a Yankee*, 157–58.

84. Kenworthy, *History of Yellow Fever in New Orleans*, 57.

85. Ibid.

86. "A Walk among the Graves," in Fossier, *New Orleans: The Glamour Period*, 57–58.

87. *Norman's New Orleans and Environs.*

88. Richard Campanella, "New Orleans: A Timeline of Economic History," Tulane University, New Orleans Business Alliance, http://richcampanella.com/assets/pdf/article_Campanella_New%20Orleans%20Timeline%20°f%20Economic%20History_NOBA.pdf.

2. TEMPLES OF LILLIPUT: THE MID-NINETEENTH CENTURY

1. Ann Merritt Masson, "The Mortuary Architecture of Jacques Nicolas Bussiere de Pouilly" (master's thesis, Tulane University, 1992), 7.

2. Ibid., 10.

3. Ann Masson, "J. N. B. de Pouilly," *KnowLA Encyclopedia of Louisiana*, ed. David Johnson, http://www.knowla.org/entry/473/.

4. Masson, "The Mortuary Architecture of Jacques Nicolas Bussiere de Pouilly," 84.

5. Peggy McDowell, "The Funerary Architecture of Jacques Nicolas Bussiere de Pouilly," *Save Our Cemeteries*, 12.

6. Edith Elliott Long, "Jacques Nicolas Bussiere de Pouilly," in Huber et al., *New Orleans Architecture, Volume III: The Cemeteries*, ed. Mary Louise Christovich (1974; New Orleans: Pelican Pub. Co., 1997), 135.

7. Masson, "The Mortuary Architecture of Jacques Nicolas Bussiere de Pouilly," 32.

8. Richard A. Etlin, *The Architecture of Death: The Transformation of the Cemetery in Eighteenth-Century France* (1984; Cambridge, MA: MIT Press, 1987), 340.

9. Masson, "The Mortuary Architecture of Jacques Nicolas Bussiere de Pouilly," 33.

10. "A Walk among the Graves," *Louisiana Courier*, June 18, 1833, in Albert E. Fossier, *New Orleans: The Glamour Period, 1800-1840: A History of the Conflicts of Nationalities, Languages, Religion, Morals, Cultures, Laws, Politics, and Economics during the Formative Period of New Orleans* (1957; New Orleans: Pelican Pub. Co., 1999), 425.

11. Benjamin Latrobe's First Bank of Pennsylvania (1798-1800) in Philadelphia and Thomas Jefferson's templelike Virginia State Capitol (1785-1789) in Richmond are examples of neoclassical buildings that were precursors to the Greek revival style.

12. Richard G. Carrott, *The Egyptian Revival: Its Sources, Monuments, and Meaning, 1808-1858* (Berkeley: University of California Press, 1978), 82-85.

13. Examples of nineteenth-century Egyptian revival prison buildings include the "Tombs" in New York City (1838), the Debtors' Apartment, Philadelphia County Prison (1835), and the New Jersey State Prison in Trenton (1836). Egyptian revival churches include First Presbyterian Church in Nashville, Tennessee (1849), by William Strickland, and Whaler's Church in Sag Harbor, New York (1843).

14. Carrott, *The Egyptian Revival*, 89.

15. The 1845 illustration, which appears on page 105 of B. M. Norman's *Norman's New Orleans and Environs*, shows thicker, nontapered columns without cavetto capitals flanking the entrance, indicating that the illustration does not depict the Cypress Grove entrance as built.

16. Masson, "The Mortuary Architecture of Jacques Nicolas Bussiere de Pouilly," 72.

17. C. W. Kenworthy, *History of Yellow Fever in New Orleans . . . Summer of 1853* (Philadelphia: C. W. Kenworthy, 1854), 50-52.

18. Ibid., 53.

19. Mark Twain, *Life on the Mississippi* (1883; New York: Signet Books, 1961), 245.

20. Jos. W. Fawcett, *Journal of Jos W. Fawcett; Diary of His Trip in 1840 Down the Ohio and Mississippi Rivers to the Gulf of Mexico and up the Atlantic Coast to Boston* (Chillicothe, OH: David K. Webb, 1944), 33.

21. G. E. Pugh, *The Day of All Saints at New Orleans* (Cincinnati: Robert Clarke & Co., 1845), 16.

22. Mary Jane Windle, "The French Graveyards in New Orleans," *Travels in the South: Selected from Periodicals of the Times,* ed. Eugene L. Schwaab (Lexington: University Press of Kentucky, 1973), 2:463.

23. James Robertson, *A Few Months in America: Containing Remarks of some of its Industrial and Commercial Interests* (London: Longman & Co., 1855), 64.

24. Twain, *Life on the Mississippi,* 242.

25. Joseph H. Ingraham, *The South-west, by a Yankee* (New York: Harper & Brothers, 1835), 154.

26. Ibid., 154–55. Lilliput was a civilization of tiny people portrayed in Jonathan Swift's *Gulliver's Travels.*

27. "All Saints—The Catholic Cemetery," *New Orleans Daily Picayune,* November 1, 1838.

28. Kenworthy, *History of Yellow Fever in New Orleans,* 68–69.

29. Ibid., 69.

30. Christopher Morgan Branyon, "An Investigation into the Ethnographic and Historical Significance of Holt Cemetery" (master's thesis, University of New Orleans, 1998), xix.

31. "Council and City Park Commission Seeking New Site for Paupers' Cemetery," *New Orleans Daily Picayune,* March 31, 1908. In 1908, the City Park Commission wanted to close Holt and find another "paupers' cemetery"; however, the plan was never carried out.

32. Jordan Andrea Krummel, "Holt Cemetery: An Anthropological Analysis of an Urban Potter's Field" (master's thesis, Tulane University, 2013), 35.

33. Ross W. Jamieson, "Material Culture and Social Death: African-American Burial Practices," *Historical Archaeology* 29, no. 4 (1995): 50.

34. Ibid., 50–51.

35. "Contrasting Scenes in the Cemeteries, Where all Classes of the Living Democracy Gather," *New Orleans Daily Picayune,* November 2, 1905.

3. THE ARCHITECTURE AND ART OF DEATH:
THE BUILDERS AND DECORATORS

1. Frank G. Matero et al., "St. Louis Cemetery No. 1: Guidelines for Preservation & Restoration" (Philadelphia: Graduate Program in Historic Preservation, Graduate School of Fine Arts, University of Pennsylvania, 2002), 17.

2. Emily Ford, informal discussion, January 18, 2016.

3. Emily A. Ford, "The Stonecutters and Builders of Lafayette Cemetery No. 1, New Orleans, Louisiana" (master's thesis, Clemson University, 2013), 64–69, http://www.oak andlaurel.com/resources.html.

4. Matero et al., "St. Louis Cemetery No. 1: Guidelines for Preservation & Restoration," 14–15.

5. USDA Soil Conservation Service, *Soil Survey of Orleans Parish* (Washington, DC: US Printing Office, 1989), 1. This source describes the soils of New Orleans as "loamy and clayey."

6. A parapet wall is taller than the roof behind it.

7. Matero et al., "St. Louis Cemetery No. 1: Guidelines for Preservation & Restoration," 15.

8. Emily A. Ford, "The Craftsman and the Gravedigger: Cemeteries in Times of Epidemic," http://www.oakandlaurel.com/blog/archives/08-2015.

9. Lawrence E. Estaville Jr., "A Strategic Railroad: The New Orleans, Jackson and Great Northern in the Civil War," *Louisiana History* 14, no. 2 (Spring 1973): 117–36; Henry Rightor, *Standard History of New Orleans, Louisiana* . . . (New Orleans: Lewis Pub. Co., 1900), 305.

10. Ford, "The Stonecutters and Builders of Lafayette Cemetery, No. 1," 68–69.

11. Ibid., 88.

12. Joan M. Martin, "*Plaçage* and the Louisiana *Gens de Couleur Libre:* How Race and Sex Defined the Lifestyles of Free Women of Color," in *Creole: The History and Legacy of Louisiana's Free People of Color,* ed. Sybil Kein (Baton Rouge: Louisiana State University Press, 2000), 59.

13. Gardner's City Directory, 1851, https://sites.google.com/site/onlinedirectorysite /Home/usa/la/orleans.

14. Gardner's City Directory, 1861.

15. Charles Lej. Mackie, "Paul Hippolyte Monsseaux: Marble Dealer," *Save Our Cemeteries* (Fall 1984): 15.

16. Leonard V. Huber, "New Orleans Cemeteries: A Brief History," in Huber et al., *New Orleans Architecture, Volume III: The Cemeteries,* ed. Mary Louise Christovich (1974; New Orleans: Pelican Pub. Co., 1997), 30.

17. The Battle of New Orleans was the final battle of the War of 1812 between the United States and Britain. It occurred two weeks after the war had officially ended because word of the war's end had not yet reached New Orleans.

18. Leonard V. Huber, *The Battle of New Orleans and Its Monument* (1983; rpr. Gretna, LA: Pelican Pub. Co., 2012).

19. Ibid., 21.

20. Joe R. Feagan, *Racist America: Roots, Current Realities, and Future Reparations* (New York: Routledge, 2014), 1–5.

21. Violet Harrington Bryan, "Marcus Christian's Treatment of *Les Gens de Couleur Libre,*" in *Creole: The History and Legacy of Louisiana's Free People of Color,* ed. Sybil Kein (Baton Rouge: Louisiana State University Press, 2000), 42–56.

22. Joseph Logsdon and Caryn Cossé Bell, "The Americanization of Black New Orleans, 1850–1900," in *Creole New Orleans: Race and Americanization*, ed. Arnold R. Hirsch and Joseph Logsdon (Baton Rouge: Louisiana State University Press, 1992), 206, 209.

23. Christopher Joseph Cook, "Agency, Consolidation, and Consequence: Evaluating Social and Political Change in New Orleans, 1868–1900" (master's thesis, Portland State University, 2012), 13.

24. Martin, "*Plaçage* and the Louisiana *Gens de Couleur Libre*," 57–70.

25. Ragan Wicker, "Nineteenth-Century New Orleans and a Carnival of Women" (master's thesis, University of Florida, 2006), 24–25.

26. Since Union forces took New Orleans in 1862, Reconstruction began earlier there than in much of the South.

27. Karen Burt Corker, "The Rise and Demise of the *Gens de Couleur Libre* Artists in Antebellum New Orleans" (master's thesis, University of Florida, 2012), 68–69.

28. Patricia Brady, "Florville Foy, f.m.c., Master Marble Cutter," *Save Our Cemeteries* (May 1989): 4.

29. Her first name may have been Azele.

30. Patricia Brady, "Florville Foy, F.M.C., Master Marble Cutter and Tomb Builder," *Southern Quarterly*, 31, no. 2 (Winter 1993): 11.

31. Obituary of Florville Foy, "The Oldest Marble Cutter in Old New Orleans," *New Orleans Daily Picayune*, March 17, 1903.

32. Sharyn Thompson, "These Works of Mortuary Masonry: The Aboveground Tombs of St. Michael Cemetery, Pensacola, Florida," *Southern Quarterly* 31, no. 2 (Winter 1993): 58–59.

33. Brady, "Florville Foy, f.m.c., Master Marble Cutter," 5.

34. Corker, "The Rise and Demise of the *Gens de Couleur Libre* Artists," 64.

35. Obituary of Florville Foy, *New Orleans Daily Picayune*, March 17, 1903.

36. Brady, "Florville Foy, f. m. c. Master Marble Cutter," 6.

37. Classified ad, *New Orleans Daily Picayune*, June 11, 1892.

38. Emily A. Ford and Barry Stiefel, *The Jews of New Orleans and the Mississippi Delta: A History of Life and Community along the Bayou* (Mount Pleasant, SC: History Press, 2012), 35.

39. Bertram Wallace Korn, "Jews and Negro Slavery in the Old South, 1789–1865," in *Strangers and Neighbors: Relations between Blacks and Jews in the United States*, ed. Maurianne Adams and John Bracey (Amherst: University of Massachusetts Press, 1999), 147–82.

40. Corker, "The Rise and Demise of the *Gens de Couleur Libre* Artists," 72.

41. Patricia Brady, "Free Men of Color as Tomb Builders in the Nineteenth Century," in *Cross, Crozier, and Crucible: A Volume Celebrating the Bicentennial of a Catholic Diocese in Louisiana*, ed. Glenn R. Conrad (New Orleans: Archdiocese of New Orleans in cooperation with the Center for Louisiana Studies, 1993), 480–88.

42. Ibid., 485–86.

43. Derik P. LeCesne, "Nineteenth-Century Black Artists, Visual Arts Sculpture," in *Louisiana's Black Heritage* (New Orleans: Louisiana State Museum, 1979), 74–78.

44. *New Orleans Daily Picayune,* December 26, 1857.

45. Corker, "The Rise and Demise of the *Gens de Couleur Libre* Artists," 79.

46. Brady, "Free Men of Color as Tomb Builders in the Nineteenth Century," 486–87.

47. Corker, "The Rise and Demise of the *Gens de Couleur Libre* Artists," 83.

48. Brady, "Free Men of Color as Tomb Builders in the Nineteenth Century," 486.

49. Ford, "The Stonecutters and Builders of Lafayette Cemetery No. 1," 89–92.

50. Ford, "The Craftsman and the Gravedigger."

51. "Burying the Dead," *New Orleans Daily Picayune,* August 9, 1853.

52. Ford, "The Stonecutters and Builders of Lafayette Cemetery No. 1," 89–92, 137.

53. Huber, "New Orleans Cemeteries: A Brief History," 61.

54. Henri A. Gandolfo, *Metairie Cemetery, an Historical Memoir: Tales of Its Statesmen, Soldiers and Great Families* (New Orleans: Stewart Enterprises, 1981), 93.

55. Ibid., 94.

56. Ibid.

57. Southeastern Architectural Archive, "Albert Weiblen Marble and Granite Company Office Records: History Biographical Note," http://seaa.tulane.edu/sites/all/themes/Howard_Tilton/docs/finding_aids/Albert%20Weiblen%20Co.pdf.

58. Alan Gauthreaux, "An Inhospitable Land: Anti-Italian Sentiment and Violence in Louisiana, 1891–1924" (master's thesis, University of New Orleans, 2007), 3–4; Richard Gambino, *Vendetta: The True Story of the Largest Lynching in U.S. History,* 2nd ed. (Toronto: Guernica Editions, 2000).

59. Peggy McDowell, "Influences on 19th-Century Funerary Architecture," in Huber et al., *New Orleans Architecture, Volume III: The Cemeteries,* ed. Mary Louise Christovich (1974; New Orleans: Pelican Pub. Co., 1997), 93.

60. "Elk's Tomb to be Erected on Fine Greenwood Cemetery Site," *New Orleans Daily Picayune,* August 7, 1911.

61. Southeastern Architectural Archive, "Albert Weiblen Marble and Granite Company Office Records."

62. Gandolfo, *Metairie Cemetery, an Historical Memoir,* 95.

4. PALACES OF THE DEAD:
SOCIETY TOMBS AND FRATERNAL CEMETERIES

1. Daniel Rosenberg, *New Orleans Dock Workers: Race, Labor, and Unionism, 1892–1923* (Albany: State University of New York Press, 1988), 62.

2. Claude F. Jacobs, "Benevolent Societies of New Orleans during the Late 19th and Early 20th Century," *Louisiana History* 21, no. 33 (1988): 23.

3. International Association of Jewish Genealogical Societies, "International Jew-

ish Genealogical Project," http://www.iajgsjewishcemeteryproject.org/louisiana-la/new
-orleans-orleans-parish.html.

4. Edward Henry Durell (H. Ditimus), *New Orleans as I Found It* (New York: Harper,
1845), 42.

5. "A Walk among the Graves," *Louisiana Courier,* June 18, 1833, in Albert E. Fossier,
*New Orleans: The Glamour Period, 1800–1840: A History of the Conflicts of National-
ities, Languages, Religion, Morals, Cultures, Laws, Politics, and Economics during the
Formative Period of New Orleans* (1957; New Orleans: Pelican Pub. Co., 1999), 427.

6. "The Sanitarians: An Interesting report from Dr. Watkins, the Asiatic Cholera, Re-
membrances from the Past and Precautions for the Future," *New Orleans Daily Picayune,*
August 21, 1885.

7. Louisiana Division, New Orleans Public Library, "Yellow Fever Deaths between
1817 and 1905," http://nutrias.org/facts/feverdeaths.htm.

8. Henry M. McKiven Jr., "The Political Construction of a Natural Disaster: The Yellow Fever Epidemic of 1853," *Journal of American History* 94 (December 2007): 734–42.

9. "Burying the Dead," *New Orleans Daily Picayune,* August 9, 1853.

10. Liliane Crété, *Daily Life in Louisiana, 1815–1830,* trans. Patrick Gregory (Baton
Rouge: Louisiana State University Press, 1981), 194.

11. "New Lusitanos Benevolent Association," *New Orleans Daily Crescent,* October 19,
1860.

12. Henry Joseph Walker, "Negro Benevolent Societies in New Orleans: A Study of
Their Structure, Function, and Membership" (master's thesis, Fisk University, 1937), 24.

13. "The Unveiling," *Daily States,* June 13, 1881.

14. Leonard V. Huber and Guy F. Barnard, *To Glorious Immortality: The Rise and
Fall of the Girod Street Cemetery, New Orleans' First Protestant Cemetery, 1822–1957*
(New Orleans: Alblen Books, 1961), 69.

15. "New Lusitanos Benevolent Association," *New Orleans Daily Crescent,* October 19,
1860.

16. Samuel Wilson Jr. and Leonard V. Huber, *The St. Louis Cemeteries of New Orleans,* 3rd ed. (New Orleans: St. Louis Cathedral, 1963), 71.

17. "The City," *New Orleans Daily Picayune,* November 2, 1859.

18. Wilson and Huber, *The St. Louis Cemeteries of New Orleans,* 71.

19. Rosenberg, *New Orleans Dock Workers,* 62; Morgan Friedman, "The Inflation
Calculator," http://www.westegg.com/inflation/.

20. "New Orleans Graveyards," *New Orleans Republican,* July 25, 1867.

21. Ibid.

22. William E. Dunstan, *Ancient Rome* (Lanham, MD: Rowman & Littlefield,
2011), 111.

23. Harold Whetstone Johnston, as revised by Mary Scott Johnston, *The Private Life
of the Romans* (1903; Scott, Foresman & Co., 1932).

24. Joseph H. Ingraham, *The South-west, by a Yankee* (New York: Harper & Brothers, 1835), 156.

25. Paul Finkelman, *Encyclopedia of African American History, 1619–1895: From the Colonial Period to the Age of Frederick Douglass* (Oxford: Oxford University Press, 2006), 48.

26. Betty M. Kuyk, *African Voices in the African American Heritage* (Bloomington: Indiana University Press, 2003), 67.

27. Robert L. Harris Jr., "Early Black Benevolent Societies, 1780–1830," *Massachusetts Review* 20, no. 3 (Autumn 1979): 613.

28. Kuyk, *African Voices in the African American Heritage*, 64.

29. Sybil Kein, "The Celebration of Life in New Orleans Jazz Funerals," *Revue française d'études américaines* 51 (February 1992): 20.

30. Anne S. Butler, "Black Fraternal and Benevolent Societies in Nineteenth-Century America," in *African American Fraternities and Sororities: The Legacy and the Vision*, ed. Tamara L. Brown, Gregory S. Parks, and Clarenda M. Phillips (Lexington: University Press of Kentucky, 2005), 70.

31. Ann DuPont, "Survival vs. Soul: The Real Battles of the Mardi Gras Indians," Saturday Juried Oral Presentation, Costume Society of America, 2013.

32. Jacobs, "Benevolent Societies of New Orleans during the Late 19th and Early 20th Century," 21.

33. DuPont, "Survival vs. Soul: The Real Battles of the Mardi Gras Indians."

34. Jacobs, "Benevolent Societies of New Orleans during the Late 19th and Early 20th Century," 23.

35. Walker, "Negro Benevolent Societies in New Orleans," 28.

36. Ibid., 35–37.

37. "Benevolent Daughters of Louisiana," *New Orleans New Republican*, November 11, 1873.

38. Walker, "Negro Benevolent Societies in New Orleans," 37.

39. C. W. Kenworthy, *History of Yellow Fever in New Orleans . . . Summer of 1853* (Philadelphia: C. W. Kenworthy, 1854), 60–61.

40. Jacobs, "Benevolent Societies of New Orleans during the Late 19th and Early 20th Century," 23.

41. Kenworthy, *History of Yellow Fever in New Orleans*, 58.

42. Kein, "The Celebration of Life in New Orleans Jazz Funerals," 22.

43. Rosenberg, *New Orleans Dock Workers*, 63.

44. Robert Florence, *City of the Dead: A Journey through St. Louis Cemetery #1, New Orleans, Louisiana* (Lafayette: Center for Louisiana Studies, University of Southwestern Louisiana, 1996), 26.

45. Joseph S. Carey, "Saint Louis Cemetery Number One" (New Orleans: Congregation of St. Louis Cathedral, 1948), 14.

46. Leonard V. Huber, "New Orleans Cemeteries: A Brief History," in Huber et al., *New Orleans Architecture, Volume III: The Cemeteries*, ed. Mary Louise Christovich (1974; Gretna, LA: Pelican Pub. Co., 1997); Florence, *City of the Dead*, 26; "Local Intelligence, All Saints' Day," *New Orleans Daily Crescent*, November 3, 1856, 1.

47. Winston Ho, "The Chinese Tomb at Cypress Grove," *Clio's Quill* 13 (2010–11): 38.

48. Ibid., 38.

49. Huber, "New Orleans Cemeteries: A Brief History," 30.

50. Ho, "The Chinese Tomb at Cypress Grove," 48; Richard Campanella, "The Lost History of New Orleans' Two Chinatowns," March 4, 2015, NOLA.com, http://www.nola.com/homegarden/index.ssf/2015/03/the_lost_history_of_new_orlean.html.

51. Emily A. Ford, informal communication with author, July 2015.

52. New Orleans Typographical Society, unpublished Union minutes (1855), Louisiana Collection, University of New Orleans, 51.

53. "Firemen's Obsequies," *New Orleans Daily Picayune*, April 27, 1841.

54. "Cypress Grove Cemetery," *New Orleans Daily Picayune*, June 6, 1841.

55. Dell Upton, "The Urban Cemetery and the Urban Community: The Origin of the New Orleans Cemetery," *Perspectives in Vernacular Architecture* 7 (1997): 142.

56. "Cypress Grove Cemetery," *New Orleans Daily Picayune*, October 3, 1840.

57. "Rural Cemetery at St. Louis," *New Orleans Daily Picayune*, June 5, 1841.

58. International Order of Odd Fellows, "About Us," http://www.ioof.org/.

59. Huber, "New Orleans Cemeteries: A Brief History," 34–35.

60. "Consecration of Odd Fellows' Rest," *New Orleans Daily Picayune*, February 27, 1849.

61. "Consecration of a Masonic Cemetery: Brilliant and Imposing Ceremonies," *New Orleans Daily Picayune*, April 4, 1868.

62. Huber and Barnard, *To Glorious Immortality*, 72.

5. SAINTS, VOODOO, AND RACISM

1. Jack Santino. "The Fantasy and Folklore of All Hallows," American Folk Center, Library of Congress, http://www.loc.gov/folklife/halloween.html.

2. British Broadcasting Channel (BBC), "All Saints' Day and all Souls' Day," http://www.bbc.co.uk/religion/religions/christianity/holydays/allsaints_1.shtml.

3. Mary Jane Windle, "The French Graveyards in New Orleans," in *Travels in the South: Selected from Periodicals of the Times*, ed. Eugene L. Schwaab (Lexington: University Press of Kentucky, 1973), 2:465.

4. "All Saints' Day," *New Orleans Daily Crescent*, November 2, 1853.

5. Leon Ronquillo, *Matters of Life and Death* (New Orleans: LFR Group, 1979), 15.

6. James Stevens Curl, *A Celebration of Death: An Introduction to Some of the Buildings, Monuments, and Settings of Funerary Architecture in the Western European Tradition* (New York: Charles Scribner, 1980), 41.

7. Ronquillo, *Matters of Life and Death*, 16–17.

8. "Paris Pencilings: Paris, November, 1878," *New Orleans Daily Picayune*, December 15, 1878.

9. G. E. Pugh, *The Day of All Saints at New Orleans* (Cincinnati: Robert Clarke & Co., 1845), 12.

10. Windle, "The French Graveyards in New Orleans," 464.

11. *The WPA Guide to New Orleans: The Federal Writer's Project Guide to 1930s New Orleans* (1938; New York: Pantheon Books, 1983), 188.

12. "All Saints' Day," *Save Our Cemeteries* (Fall 1984): 9–10.

13. "Contrasting Scenes in the Cemeteries, Where All Classes of the Living Democracy Gather," *New Orleans Daily Picayune*, November 2, 1905.

14. Pugh, *The Day of All Saints*, 12.

15. A. Oakey Hall, *The Manhattaner in New Orleans; or, Phases of "Crescent City" Life* (New York: J. S. Redfield, Clinton Hall, 1851), 109.

16. Windle, "The French Graveyards in New Orleans," 464.

17. "The City: All Saint's Day," *New Orleans Daily Picayune*, November 1, 1869, 2.

18. "Contrasting Scenes in the Cemeteries, Where All Classes of the Living Democracy Gather," *New Orleans Daily Picayune*, November 2, 1905.

19. Lafcadio Hearn and Joseph Pennell, *Historical Sketch Book and Guide to New Orleans and Environs* (New York: Will H. Coleman, 1885), 224.

20. "The City: The City of the Dead," *New Orleans Daily Picayune*, November 2, 1864.

21. John H. B. Latrobe, *Southern Travels: Journal of John H. B. Latrobe, 1834*, ed. Samuel Wilson Jr. (New Orleans: Historic New Orleans Collection, 1986), 168.

22. Elizabeth Fussell, "Constructing New Orleans, Constructing Race: A Population History of New Orleans," *Journal of American History* 94 (December 2007): 847.

23. Michael A. Gomez, *Exchanging Our Country Marks: The Transformation of African Identities in the Colonial and Antebellum South* (Chapel Hill: University of North Carolina Press, 1998), 55.

24. Robin Law, "Dahomey and the Slave Trade: Reflections on the Historiography of the Rise of Dahomey," *Journal of African History* 27, no. 2 (1986): 242.

25. Jordan Andrea Krummel, "Holt Cemetery: An Anthropological Analysis of an Urban Potter's Field" (master's thesis, Tulane University, 2013), 27.

26. Carolyn Morrow Long, "Voodoo-Influenced Rituals in New Orleans Cemeteries and the Tomb of Marie Laveau," *Louisiana Folklore Miscellany* 19 (1999): 2.

27. Ina J. Fandrich, "Yorùbá Influences on Haitian Vodou and New Orleans Voodoo," *Journal of Black Studies* 37, no. 5 (May 2007): 775–91.

28. Gomez, *Exchanging Our Country Marks*, 55; Zora Hurston, "Hoodoo in America," *Journal of American Folklore* 44, no. 174 (October–December 1931), 318.

29. Yvonne P. Chireau, *Black Magic: Religion and the African American Conjuring Tradition* (Berkeley: University of California Press, 2003), 37.

30. Hurston, "Hoodoo in America," 3.

31. Emily Anna Monitz, "Voodoo in the Vieux Carré: Consumption, Identity, and Afro-Caribbean Religion in New Orleans," 4, http://www.academia.edu/2046421/Voodoo

_in_the_Vieux_Carr%C3%A9_Consumption_Identity_and_Afro-Caribbean_Religion
_in_New_Orleans.

32. Monitz, "Voodoo in the Vieux Carré," 5.

33. Krummel, "Holt Cemetery," 28.

34. Monitz, "Voodoo in the Vieux Carré," 6.

35. Ina J. Fandrich, "Defiant African Sisterhoods: The Voodoo Arrests of the 1850s and 1860s in New Orleans," in *Fragments of Bone: Neo-African Religions in a New World*, ed. Patrick Bellegarde Smith (Urbana: University of Illinois Press, 2005), 196.

36. Chireau, *Black Magic*, 48.

37. Hurston, "Hoodoo in America," 397.

38. Ibid., 378.

39. Ibid., 361.

40. "Proposed Colored Demonstrations," *New Orleans Times*, September 27, 1868.

41. "Exhumed Body: Old Negro Sexton Thought to Practice Voodoo Rites," *New Orleans Times-Picayune*, March 7, 1914, 4.

42. Long, "Voodoo-Influenced Rituals in New Orleans Cemeteries," 5.

43. "Voodoos Still Worship Snake in Weird Rite," *New Orleans Times-Picayune*, February 25, 1938, 67.

44. Long, "Voodoo-Influenced Rituals in New Orleans Cemeteries," 4.

45. Anthony J. Stanonis, "Dead but Delightful: Tourism and Memory in New Orleans Cemeteries," in *Destination Dixie: Tourism and Southern History*, ed. Karen L. Cox (Gainesville: University Press of Florida, 2012), 257.

46. Matthew Brennan, "Freed from All Constraint: Voudou and the Black Body in New Orleans, 1850–1865" (master's thesis, Tulane University, 2013), 1.

47. "Girod Cemetery Desecrated, Probably by Voodoos Looking for Grewsome [*sic*] Charms," *New Orleans Daily Picayune*, November 4, 1906.

48. Barbara Rosendale Duggal, "Marie Laveau: The Voodoo Queen Repossessed," in *Creole: The History and Legacy of Louisiana's Free People of Color*, ed. Sybil Kein (Baton Rouge: Louisiana State University Press, 2000), 63.

49. Carolyn Morrow Long, *A New Orleans Voudou Priestess: The Legend and Reality of Marie Laveau* (Gainesville: University Press of Florida, 2006), introduction.

50. Ibid., 123. In 1869, the *Commercial Bulletin* reported that Marie Laveau had reached the age of seventy and was being replaced by a "new voodoo queen" at a Voodoo ceremony on St. John's Eve of that year.

51. Long, *A New Orleans Voudou Priestess*, 123, 166.

52. Ina J. Fandrich, "The Birth of New Orleans' Voodoo Queen: A Long-Held Mystery Resolved," *Louisiana History* 46, no. 3 (Summer 2005): 299.

53. Long, *A New Orleans Voudou Priestess*, 209.

54. Maude Wallace, "Voodooism," interview of Lela, February 9, 16, 21, 1940, WPA Writers' Project, 2.

55. Ibid., 3.

56. Robert Florence, "The Truth about Those X's," *Save Our Cemeteries* (August 1997): 2.

57. Long, *A New Orleans Voudou Priestess*, 177.

58. "In Old St. Louis Cemetery No. 2," *New Orleans Times-Picayune*, February 26, 1921, 18.

59. "Cities within the City: Down the Lanes of Memory Where the Dead Live On," *New Orleans Daily Picayune*, February 25, 1938.

60. Robert Tallant, *Voodoo in New Orleans* (1946; rpr. Gretna, LA: Pelican Pub. Co., 1990), 129.

61. Florence, "The Truth about Those X's," 1.

62. Long, "Voodoo-Influenced Rituals in New Orleans Cemeteries," 5.

63. Florence, "The Truth about Those X's," 2.

64. Leonard V. Huber, "Cities of the Dead," *New Orleanian*, September 2, 1930, 18.

65. "Voodoo Crosses Found on Grave of Noted 'Queen,'" *Baton Rouge Morning Advocate*, June 23, 1936.

66. Ralston Crawford, photograph, Box 9, #38, Ralston Crawford Collection, William Ransom Hogan Archive of New Orleans Jazz, Howard-Tilton Memorial Library, Tulane University, New Orleans.

67. Douglas W. Owsley et al., "Demography and Pathology of an Urban Slave Population from New Orleans," *American Journal of Physical Anthropology* 74, no. 2 (October 1987): 185.

68. "Board of Health: Record of Interments," *Courrier de la Louisiane*, March 3, 17, 1823.

69. Timothy Flint, *Recollections of the Last Ten Years, Passed in Occasional Residences and Journeyings in the Valley of the Mississippi* . . . (Boston: Cummings, Billiard & Co., 1826), 313.

70. Hearn and Pennell, *Historical Sketch Book and Guide to New Orleans*, 226.

71. National Association for the Advancement of Colored People, "Black History Tour Guide: New Orleans Black History Tour: St. Louis II Cemetery, Square 3," *Save Our Cemeteries* (March 1990 [1980]).

72. "The City: Our Cemeteries and Their History," *New Orleans Daily Picayune*, October 30, 1859, 3.

73. "Lafayette Cemetery Number II," http://www.saveourcemeteries.org/lafayette-cemetery-no-2/.

74. "Race Question in the Cemeteries: Mrs. Leathers Sues Odd Fellows Cemetery for Ejecting Black Mammy's Body," *New Orleans Daily Picayune*, December 4, 1912, 7.

75. "A Plea for the Dead," *New Orleans Times-Picayune*, May 11, 1924, 36.

76. *The WPA Guide to New Orleans*, 189.

6. SUBURBS OF THE DEAD:
THE VICTORIAN GARDEN CEMETERY IN NEW ORLEANS

1. *New Orleans Republican*, May 5, 1872.

2. Marilyn Yalom, *The American Resting Place: Four Hundred Years of History*

through Our Cemeteries and Burial Grounds (Boston: Houghton Mifflin, 2008), 45–47.

3. James Dietz, *In Small Things Forgotten: An Archaeology of Early American Life,* exp. and rev. ed. (New York: Anchor, Doubleday, 1996).

4. Blanche Linden-Ward, "Strange but Genteel Pleasure Grounds: Tourist and Leisure Uses of Nineteenth-Century Rural Cemeteries," in *Cemeteries and Gravemarkers: Voices in American Culture,* ed. Richard E. Mayer (Logan: Utah State University Press, 1992), 305.

5. Laurel Hill Cemetery, "History," http://www.thelaurelhillcemetery.org/index .php?flash=1.

6. Linden-Ward, "Strange but Genteel Pleasure Grounds," 317.

7. Peggy McDowell and Richard E. Mayer, *The Revival Styles in American Memorial Art* (Bowling Green, OH: Bowling Green State University Popular Press, 1994), 14.

8. Joseph H. Ingraham, *The South-west, by a Yankee* (New York: Harper & Brothers, 1835), 150.

9. Ibid., 152.

10. *New Orleans Commercial Bulletin,* July 10, 1833.

11. Fredrika Bremer and Mary Howitt, *Homes of the New World: Impressions of America* (New York: Harper & Brothers, 1853), 214–15.

12. "Old Metairie Track: From Racecourse to Cemetery," Old New Orleans, http://old -new-orleans.com/NO_MetairieRaceCourse.html.

13. A. G. Durno, "Old Burial Places," in *Standard History of New Orleans, Louisiana,* ed. Henry Rightor (Chicago: Lewis Pub. Co., 1900), 264.

14. *The Picayune's Guide to New Orleans,* 3rd ed. (New Orleans: The Picayune, 1897), 95; "The New Metairie Cemetery," *New Orleans Daily Picayune,* November 9, 1873. The *Daily Picayune* article cites the cemetery's architect as "Mr. Harrod, the gentleman in charge of the improvements."

15. Ari Kelman, "The Cat Became the Champion of the Crawfish: Struggling to Drain New Orleans' Wetlands," *Historical Geography* 32 (2004): 165; Henri A. Gandolfo, *Metairie Cemetery, an Historical Memoir: Tales of Its Statesmen, Soldiers and Great Families* (New Orleans: Stewart Enterprises, 1981), 17. In "New Orleans Cemeteries: A Brief History," in Huber et al., *New Orleans Architecture, Volume III: The Cemeteries,* Leonard V. Huber writes that the designer of the cemetery was Benjamin F. Harrod; however, an archival search found no evidence of an architect of that name ever having worked in New Orleans, and sources citing "Benjamin F. Harrod" as the architect of Metairie Cemetery cite Huber, indicating that "Benjamin F. Harrod" was a typographic error of "Benjamin M. Harrod."

16. Benjamin D. Maygarden et al., "National Register Evaluation of New Orleans Drainage System, Orleans Parish, Louisiana" (Washington, DC: National Park Service, 1999), 71; "Maj. B. M. Harrod Called by Death: Celebrated Engineer, Former Member of River and Canal Commissions," *New Orleans Daily Picayune,* September 8, 1912, 9.

17. *The Picayune's Guide to New Orleans,* 95. This guide attributes the design of the Metairie Cemetery to "Major B. M. Harrod."

18. *New Orleans Republican,* May 5, 1872.

19. "Metairie Cemetery," *New Orleans Daily Picayune,* November 13, 1873.

20. "All Saints' Day: Yesterday's Visitations at the Homes of the Dead," *New Orleans Daily Picayune,* November 2, 1877.

21. *The Picayune's Guide to New Orleans, Revised and Enlarged,* 6th ed. (New Orleans: The Picayune, 1904), 153.

22. "What the City Has Been Doing: Public Buildings and Schoolhouses Erected during the Year," *New Orleans Daily Picayune,* September 1, 1897.

23. Leonard V. Huber, "Cities of the Dead," *New Orleanian,* September 2, 1930, 32.

24. Gandolfo, *Metairie Cemetery, an Historical Memoir,* 42.

25. Stephanie Bruno, "Eternal Homes: In New Orleans' Historic Cemeteries, the Tombs Echo Trends in Architecture," NOLA.com, http://www.nola.com/homegarden /index.ssf/2010/10/eternal_homes_in_new_orleans_h.html.

26. Mathew A. Speiser, "Origins of the Lost Cause: The Continuity of Regional Celebration in the White South, 1850–1872," Department of History, University of Virginia: Essays in History, http://www.essaysinhistory.com/articles/2011/6.

27. *The Creole Tourist's Guide to the City of New Orleans, with Map* (New Orleans: Creole Pub. Co., 1910–11), 109.

28. Durno, "Old Burial Places," 265.

29. Gandolfo, *Metairie Cemetery, an Historical Memoir,* 42.

30. *The WPA Guide to New Orleans: The Federal Writers' Project Guide to 1930s New Orleans* (1938; New York: Pantheon Books, 1983), 195.

31. Huber, "Cities of the Dead," p. 32.

32. Huber, "New Orleans Cemeteries: A Brief History," 51.

33. David Charles Sloan, *The Last Great Necessity: Cemeteries in American History* (Baltimore: Johns Hopkins University Press, 1991), 159.

34. Anthony J. Stanonis, "Dead but Delightful: Tourism and Memory in New Orleans Cemeteries," in *Destination Dixie: Tourism and Southern History,* ed. Karen L. Cox (Gainesville: University of Florida Press, 2012), 249.

7. SLUMS OF THE DEAD:
DECAY AND CEMETERY PRESERVATION

1. "A Tomb has Justly been Remarked is a Monument Situated on the Confines of Both Worlds," *New Orleans Commercial Bulletin,* November 3, 1835.

2. G. E. Pugh, *The Day of All Saints at New Orleans* (Cincinnati: Robert Clarke & Co., 1845), 12.

3. A. Oakey Hall, *The Manhattaner in New Orleans; or, Phases of "Crescent City" Life* (New York: J. S. Redfield, Clinton Hall, 1851), 109.

4. "Commentary," *New Orleans Daily Picayune,* September 1, 1844.

5. Emily A. Ford, informal interview, January 18, 2016.

6. Mary Jane Windle, "The French Graveyards in New Orleans," in *Travels in the South: Selected from Periodicals of the Times*, ed. Eugene L. Schwaab (Lexington: University Press of Kentucky, 1973), 2:466.

7. Mark Twain, *Life on the Mississippi* (1883; New York: Signet Books, 1961); *The WPA Guide to New Orleans: The Federal Writers' Project Guide to 1930s New Orleans* (1938; New York: Pantheon Books, 1983), 245.

8. Leonard V. Huber, "Cities of the Dead," *New Orleanian*, September 2, 1930, 19.

9. Judith Alleyne Peters, "Modeling of Tomb Decay at St. Louis Cemetery No. 1: The Role of Material Properties and the Environment" (master's thesis, University of Pennsylvania, 2002), 19.

10. "Commentary," *New Orleans Daily Picayune*, July 7, 1839.

11. "The City: Our Cemeteries and Their History," *New Orleans Daily Picayune*, October 30, 1859, 3.

12. Lafcadio Hearn, *Creole Sketches*, ed. Charles Woodward Hutsun (1880; Boston: Houghton Mifflin, 1924), 136.

13. Peters, "Modeling of Tomb Decay at St. Louis Cemetery No. 1," 20.

14. Lafcadio Hearn and Joseph Pennell, *Historical Sketch Book and Guide to New Orleans and Environs* (New York: Will H. Coleman, 1885), 226.

15. A. G. Durno, "Old Burial Places," in *Standard History of New Orleans, Louisiana*, ed. Henry Rightor (Chicago: Lewis Pub. Co., 1900), 257.

16. "Girod Cemetery Desecrated Probably by Voodoos Looking for Charms," *New Orleans Daily Picayune*, November 4, 1906.

17. *The Creole Tourist's Guide to the City of New Orleans, with Map* (New Orleans: Creole Pub. Co., 1910–11), 109.

18. "Ancient Tombs Society Grows: Will Preserve Historic Burial Places," *New Orleans Times-Picayune*, May 7, 1923.

19. Ibid.

20. "Notables in New Orleans Sleep in Wretched Tombs," *New Orleans Times-Picayune*, February 3, 1924.

21. Joseph S. Carey, *Saint Louis Cemetery Number One* (New Orleans: Congregation of St. Louis Roman Catholic Cathedral, 1948), 5.

22. Eugène-Emmanuel Viollet-le-Duc, *The Foundations of Architecture: Selections from the Dictionnaire raisonné*, trans. Kenneth D. Whitehead (1854; New York: George Braziller, 1990), 195.

23. E. Viollet-le-Duc, *On Restoration* (London: Sampson Low, 1875), 9.

24. John Ruskin, *The Seven Lamps of Architecture* (New York: Wiley & Halsted, 1857), 161.

25. *The WPA Guide to New Orleans*, 194.

26. Ryan M. Seidemann, "Do Not Disturb: A Practical Guide for What Not to Do around Cemeteries and Human Remains for the Louisiana Energy and Land Use Practitioner," *LSU Journal of Energy Law and Resources* 2, no. 2 (Spring 2014): 247.

27. Joyce M. Davis, "Slums of the Dead: Archdiocesan Director Reveals Plans to Demolish St. Louis No. 2 Cemetery," *New Orleans Times-Picayune*, December 4, 1974, sec. 1.

28. Ibid.

29. "Cemeteries," http://www.saveourcemeteries.org.

30. American Architectural Foundation, "Important Research and Analysis of St. Louis Cemetery No. 1 Aided by a Save America's Treasures Grant," http://www.archfoundation.org/2013/11/important-research-and-analysis-of-st-louis-cemetery-no-1-aided-by-a-save-americas-treasures-grant/.

31. Marilyn Yalom, *The American Resting Place: Four Hundred Years of History through Our Cemeteries and Burial Grounds* (Boston: Houghton Mifflin, 2008), 144.

32. According to SOC's financial statements, in 2014 it spent $20,581 on restoration, representing 7.4 percent of its budget; in 2013 it spent $2,507, representing 1.2 percent of its budget; in 2012 it spent $4,355, representing 2.2 percent of its budget; and in 2011 it spent $3,553, representing 2.0 percent of its budget ("Financials," http://www.saveourcemeteries.org/financials/). As of this writing, the SOC website listed just one cemetery restoration initiative, called the "Open Tombs" Project at Lafayette Cemetery No. 2, which took place in July 2015 ("Preservation," http://www.saveourcemeteries.org/cemetery-preservation/).

33. Frank G. Matero et al., "St. Louis Cemetery No. 1 Guidelines for Preservation & Restoration," Graduate Program in Historic Preservation Graduate School of Fine Arts, University of Pennsylvania (July 2002), http://www.nis.cml.upenn.edu/nola/pdfs/GuidelinesIntroHistory.pdf, 22.

34. Emily A. Ford, informal interview, July 15, 2015.

35. Leonard Victor Huber and Guy F. Barnard, *To Glorious Immortality: The Rise and Fall of the Girod Street Cemetery, New Orleans' First Protestant Cemetery, 1822–1957* (New Orleans: Alblen Books, 1961), 68.

36. "Dark Deeds: A Graveyard Violated," *New Orleans Daily Picayune*, May 1, 1864; "Girod Cemetery Desecrated, Probably by Voodoos Looking for Grewsome [*sic*] Charms," *New Orleans Daily Picayune*, November 4, 1906; "Tomb Smashers," *New Orleans Daily Picayune*, June, 18, 1912; "Clambering Tourists Damage Old Tomb," *New Orleans Times-Picayune*, January 25, 1931.

37. Emily A. Ford, "The Stonecutters and Builders of Lafayette Cemetery No. 1, New Orleans, Louisiana" (master's thesis, Clemson University, 2013), 46.

38. "The Graveyard Shift," *New Orleans Times-Picayune*, July 13, 2015.

39. Channel 12 KSLA News, "Cemetery Bones Stolen for Black Magic Rites," December 16, 2015, http://www.ksla.com/story/30768741/cemetery-bones-stolen-for-black-magic-rites. The same story was reported on New Orleans television station WWL on December 14, 2015.

40. Richard A. Webster, "New Rules Limiting Access to St. Louis Cemetery No. 1 Receive Mixed Reaction," NOLA.com, http://www.nola.com/business/index.ssf/2015/01/new_rules_limiting_access_to_s.html.

41. Susan Langenhennig, "Because of Vandalism, Only Tours Will Be Allowed in St. Louis No. 1 Cemetery," NOLA.com, http://www.nola.com/homegarden/index.ssf/2015/01/because_of_vandalism_only_tour.html.

42. Jill Smolowe, "The Big Uneasy," *People* 51, no. 16 (May 3, 1999), http://www.people.com/people/archive/article/0,,20128078,00.html.

43. Matero et al., "St. Louis Cemetery No. 1 Guidelines for Preservation & Restoration." To assist those engaged in restorations of all kinds of historic structures, the National Park Service publishes a set of national standards called *The Secretary of the Interior's Standards for Restoration,* which are guidelines on how to retain historic integrity when refurbishing most types of historic structures. Also, the State of Louisiana has created design guidelines for use in restoration projects in historic cemeteries. Even more specific to New Orleans is the detailed restoration guide for restoring tombs in St. Louis Number 1 called "St. Louis Cemetery No. 1: Guidelines for Preservation and Restoration" cited above, which is available online. Because of the difficulty in determining which repairs are necessary and the complexities of using the correct restoration methods, tomb owners should hire a qualified historic tomb restoration specialist to perform and/or supervise all but the most rudimentary maintenance and restoration projects.

44. In 2015, tour guides and tour companies were required to pay $450 a month, $1,200 quarterly, or $4,500 a year to be allowed to take tourists through the cemetery.

45. Webster, "New Rules Limiting Access to St. Louis Cemetery No. 1 Receive Mixed Reaction."

46. Emily A. Ford, informal interview, January 18, 2016.

47. Glasnevin Trust, "Glasnevin Cemetery," http://www.glasnevintrust.ie/.

48. Friends of Laurel Hill Cemetery, "Friends of LHC," http://www.thelaurelhillcemetery.org/index.php?m=7&p=1&s=10.

49. "Cemeteries," City of Savannah website, http://www.savannahga.gov/index.aspx?NID=498.

50. Sam Beetler, preservation specialist for the City of Savannah Department of Cemeteries, interview with author, January 21, 2016.

51. The City of New Orleans owns and maintains Lafayette Cemeteries Numbers 1 and 2, and the Carrollton, St. Mary's, Valence, and Holt cemeteries, all of which suffer from neglect.

52. "BHS," Bonaventure Historical Society website, http://www.bonaventurehistorical.org/bonaventure/bhs.

53. Beetler, interview with author, January 21, 2016.

54. Ibid.

55. Ford, informal interview, January 18, 2016.

APPENDIX A

1. Lloyd Vogt, *New Orleans Houses: A House Watcher's Guide* (Gretna, LA: Pelican Pub. Co., 1992), 15–24.

APPENDIX B

1. Leonard V. Huber, "New Orleans Cemeteries: A Brief History," in *New Orleans Architecture, Volume III: The Cemeteries,* ed. Mary Louise Christovich (1974; New Orleans: Pelican Pub. Co., 1997), 10.

2. "Cemeteries," http://www.saveourcemeteries.org/cemeteries/.

3. Huber, "New Orleans Cemeteries: A Brief History," 34.

4. Emily Ford, "Llulla's Louisa Street Legacy: St. Vincent de Paul Cemetery and Its Famous Founder," http://www.oakandlaurel.com/blog.

5. Huber, "New Orleans Cemeteries: A Brief History," 32.

6. Ford, "Llulla's Louisa Street Legacy."

7. Edward Branley, "NOLA History: 6 Interesting New Orleans Cemeteries," http://gonola.com/2014/10/20/nola-history-6-interesting-new-orleans-cemeteries.html.

8. Huber, "New Orleans Cemeteries: A Brief History," 60–61.

9. Ibid., 34–35.

10. Emily A. Ford, informal interview, January 18, 2016.

11. Huber, "New Orleans Cemeteries: A Brief History," 45.

12. International Association of Jewish Genealogical Societies, "International Jewish Genealogical Project," http://www.iajgsjewishcemeteryproject.org/louisiana-la/new-orleans-orleans-parish.html.

13. Robert Florence, *New Orleans Cemeteries: Life in the Cities of the Dead* (New Orleans: Batture Press, 1997).

14. George E. Warring and George Washington Cable, *History and Present Condition of New Orleans, Louisiana, and Report on the City of Austin, Texas* (1880; London: ReInk Books, 2015), 72.

15. Branley, "NOLA History: 6 Interesting New Orleans Cemeteries."

16. International Association of Jewish Genealogical Societies, "International Jewish Genealogical Project."

17. Warring and Cable, *History and Present Condition of New Orleans, Louisiana,* 72.

18. Find a grave, "Saint John Cemetery," http://www.findagrave.com/cgi-bin/fg.cgi?page=cr&CRid=1960962

19. "The New Metairie Cemetery," *New Orleans Daily Picayune,* November 9, 1873. This article cites the cemetery's architect as "Mr. Harrod, the gentleman in charge of the improvements." *The Picayune's Guide to New Orleans,* 3rd ed. (New Orleans: The Picayune, 1897), 95.

20. *The Picayune's Guide to New Orleans, Revised and Enlarged,* 6th ed. (New Orleans: The Picayune, 1904), 153.

21. Huber, "New Orleans Cemeteries: A Brief History," 60.

22. Christopher Morgan Branyon, "An Investigation into the Ethnographic and Historical Significance of Holt Cemetery" (master's thesis, University of New Orleans, 1998), xix.

23. "Council and City Park Commission Seeking New Site for Paupers' Cemetery," *New Orleans Daily Picayune,* March 31, 1908.

INDEX

African Americans: arrival in New Orleans, 16; burial societies of, 100–104; burial traditions of, 63–64; burials in St. Peter's Cemetery and, 16; Catholic control of burials of, 16; death rates compared with whites, 101; as enslaved tomb craftspeople, 69; grave goods of, 6, 63–65, 227; importance of funerals to, 100–101; influences on burial practices, 16; life expectancy compared with whites, 101; as stone cutters and tomb builders, 72; tradition of burial societies and, 100–101

Ahavas Sholem Cemetery, New Orleans: founding of, 225; location of, 225; Orthodox Jewish immigrants and, 225

Albert Weiblen Marble & Granite Company, 88

All Saints' Day: African American graves and, 64; All Souls' Day and, 116; ancient Roman origins of, 22–23, 115; carnival atmosphere of, 117–118; Celtic origins of, 114–115; charitable activities and, 95, 119; connection between living and dead and, 125; decoration of graves and, 64, 116–118; integration of race and class and, 118; medieval origins of, 115; melancholia and, 119; newspaper reports and, 116; orphans and, 119; Paris and,

116; prayers at graves on, 115–116; preparation of tombs for, 116–117; Protestants and, 116; spectacle of, 115–118; tomb preservation and, 119; as unifying event for city, 118–119, 189

All Souls' Day, 116

ancient Greek orders, 52

The Antiquities of Athens (Stuart and Revett), 19

Antiquities of Herculaneum, 19

Antoine Abat family tomb, 79

Archdiocese of New Orleans, 167, 173, 180, 186–187, 218; and architectural innovation, 44; pre-industrial aesthetic of, 55

Arlington, Josie, 153, 155

Army of Northern Virginia monument, Metairie Cemetery, 86, 150–152

Aubrey, Eloise, 78

Augustus (emperor), 24

Baron Carondelet canal, 12

barrel-vaulted tomb, 200

Bates, Katherine, 28

Battle of New Orleans, 74, 78, 235n17

Battle of New Orleans monument, Chalmette, 74

Beauregard-Larendon tomb, 146–148, 216

Beaux-Arts style, 210, 215

fenced grave, 204
Feralia, 22
Ferry, Irad, 109, 219
filles à la cassette. See casket girls
Fireman's Cemetery, New Orleans. *See* Cypress Grove Cemetery Number 1, New Orleans
Fireman's Charitable Benevolent Association, 109–111, 219, 223
Firemen's Monument, 223
Flint, Timothy, 32, 36
four, 28, 30, 194. *See also* oven tomb
Four Books of Architecture (Palladio), 19
Foy, Florville: ancestry of, 78; artistry of designs and, 79; death of, 81; education of, 78; as employer of Daniel Warburg Jr., 83; as farmer, 81; French-speaking clients of, 85; marriage of, 80; success as tomb designer, 78–80; training as marble cutter, 78; working relationship with de Pouilly, 78; work outside of New Orleans, 79–80
Foy, Prosper, 78
France: decree banning cemeteries within cities and, 18; development of cemeteries and, 17; economic bubble and, 2; founding of New Orleans and, 1; revolution of, 47
fraternal societies: examples of, 89; segregation of, by gender, 89
Free Masons, 89, 107
free people of color: burial societies and, 103–104; emancipation and, 76, 81; immigration from Haiti and, 76; interracial unions and, 76–77, 80; loss of status after Reconstruction, 77–78; numbers in antebellum Louisiana, 76; numbers in antebellum New Orleans, 76; *plaçage* and, 77; quadroon balls and, 77; racial definitions and, 76; roles within nineteenth-century New Orleans society, 75–77; as stone cutters and tomb builders, 72
French Empire style, 56

"French Hospital" benevolent society tomb, 107–108, 224
Friends of Laurel Hill Cemetery, 184
Funerals, cost of, 96

Gallier Cenotaph, 222
Garbeille, Philippe, 82
garden cemeteries: compared with historic New Orleans cemeteries, 140; description of, 139–140; etiquette and, 139; Père Lachaise and, 44; popularity of, 139–140; serenity of, 141; tourism and, 138–139
Gates of Mercy Cemetery, New Orleans, 38, 65, 224–225
General Cemetery, Santiago, Chile, 32, 146
German Washington Benevolent Association, 94–95
Girod Street Cemetery, New Orleans: African American society tombs within, 101, 103–104; charitable activities at, 95; demolition of, 165–166; historical descriptions of, 36–38; New Lusitanos tomb and, 95; oven tombs within, 30–31, 34, 103; poor condition of, 37, 112, 160–163, 165; slavery and, 131; vandalism and, 163, 175; Voodoo and, 125
Glasnevin Cemetery, Dublin, Ireland, 181–182
Glasnevin Trust, 181
Good Friday fire, 8
gothic revival style, 51, 53–56, 213
Graceland Cemetery, Chicago, Ill., 146
Grailhe family tomb, 56–57, 59, 73, 176–177
Granada Municipal Cemetery, Spain, 28
Grandjean, George H., 144, 226
Grand Tours, 19–20
grave goods, 6, 64–65
graves: coping grave, 203, 223–224; fenced grave, 204; headstone marker, 208; ledger stone marker, 209; pedestal monument, 207; table grave, 202
Greek revival style, 51–53, 211, 233n11

plantings and, 143; praise for, 143; society tombs and, 145–146; tomb forms and, 145; visitation and, 157, 183

Metairie Cemetery Association, 141, 143

Metairie Race Course, 141, 226

Metairie Ridge, 141

Mills, Robert, 74

Mississippi brick, 67

"Mississippi bubble," 4

Mississippi River, 1, 67, 141, 221, 226

Monsseaux, Paul Hippolyte, 72–73, 75, 80, 84, 85

monument tomb, 206

Morales tomb, 153, 155

Moriarty, David, 152

Moriarty monument, 152–154

Mount Auburn Cemetery, Boston, Mass., 56, 111: creation of, 134–137, 159; description of, 134–136, 138; picturesque qualities of, 137–138; pleasure garden and, 138; praise of, 140; visitation and, 138

National Register of Historic Places, 167–168; benefits of listing, 168

Native Americans: as enslaved, 4; burial of, 6; New Orleans and, 16

neoclassical style, 18–21, 31, 43–44, 47, 210

Neo-Grec architecture, 43–44, 47, 50, 55

New Lusitanos Benevolent Association, 93–95; charitable activities of, 95; disbanding of, 95; membership of, 95; tomb of, 95

New Orleans, after Louisiana Purchase: aboveground burial and, 16, 28–31, 96; city council and, 14; death rate and, 70; economic expansion of, 38–39, 41; epidemics and, 35–36, 70–71, 84–85, 92, 161, 189; flooding and, 36, 39, 169; French influence and, 42; geography of, 39, 67; high water table and, ix, 4, 12, 15; immigration to, 32–33, 41, 76, 90, 106; lack of native building stone and, 67; local nineteenth-century brick types and,

67; nineteenth-century architecture of, 42; population growth and, 26, 32–33, 120; racial identities and, 76; social status of women and, 77; tomb vaults and, 49–50, 97–98; transportation to and from, 67, 71–72

New Orleans, colonial: African American immigration and, 120; burial underground and, 15; disease and, 1, 4, 8–9; economic growth and, 15; expansion of, 4–5; fires and, 8; first cemeteries in, 5; flooding and, 1, 8, 10; isolation of, 1; maps of, 6, 10; marriage and, 77; population of, 4–5; racial identities and, 76; slavery and, 4; social status of women and, 77; strategic location of, 2; women and, 4, 76–77

New Orleans Bee, 78

New Orleans Italian Mutual Benevolent Society mausoleum, 105–106

New Orleans Typographical Union, 107

Notre Dame Cathedral, Paris, 54, 165

Odd Fellows Rest Cemetery, New Orleans, 61; abandonment of, 180; cost of land and, 112; deterioration of, 180, 221; formation of, 112, 221; Howards society tomb and, 221; location of, 221; National Register of Historic Places and, 167; opening ceremony and, 112; ownership and, 221; public access to, 180; racial segregation and, 132

Orleans, Charles A.: death of, 86; early career of, 85; financial difficulties of, 86; as prolific tomb builder, 85; tombs designed by, 86, 223; use of granite in tombs and, 85–86

Orso, Anthony, 14

Ottoman Empire, 51

oven tomb, 194; affordability of, 40, 103; cost of interment and, 103; in Cuba, 31–32; in Cypress Grove Cemetery, 111; described as ghoulish, 30; in Girod Street Cemetery, 30–31, 165; historical

oven tomb (*continued*)
descriptions of, 28–31; in Latin America, 31–32; location of, in cemeteries, 194; origins of, 25–28; reuse of, 28, 32; Spanish examples and, 28; Spanish influence and, 26–28

Palladio, Andrea, 19
parapet tomb, 198
Paris, France: catacombs and, 18; cemeteries of, 9, 17–18; Cemetery of the Holy Innocents, 17–18; epidemics and, 9; fires and, 9
Pauger, Adrien de, 3, 6
pedestal monument, 207
pediment tomb, 65, 197
Peñalver y Cárdenas, Don Luis de, 10
Peniston-Duplantier tomb, 52–53, 73
Père Lachaise Cemetery, Paris, France, 18, 44–49, 109, 134, 140, 159
Perseverance Benevolence and Mutual Aid Association of New Orleans, 100
Philippe II (Duc d'Orléans), 2
Pintard, John, 12–15, 17, 26
Piranesi, Giovanni Battista, 19–20, 26
Place d'Armes, New Orleans, 5
platform tomb, 65, 199
Plessy, Homer, 131, 217
Poincy, Paul F., 80
Pointe Du Mardi Gras, 1
Pompeii, 19
Pontchartrain brick, 67
Port-au-Prince cemetery, 9
potter's fields, 61–65, 77, 96, 99–100
Pouilly, Jacques Nicholas Bussière de: architectural career of, 42; architectural training of, 42; association with P. H. Monsseaux, 73; influence on New Orleans tomb design, 24, 39, 41–44, 47–48, 50–54, 56–57, 65, 75, 85, 95, 109, 188; innovation and, 50–51; materials used by, 70; sketchbook of, 50, 73, 109; tomb design limits and, 48; working relationship with Florville Foy, 78

preservation, historic, xi; cemetery advocacy groups and, 187; cemetery tourism and, 179–187; climate of New Orleans and, 169–170, 186; descendants and, 168; flooding and, 169–170; Glasnevin Cemetery and, 181–182; historical integrity and, 178–179; Hurricane Katrina and, 169–170; Laurel Hill Cemetery and, 184–185; looting of tombs and, 160, 176–177; maintenance of tombs and, 161; neglect of tombs and, 160–163, 168; New Orleans cemetery office and, 185; practices of, 173–175, 177; program of, 190; restoration philosophies and, 164–165; Ruskin and, 165; Savannah (Ga.) Department of Cemeteries and, 184–186; Save Our Cemeteries and, 166–167, 247n32; *The Secretary of the Interior's Standards for Restoration* and, 248n43; Society for the Preservation of Ancient Tombs and, 163; "St. Louis Cemetery No. 1: Guidelines for Preservation and Restoration" and, 248n43; tomb restoration standards and, 248n43; vandalism of cemeteries and, 160, 175–176; Viollet-le-Duc and, 164–165
Protective Order of Elks, 89, 107
public health: cemeteries as threats to, 8–9, 17–18, 21, 31, 33–35
Pugh, G. E., 116–117
Pugin, A. W. N., 53

quadroon balls, 77

racial segregation: burial societies and, 89; Jim Crow era and, 77–78, 129, 132; Lafayette Cemetery Number 1 and, 218; Lafayette Cemetery Number 2 and, 132; Lost Cause and, 149; Odd Fellows Rest and, 132; St. Louis Cemetery Number 2 and, 34, 131–132, 218; St. Peter's Street Cemetery and, 6; Voodoo and, 122–123
racism, 76, 82, 101, 103–104, 125, 129
railroads: arrival in New Orleans, 65, 71–72

Reconstruction, 77, 132
Renaissance revival style, 215
reuse of tombs, 49–50, 97–98, 194
Richards, Newton, 73–75, 88
Robinson family tomb, 75
Roffignac, Joseph, 33
Romanesque revival style, 214
Romantic movement, 43, 55, 137
Rome, ancient, 21–22, 24–25, 31
Rousseau, Jean-Jacques, 43
rural cemetery movement, 137, 140–141,
 189
Ruskin, John, 54, 165

Saint-Domingue: cemetery and, 9; emigration to New Orleans, and 16–17, 23–
 33, 77–78; revolution of, 9
Samhain, 114–115
San Isidro Cemetery, Madrid, Spain, 28
sarcophagus, 201
sarcophagus tomb, 201
Savannah (Ga.) Department of Cemeteries, 184–185
Save Our Cemeteries, 166–167, 183, 186,
 247n32
*The Secretary of the Interior's Standards
 for Restoration,* 248n43
Section 106 process, 168
Sedella, Antonio de, 8
segregation. *See* racial segregation
slavery, 2, 76; burial places of enslaved
 individuals, 77, 103–104, 131; burial societies of the enslaved, 100, 103–104;
 St. Peter's Street Cemetery and, 129;
 Voodoo and, 120–122
slave trade, 101, 120
Sociedad Iberia de Beneficencia Mutual
 mausoleum, 73
Society for the Preservation of Ancient
 Tombs, 163, 166
society tomb: affordability of, 40, 189;
 ancient Rome and, 99; burial within
 viewed as unacceptable, 98; Cypress
 Grove Cemetery and, 219; descriptions

of, 58, 89, 205; deterioration of, 113;
 early history of, 99; efficient means of
 interring victims of epidemics and, 93;
 elevation of social status of those buried
 within, 104; large numbers built, 92;
 scale of, within cemeteries, 104–105; unmarked graves and, 98
Soon On Tong Association tomb, 106–107
South Park Street Cemetery, Calcutta, India, 9
Spain: acquisition of Louisiana, 8; competition for Louisiana conquest and, 1;
 effort to Christianize slaves by, 16; influence of, on New Orleans tombs, 26
Spring Grove Cemetery, Cincinnati, Ohio,
 139
St. Bartholomew and St. Mary Cemeteries, New Orleans: acquisition by
 the city, 222; Duverje family and, 221;
 founding of St. Bartholomew Cemetery,
 221; founding of St. Mary Cemetery,
 221–222; locations of, 221; tomb types
 and, 222
St. Bonaventure Cemetery, Savannah, Ga.,
 184–186
St. John Cemetery, New Orleans: founding
 of, 226; Hope Mausoleum and, 226; location of, 226; Victor Huber and, 226
St. Joseph Cemeteries Numbers 1 and 2,
 New Orleans: chapels and, 223; coping
 graves and, 223; deterioration of, 223;
 founding of, 223; location of, 223; Sisters of Notre Dame and, 223
St. Louis Cathedral: burials forbidden in,
 14; remodeling of, by de Pouilly, 42
St. Louis Cemetery Number 1, New Orleans: aboveground burial in, 14, 26; All
 Saints' Day and, 119; Antoine Bonabel
 marker in, 12–13; appearance of tombs
 and, 67; belowground burial in, 12, 26;
 Caribbean influences and, 32; changes
 to, 34–35, 217; compared with Cypress
 Grove Cemetery, 111; compared with
 other cemeteries, 18, 28–30, 44; com-

Thevis, Peter Leonard, 227
Thierry, Camille, 80
Thompson, Samuel, 124
Thoreau, Henry David, 43
tomb builders: backgrounds of, 72, 88; dangers of catching disease and, 71; large number in New Orleans, 72; as newcomers to New Orleans, 88; overcoming social barriers, 88; special skills of, 69
Tomb of the Army of Tennessee, 151, 153
tombs: abandonment of, 161, 163, 168; ancient Rome and, 21–22, 24; architectural description of, 60–61; artistic qualities of, 70; barrel-vaulted tomb, 200; block vault tomb, 196; box tomb, 65, 192; building materials used in, 41, 43, 49–50, 52, 58, 65, 67–69, 71–73, 75, 85–86, 169, 188, 192, 194–195, 197–201, 205–206; construction methods and, 68–70, 86, 194; contemporary mausoleums, 157–158; designed to prevent hauntings, 22, 101; deterioration of, due to elements, 169; Egyptian revival style, 212; as follies, 48; free expression of architectural concepts and, 44; Gothic revival style, 213; Greek revival style, 211; as indicators of social class, 77, 144; industrialized production of, 86; maintenance of, 170–173; manmade threats to, 173–179; medieval Europe and, 15; melancholia and, 119; monument tomb, 206; natural threats to, 169–172; neglect of, 160–163, 168; neoclassical style, 210; New Orleans tradition and, 159; offerings and, 22–23; oven tomb, 194; parapet tomb, 198; pediment tomb, 65, 197; platform tomb, 65, 199; as point of contact with dead, 22, 116; as points of memory, 55, 119; Renaissance revival style, 215; restoration guidelines for, 248n43; restoration specialists and, 248n43; reuse of, 49–50, 97–98, 194; Romanesque revival style, 214; sarcoph-

agus tomb, 201; society tomb, 205; as status symbols, 16, 38, 41, 44, 57–58, 66, 96, 104, 144; step tomb, 65, 193; style (definition) of, 191; taxing of, 14; type (definition) of, 191; vandalism of, 175–176; vernacular architecture and, 23–24; vulnerability of, 160; wall vault tomb, 195
Trudeau, Carlos, 10
Twain, Mark, 58, 161

Uncle Tom's Cabin (Stowe), 83, 104
Ursuline Convent, 4

Varney tomb, 56, 162, 212
Victorian death customs, 138
vigilantism, 86–87
Viollet-le-Duc, Eugène Emmanuel, 164–165
Vitruvius Pollio, 19
Voodoo: Catholicism and, 120–121; cemeteries and, 122–125; contrasted with Hoodoo, 121; evidence of, in cemeteries, 124–125; Ewe, Yorba, and Fon cultures and, 120; female practitioners of, 122–123, 125–129; gris-gris and, 122, 125; "goofer dust" and, 123, 125; grave robbing and, 125; graves used in spells and, 123–125, 180; Haitians and, 17, 120; magic and, 121–124, 127–128; Marie Laveau and, 125–127; misunderstood, 123; offerings at graves and, 120, 127–128; origins of, 120; Palo Mayombe and, 122; racism and, 125, 129; Santaria and, 122; spirits of the dead and, 121; St. John's Eve and, 124, 126, 129; suppression of, 122–123; Voodoo doll, 121; Voodoo meetings, 122–123; "Wishing Vault" and, 127–128; X marks on tombs and, 124–125, 127–130

wall vault tomb, 195
Warburg, Daniel: career as tomb builder, 83; childhood of, 81; education of, 81–82; examples of tombs, 83

Warburg, Daniel, Jr., 83
Warburg, Daniel Samuel, 81
Warburg, Eugene: career as tomb builder, 82; career in fine sculpture, 82–83; childhood of, 81; death of, 83; education of, 81–82; emigration to Europe, 82; as slave owner, 82
Washington Monument, 74
water table, ix, 4, 21, 159, 188
Weiblen, Albert, 83, 153: death of, 88; as designer of David C. Hennessey monument, 86; as designer of Elk's tomb, 223; early career of, 86; purchase of Metairie Cemetery and, 88; sources of building stone used by, 88; use of industrial machinery in tomb building, 86, 88
West African democratic and patriotic societies, 100

Whittaker, Louisa, 80–81
Widow Paris tomb, 120, 124–125, 127, 130–131, 175–176, 180, 217
Wilkinson, Frederick, 56, 110
Williams tomb, 212
Woodlawn Memorial Park. *See* Lake Lawn Memorial Park, Metairie
Woodmen of the World, Palmetto Camp No. 2 tomb, 96

yellow fever: cause of, 93; nineteenth-century treatments of, 93; numbers of people killed by, 93; outbreaks of, 35, 93; role of, in cemetery creation, 35; St. Louis Cemetery Number 3 and, 222; St. Roch Cemetery and, 227; symptoms of, 93